Foreword

My name is Dan (@DanBennett3) and I've been playing this fascinating game called Fantasy Premier League (FPL) for 15 seasons. I have finished inside the top 10k on ten occasions with a personal best finish of 917 in the 2014/15 season. As the popularity of the Premier League grows, the number of managers playing the game has increased season-on-season. This has led to a rise in the quantity, and quality, of FPL related content as we all seek to find an edge on our rivals. There are YouTube channels, podcasts, Twitter threads, Discord channels and more, but nothing beats a good, old-fashioned book.

I've been interacting with Paul on Twitter for a few years now. His regular Twitter threads, polls and other FPL related posts are always on topic and extremely useful. He knows FPL inside and out. Paul's first book, *Taking a Hit: The Key To Success,* was a comprehensive and insightful look into one of the most important parts of the game. The amount of research, time and effort that went into it was clear to see. Therefore, I had very high expectations when Paul told me he was writing a second FPL related book. *Chasing Green Arrows* lives up to those expectations and surpasses them. We all love a green arrow at the end of each gameweek, whether it's in the overall ranks, or in your work mini league. *Chasing Green Arrows* leaves no stone unturned in this aim. From selecting your initial squad, to transfer strategy, picking your captain and, of course, the best way to utilise your chips.

Whether you're a veteran of the game, or a relative newcomer, your understanding of the game will benefit from reading this book. Whatever your current playing style, be it risk averse or upside chasing, you'll find new ideas to help chase the next green arrow. It's the most comprehensive FPL book I've ever read (and I've read plenty). Paul's writing style makes it an engaging read, which is not an easy feat when discussing some of the finer points of the game. The section on psychology is a helpful reminder to remain positive when variance takes a wrong turn.

As with Paul's first book, there is a section on the 'Top One Hundred Managers and The Elite'. I was honoured to be among the contributors to this section previously. There are new names providing the insights this time and they are not to be missed. These managers are among the best to have played the game. It's the perfect way to finish the book.

Thank you to Paul for giving me the opportunity to write this foreword. I'm far from a writer myself, but just penning these few hundred words has given me an even greater appreciation for the magnificent job Paul has done in producing this amazing book. In my opinion, it's the ultimate handbook for every FPL manager. I'm sure you'll enjoy it as much as I did.

Fantasy Premier League

FPL

CHASING GREEN ARROWS

FPL Strategies and Tips to Succeed

First Edition

Cover design by: Unboxing Studio

ISBN (paperback): 978-1-7398608-4-4

ISBN (ebook): 978-1-7398608-5-1

Published by Arrowcroft Press

ARROWCROFT
PRESS

Contents

Preface

"Success is no accident. It is hard work, perseverance, learning, studying, sacrifice and most of all, love of what you are doing or learning to do." – Pelé

Football is the most popular sports game in the world and, deriving from the 'beautiful game', is Fantasy Premier League (FPL). An enthralling football prediction game which tests the managerial skills of the players who are participating in an extremely challenging competition. FPL managers pit their wits against like-minded players from across the globe with one aim in mind – to succeed. A totally unpredictable and gripping game which is loved by 11m players worldwide, FPL is an emotional rollercoaster, delivering both highs and lows regularly. The exceptional Gameweeks (GWs) re-energise your appetite for the game, while the lows make you question your participation in such a prolonged campaign. Yet, season after season, whether you're a novice or a seasoned campaigner, millions eagerly await the start of a new challenge.

Having enjoyed Fantasy Premier League for years, I have been a part of the FPL community on Twitter since 2020. I regularly write FPL threads for the community. Writing articles for FPL Connect and The FPL Way has also been a pleasure. My passion for FPL and fascination with additional transfers inspired me to write a book entitled *Taking a Hit: The Key to Success Plus The Top One Hundred Managers and The Elite*, which was published in December 2021. The book explores additional transfers and discusses the outcomes of a comprehensive study. Furthermore, an analysis of the Top One Hundred Managers from the 2020/21 season and a group of Elite Managers is revealed within. A combination of these 12 outstanding managers provides a fascinating insight into their game.

Chasing Green Arrows is a guide to FPL; a book designed to take your game to the next level. Useful tips to help you succeed are in abundance, plus all the main aspects associated with FPL are explored with a view to helping you find your optimum team. Furthermore, there are some relevant and interesting findings from the extensive research that I have conducted over the past two seasons. My research has focused on strategies and additional transfers. The aim was to establish whether my research from the 2021/22 season was consistent with the findings originating from the previous season. In many instances, the data from both seasons has been compared to determine if there are any consistent patterns or trends.

This book incorporates the expertise of some of the best players in the game. We explore the strategies that the top players have adopted to deliver an outstanding overall rank and propel them to the top of the FPL summit. We hear from managers who are either regarded as Elite players for their consistently high finishes, or those who have fought off the challenge of over nine million other players to finish in the Top One Hundred Managers in the world during the 2021/22 campaign. The Elite Managers consistently perform at the highest level, achieving an impressive rank season after season. They become elite players for a reason and that's because they have the attributes to succeed. Their strategies are spot on. They identify the best players to select, excel at captaincy picks, know when to attack and defend, and when to make additional transfers. They also identify optimal fixture patterns and plan their game meticulously.

Analysing the performance of the top managers will enable you to identify the best strategies to adopt in order to succeed. A combination of Elite and Top One Hundred Managers provides a fascinating and revealing insight into the strategies that have propelled them to the top of the FPL ladder. Invaluable information and advice which will undoubtedly assist you in your quest for FPL glory. Additionally, all the top tips are discussed, which will help you in your FPL journey and take your game to the next level. Players rely on some good fortune in order to achieve their goal, but it's essential that managers possess the knowledge and skill necessary to succeed. There is overwhelming evidence to demonstrate that anyone can excel at FPL and there is nothing preventing you from following in the footsteps of the top managers. Whether your goal is to climb to the top of the FPL pyramid or to top your mini-leagues, it's achievable.

This FPL guide will provide you with the tools to help you unlock the door, improve your overall game, and for you to become a successful manager. Unquestionably, the content of this book will ensure that those aspirations are achieved. Information that will not only make you a better player, but many of the tips and strategies are reinforced by my research and insight from the top players. Chasing green arrows is our ultimate goal in achieving a top rank. Green arrows in abundance will lead to the success you crave. Good luck with the seasons ahead and in your quest to reach the summit.

"If my mind can conceive it and my heart can believe it, then I can achieve it." – Muhammad Ali

Introduction

"Some people think that football is a matter of life and death. I assure you, it's much more important than that." – Bill Shankly

Football is a game enjoyed by countless fans worldwide and there is a true saying; you cannot beat the beautiful game. Fantasy football is a game that brings people together, a game which is played for enjoyment, whether you are a novice or seasoned campaigner. Deep down, it seems that we are all budding football managers, ready to pit our wits against liked-minded individuals. Fantasy Premier League is the most popular fantasy football game in the world, which offers players the chance to battle it out with family, friends, and fellow managers around the globe. A football prediction game with managers picking a virtual squad composed of 15 real-life Premier League players. Those players accrue FPL points over a gruelling 38 Gameweek (GW) season that generally runs from August to May.

Millions of people have joined the fantasy football phenomenon, which started with games in the national press in the 1990's. Fantasy Premier League has since developed into the world's premium fantasy football online game. A totally exhilarating and addictive game which has been highly successful. Since its launch in 2002, FPL has become a magnet for football fans from across the globe, all bidding to become the top manager in the world. To highlight the game's global appeal, just take into consideration the top One Hundred FPL Managers over recent seasons. Remarkably, 35 different countries were represented by those top managers during the 2020/21 season and 33 countries in the following campaign. Players originate from each continent, including small islands like the Falkland Islands and Christmas Island. The game has grown exponentially and continues to evolve year-on-year. We cannot get enough of fantasy football.

FPL is a game of skill, patience, planning, dedication and self-discipline. A good management style, motivation, a sound temperament, and excelling at decision-making are all beneficial. They are all key attributes for becoming a successful FPL manager. You also need a slice of good fortune to help you on your way. Whether it be deflected goals, goal-line clearances, a fit squad, goals off the post, the woodwork saving you, or favourable VAR decisions. It's a game of fine margins. As an FPL manager, finding and adopting the right strategies is the key to unlocking the door to success. Strategies are a fundamental part of this utterly immersive and dynamic game. For many, FPL is a hobby. For others, it's a passion. The most committed players devote a considerable amount of their time in pursuit of perfection. In-between Gameweeks, many are frantically catching up with extended highlights, studying underlying statistics, listening to podcasts or reading FPL material. Being a football expert is not compulsory, but having some knowledge of the game is advantageous.

The beauty of the game is its unpredictability; not knowing what's around the corner. This makes the game so compelling. Regardless of whether you're a novice or seasoned campaigner, ranked 10m or in the top 10, everyone is prone to a poor Gameweek. No manager is immune to mediocre weeks and even the most diligent of FPL managers can have a shocker – the same fate applies. A game that offers both immense joy and profound sadness in a short space of time. You can experience the highs with some sublime Gameweeks, followed by the lows, which bring you back down to earth with a bump. One week you could break the 100-point barrier, swiftly followed by a week where you struggle to muster 30 points. Weekly, the game can produce huge fluctuations in rank; an exceptional Gameweek and a green arrow can see your rank soar dramatically. Conversely, an awful score and a red arrow can cause your rank to plummet. One minute you're riding the crest of a wave and the next, a period of adversity.

This pulsating game is full of drama and produces both magical and damaging moments each Gameweek. From celebrating your striker completing his hat-trick one moment and the next, your defender could be conceding a 95th minute 'clean sheet wipeout' at the opposite end of the pitch. For those not familiar with the expression, a wipeout occurs when a team concedes a goal and, as a result, the goalkeeper and each defender lose their four clean sheet bonus points. Experiencing a clean sheet wiped out right at the death is certainly demoralising. If you are unfortunate to own two defensive assets from the same team, it may be double the pain. It's also common to have two of your assets playing for opposing teams. This is when it gets tricky, particularly if one of your forwards is facing one of your defensive assets. You eagerly try to determine what would be the best outcome for your team. Sound familiar?

For FPL managers, there are few things more excruciating than the annual wait for the end of the summer recess and for a new season to commence. It's late June and, after a period of rest and recuperation, FPL fans re-ignite their enthusiasm for the beautiful game as a new season is on the horizon. Football pitches are looking pristine and FPL managers relish the start of the upcoming campaign. Rejuvenated and full of optimism, the most committed and highly motivated managers start to monitor any transfer activity or football gossip, relishing the prospect of another exciting season. One's enthusiasm for the beautiful game starts to grow for the new challenge ahead. Within weeks, the most popular sport in the world will once again be entertaining football fans worldwide. That includes excited FPL managers who eagerly await to put their skills to the test once again in their quest for glory.

The much-anticipated fixture schedule is released and the most devoted players have inevitably started to make a mental note of the teams and players to target for the opening set of fixtures. Player price reveals have been made and the day finally arrives. The game goes live and you are presented with a blank canvas; the chance to pick your ultimate 15-man squad. Countless enthusiasts starting equal but with the same goal in mind – to win the coveted title. The sole aim is to maximise your points potential to top mini-leagues and global rankings. Bragging rights are at stake. A new FPL season is upon us. The desire and passion to succeed and win the prestigious title reaches epic proportions. We can all hold on to those dreams:

"If you can dream it, you can do it." – Walt Disney

Over the following weeks, you merrily tinker away as the pre-season friendly games reveal endless clues for the season ahead. Pre-season provides managers with the ideal opportunity to assess any new signings, how teams line up, what formations are being adopted, and which players look sharp. The goal is to pack your team with players that are likely to start, possess goal threat, deliver assists, and have a favourable run of opening fixtures. After some serious deliberations, you're finally content with your 15-man squad and millions of others are waiting in anticipation for the Gameweek 1 deadline, which is nearly upon us. Avid FPL players are all set for another season on the rollercoaster ride that is Fantasy Premier League. Although the start of a new Premier League season is eagerly anticipated, no one knows how the season is going to begin, whether all your players will start – or be in-form – or which teams will hit the ground running. These are nervous times. As the season progresses, we find out if the hours of preparation have been worthwhile. How many template players do you own? Have you uncovered any hidden gems? Managed to make a promising start? The questions will soon be answered.

The Gameweek kicks-off and, as an FPL enthusiast, you cannot sit down in the comfort of your own home, bar or cafe and enjoy a game of Premier League football. These are anxious times as we become engrossed in the game. You're guaranteed to be on the edge of your seat as you watch the drama on the field unfold, urging your players to perform and deliver the substantial number of points that you crave. On top of your wish list is that your players produce goals, assists and clean sheets. They are all highly desirable and every point counts. We have a vested interest in every fixture and, undoubtedly, we all ask ourselves the same question before each match kicks off. Which players do we have playing in this game? Will they start? Will they complete 60 minutes? Who will net a points haul? Will our captain score? What players can damage our rank? Let the game begin.

This is a time to abandon your loyalty and, instead of focusing on your favourite team, you need to concentrate on your FPL assets. Even if it means they are on the opposing team. Your captain, Erling Haaland, is just about to pull the trigger in your favourite team's penalty box: do you want your defenders to tackle him or are you secretly hoping for a Haaland goal? The question is: what's more important to you, team loyalty or your FPL team? A dilemma that countless fans will encounter frequently. If we don't own any assets from our favourite club, we may want them to concede the odd goal to ensure a clean sheet wipeout, but still do enough to win the game. Undoubtedly, the drama of FPL is played out throughout many homes around the globe every week; a game that unites football fans and is unrivalled.

If none of your team feature in the televised game, there are further considerations. Firstly, the 'eye test'. You're on a scouting mission looking for potential new signings. Which players look in form? Are any hidden gems emerging? Managers will be making a mental note for their forthcoming team selections as they scout new talent. Then, for the sake of your rank, you are silently wishing for both teams to score to ensure a clean sheet wipeout. A goal not only secures a wipeout, but it also damages the chances of those players receiving extra bonus points based on their performance. If both teams manage to score, it is a huge relief for those not owning any of the defensive players involved. Additionally, it's a bonus if both teams only score the odd goal. A clean sheet wipeout is pleasing, but you don't want your rivals benefiting from more goals and assists. Needless to say, that one goal for both teams suffices!

Naturally, those managers who can't get to a television screen will have another device to hand in order to follow the live action while also having one eye on other match updates. Continually refreshing their screens at every conceivable moment to obtain details of the latest goal, goal scorer, assister, plus their latest points tally and rank. With the advent of social media, game updates are spontaneous. This allows the most eager of managers to dissect every goal or assist that is unfolding in front of them. As soon as the first whistle is blown and the Gameweek commences, the FPL community on Twitter is whipped up into a frenzy, as managers follow the live action. The conversation is not centered on the title or relegation battles, but instead, there is serious debate as to whether a goal should be allowed and, if so, who got the final touch and who got the assist. Every FPL point is fought for and precious. It could be the difference between winning your mini-league or not.

In-between deadlines, the most devoted managers are frantically tinkering away to ensure that they own the ultimate squad, a squad that will deliver them glory. There are a multitude of ways to aid preparation, analysing data, watching games and videos, listening to podcasts, reading FPL material, and interacting with fellow FPL players. Managing your virtual team provides you with the sensation of being out on the pitch and kicking every ball with your players. You experience both ends of the spectrum; the lows followed by the highs. One of your players is subbed off in the 59th minute while another collects a booking. Moments later, a few goals or assists for your team are accompanied by an adrenaline rush and your Gameweek is back on track. The most ardent FPL players will continually monitor their GW score, culminating in the despair of a red arrow or the joys of a green arrow.

It was an absolute pleasure to watch the drama unfold on the final day of the 2021/22 season. A number of major outcomes were still to be decided. Both Manchester City and Liverpool could win the Premier League title. Tottenham and Arsenal were fighting it out for the final Champions League spot, whilst Burnley and Leeds were battling for their Premier League status. One of the two had to be relegated to the Championship. The beauty of this day was the fact that all 10 games kicked off simultaneously and many were televised. Many fans indulged in an afternoon of football by monitoring multiple games via television and other devices. It was sheer joy as the goals started to fly in and the points started to accumulate. This provided the last opportunity to overhaul the leader of your mini-league or make a late surge for your desired rank.

All the drama of a normal Gameweek was present but crammed into a joyous 90 minutes of exciting football. Goals, assists, clean sheets, wipeouts, yellow cards, red cards and own goals. It was all there, an intense afternoon of scintillating football. It was a tense finish to another excellent season. Manchester City were stunned by Aston Villa as they fell two goals behind to The Villains at the Ethiad, whilst Liverpool stormed into a lead against Wolves. However, like true champions, City turned the game around with three goals in the space of five minutes. They went on to comfortably win the game 5-2 and were crowned champions for the fourth time in five seasons. In the two other crucial games, Burnley fell to a 2-1 defeat at home to the resurgent Newcastle Utd, whilst Leeds' Premier League status was in the balance until the 94th minute when a late goal ensured their safety for another season. During the second half of the games, all options were still unresolved. It was a day of despair and heartbreak or of joyous celebration as the season finally came to an end. Another memorable finale to a chaotic season.

FPL is an extremely competitive game and if you are fortunate enough to be crowned the world's number one, you receive the acclaim that you richly deserve. To be the top Fantasy Premier League Manager in the world is the ultimate accolade and a feat that we would all like to emulate. The most recent winner is Jamie Pigott from the United States who took the 2021/22 crown with a record points total of 2,844. Jamie went into GW38 just one point ahead of his nearest rival. It was a monumental achievement by Jamie, who received mass media exposure and the recognition that now comes with winning the coveted title. We can all carry that dream forward.

My research has not only focused on the Top One Hundred Managers from recent seasons, but I have also analysed a group of 'Elite' managers. These are exceptional managers who consistently climb to the top of the FPL pyramid. They possess all the key traits, have the ability to excel at the game, and have performed at the highest level throughout their FPL careers. I have had the privilege of communicating with six of the finest FPL managers in the world. Some great minds provide a fascinating insight into their game. You will learn about their career backgrounds, sources of information, the strategies that they have adopted to succeed, and they also offer some top advice. Their expertise will undoubtedly help to elevate your game and assist you in your quest for glory.

Managers continually chase the green arrows, which ensures a rise in rank and your mini-league standing. *Chasing Green Arrows* is an appropriate name for a book which is aimed at improving your game and helping you become a successful FPL manager. A succession of green arrows will propel your team towards the FPL summit. It's very satisfying and rewarding to collect a green arrow, seeing your overall rank improve and your team rocketing up your mini-leagues. Fantasy Premier League can be both exciting and disheartening, a game which plays on your emotions. It delivers both the highs and the lows. It is an emotional rollercoaster, so buckle up and enjoy the ride...

"You have to fight to reach your dream. You have to sacrifice and work hard for it." – Lionel Messi

Part 1: The Evolution of Fantasy Premier League

The Evolution of Fantasy Premier League

"The only one who can tell you 'you can't win' is you and you don't have to listen." – Jessica Ennis-Hill

The origins of fantasy football date back to 1963, when the game was first introduced in America. Will Wickenbach (part-owner of the American football team, the Oakland Raiders), Bill Tunnell (a Raiders PR man) and Scotty Stirling (a sports reporter for the Oakland Tribune) founded the Greater Oakland Professional Pigskin Prognosticators League (POPPPL). Initially, the game was made exclusively for Oakland Raiders affiliated members, but in 1969, the game was made available to everyone. Fantasy football was born... It wasn't until 1990 that fantasy football finally arrived in Europe when journalist, Riccardo Albini, developed the Fantacalcio (Italian Fantasy Football). A year later, fantasy football was officially introduced in the UK by Andrew Weinstein when he established 'Fantasy League Ltd'. In 1993, in association with Fantasy League Ltd, The Daily Telegraph became the first national daily newspaper to run a fantasy football competition. The game was launched in readiness for the 1993/94 season and it is still going strong today. Such was its success that, shortly afterwards, many of the tabloid press joined the fantasy football revolution. Fantasy football grabbed the public's imagination and it provided football fans with the opportunity to pitch their custom-built team against other fans' teams.

To highlight the game's development, initially the Gameweek deadline was set for Friday lunchtime. Managers either had to make their team selections and transfers by using a premium telephone number or via the postal service. At that time, an online game was purely a distant dream. The game exploded into life and was catapulted into the spotlight in the UK in 1994 when a new television programme took to our screens. Fantasy Football League, a football-based comedy programme hosted by comedians Frank Skinner and Daniel Baddiel, propelled fantasy football to a new level and its popularity soon grew with a cult following. The programme had been inspired by the fantasy football phenomenon, which had started several years earlier. Fantasy football was transformed in 1997 with the introduction of the first website devoted to the game. Initially, the American news channel CBS launched their website, which proved an instant success. Such was the interest, that it forced all the other major sports news companies in the Unites States to follow suit. Fantasy football finally made its online debut in the UK in 2002 when Fantasy Premier League was born.

In its inaugural season, FPL attracted just under 76k participants and since then, the game has grown exponentially, culminating in 9,167,407 players participating in the 2021/22 season. That number snowballed to 11.3m players during the 2022/23 season, a record number for a game which attracts a worldwide audience. The game continues to thrive and with the number of entrants increasing annually; the competition is fierce. The official FPL Twitter account also continues to grow and currently the site has 5.1m followers. During those early years, not many would have imagined that FPL would be so popular and go on to become the fantasy football phenomenon it is today. The rapid growth in this rollercoaster of a game is evidenced below and undoubtedly, those numbers will continue to grow for the foreseeable future.

Year	FPL Managers
2002	75k
2006	1.3 million
2008	1.9 million
2010	2.4 million
2013	3.2 million
2016	4.5 million
2017	5.2 million
2018	6.3 million
2019	7.6 million
2020	8.2 million
2021	9.1 million

The game has evolved since its inception and, although many fantasy football games still exist, it's Fantasy Premier League that captivates the audience. FPL is the King of Kings; it is the biggest fantasy football game in the world and nothing can compete with it. The game has been an enormous success, but why is it so popular and what is triggering its continual growth? The growth of FPL can probably be attributed to a number of factors. Firstly, the Premier League is a world-class product, which has huge global appeal, and the game has flourished over many years. It's a brand which is recognised on every continent and is engaging fans like never before. Games are easily accessible and can be viewed either by watching the matches live or via a highlights package. Increasing numbers are watching the games on offer, partly due to the success of FPL. The recruitment of the top-quality players that now grace the Premier League has made the game of football far more appealing to fans. The league is renowned for being a playground for many of the world's top players. With a large pool of high calibre players consistently displaying their incredible skills on pitches weekly, it's only natural that fans who love the beautiful game are going to be attracted by what's on offer.

The exhilarating football on offer, positive rule changes, accessibility and good marketing have all contributed to the game's success. The advent of the internet has made FPL more accessible and it is now readily available worldwide. It provides football fans with the opportunity to test their managerial skills against other aspiring football managers. What's also appealing is the fact that you can either create or join other mini-leagues which will enable you not only to compete with competitors worldwide, but also your family, friends, and work colleagues. Bragging rights are on offer.

A vast amount of money is invested in football. Finances from external sources are driving the game as clubs continue to invest heavily in building bigger and more powerful squads with greater depth than ever before. Televised games attract big investors and the revenue continues to strengthen the beautiful game. A combination of attractive football and an absorbing fantasy football game is a winning formula.

FANTASY PREMIER LEAGUE – CHASING GREEN ARROWS

The game's development can be clearly seen in the pricing structure and quality of players on offer in comparison to a decade ago. England goalkeeper Joe Hart was available at 7m. Today, a premium keeper can be bought for as little as 5.5m. FPL managers have a bigger pool of players to choose from. Hence, the pricing structure is more competitive. Some mouth-watering bargains can be picked up. Vincent Kompany was the highest priced defender at 7.5m, the same price point as Trent Alexander-Arnold is today, but you can't compare the two as FPL assets. The Liverpool defender is an FPL points magnet who frequently produces clean sheets, goals and assists, but the same couldn't have been said about Vincent Kompany. Just 28 goals and 8 assists in 265 appearances for Manchester City.

Since its inaugural season, the rules have been continually updated. While FPL was in its infancy, you could decide who your vice-captain would be based on price or form. If called upon, the player with the highest price or best form would become your captain. The term 'chip' was unheard of and the only feature in existence was a Wildcard, which could be used in January.

Planning for double Gameweeks and registering huge scores was just a distant dream. Double and blank GWs were infrequent and not targeted as they are today. The 2015/16 season heralded a new dawn with some major restructuring. It was intriguing to see three new chips being introduced simultaneously, which added an extra tactical element to the game. Chips transformed the way that we play the game and it's likely to have benefited the stronger performing managers.

The introduction of the All Out Attack, Bench Boost (BB) and Triple Captain (TC) chips were designed to enhance the game. They were a welcome addition to a player's armoury. The changes not only made the game more appealing, but they allowed fantasy managers to achieve unprecedented Gameweek scores. The added elements rewarded the stronger players as the points difference between the stronger and weaker performing players grew. An additional Wildcard was also made available. This allowed managers to activate one in each half of the season. The All Out Attack chip allowed you to field a 2-5-3 formation for one Gameweek. An ideal scenario for when your defenders faced a difficult fixture and your attacking assets a favourable game. However, the chip didn't last long and was replaced prior to the 2017/18 season by the Free Hit chip.

Bonus points have been an integral part of FPL since its launch in 2002. Initially, three bonus points were awarded by the Press Association to the player(s) who was adjudged to have made the most significant contribution to a game. The Actim Index Bonus was introduced prior to the 2005/06 season, although the index was compiled and distributed by PA Sport, a subsidiary of the Press Association. The Actim Index was the official player rating system of the Barclays Premiership, a system which used a complex mathematical formula. Three, two and one bonus points were awarded to players, although they were not allocated for several days afterwards. Eventually, that was reduced to 48 hours after the last match in that Gameweek.

Prior to the start of the 2007/08 season, the Press Association were re-instated and bonus points were awarded an hour after the last match on each game day. Ex-professional footballers fulfilled the role of analysts for the PA until the 2011/12 season when the EA Sports Player Performance Index was introduced. The new system remained in place for several seasons until the Opta Bonus Points System (BPS) was introduced, relying upon their own metrics. The BPS system has since been updated but has now remained unchanged since the 2015/16 season. The BPS allowed for greater transparency and made it easier to determine how bonus points are awarded.

With FPL continually evolving, players have become accustomed to game changes. The Covid pandemic caused the late completion of the 2019/20 season. Consequently, the start of the following campaign was delayed by a month and the first Wildcard deadline was brought forward to GW16. In an effort to combat the number of leaked team sheets on social media, the time of the Gameweek deadline was also changed. The one-hour GW deadline was extended to 90 minutes. However, since the change, the official FPL website has experienced technical glitches which have caused mayhem. Occasionally, late team leaks have been made available on social media. Accordingly, the website has been unable to cope with player demand and on occasions the site has crashed minutes before the GW deadline. Countless eager managers trying to react to the leaked information were unable to make transfers or change their captaincy options and were left disappointed. Many argue that the GW deadline should be timed to coincide with the kick-off of the first match. Besides the glitches, the official website continues to improve with ongoing development. For example, prior to the 2021/22 season commencing, live points/rank updates were made available shortly after each game. However, several alternative websites, including www.livefpl.net provide instant updates (points/rank/bonus points, etc.) as the action unfolds.

FPL is continually adapting to changing circumstances. For example, during the 2021/22 season there was a unique number of chips in operation. Such was the impact of the Covid pandemic that an extra Free Hit chip was made available to players to tackle the unprecedented number of fixture postponements. Undoubtedly, the extra chip contributed to the record number of points attained by the top team. Another example being the arrangements surrounding the 2022 World Cup in Qatar. Due to the staging of the competition during the winter months, the first Wildcard (WC1) deadline was brought forward to GW16. Furthermore, managers were provided with the opportunity to make an unlimited number of transfers during the World Cup break between Gameweeks 16-17. In effect, it was an additional Wildcard.

FPL has transformed the way people watch football. It's not merely watching an exciting game of football on a grass pitch. For FPL enthusiasts, it's an ultra-competitive and addictive game which draws your attention and demands your participation. Managers have high expectations of their FPL assets producing significant point hauls. Therefore, each GW is eagerly anticipated. In all likelihood, many fans have been attracted to the game of football purely because of fantasy football. There is no big cash prize on offer, yet people partake because it's a combination of watching quality football while also relishing the gripping fantasy game. Besides enjoying the beautiful game, players strive to become a successful FPL manager. Their goal is to top mini-leagues, climb the global rankings and the pinnacle would be winning the coveted title. The game is also very popular amongst many current or past Premier League footballers.

Regardless of what football team you support, team loyalty goes out of the window. The focus is on your FPL team performing and producing the green arrows to propel you to the top. Managers strive to continually improve their overall performance by investing a great deal of their time in the game. They endeavour to become more knowledgeable at every opportunity and a better player for it. The desire for people to succeed has fuelled a sharp increase in the number of content creators to appease the appetite of FPL players. A vast array of information is now available via many different mediums. FPL is already very competitive, but the information on offer is driving the game to a completely new level. Hence the record scores that have recently been achieved.

FPL is unrecognisable in comparison to its launch when the amount of information available to assist players was limited. The emergence of Podcasts, YouTube channels, blogs and written material can all be absorbed by the most committed managers. FPL players also have information and advice at their disposal via social media, a medium which has had a huge impact on accessibility to all the essential information that we crave. There are thriving FPL communities on Twitter, Reddit, etc. where all the talk is FPL. In preparation for a Gameweek, many managers will interact on social media, watch match highlights and conduct thorough research. Useful information that you need to enhance your game can be found on dedicated FPL websites like Fantasy Football Scout, Fantasy Football Hub, Fantasy Football Fix and Fantasy Premier Tools. Websites are a valuable source of information which can aid your performance. Articles, in-depth analysis, fixture tickers, Opta statistics and predicted points, etc. are in plentiful supply; all designed to assist players of differing abilities. Several other websites, like FPL Review, FPL Gameweek and FPL Optimized, also offer informative FPL material, while FBref and Understat produce every conceivable football statistic imaginable. There is an abundance of data to aid managers in their decision-making process. These are all relevant factors which could be driving growth.

Besides playing the game for enjoyment, the primary aim at the start of each season is to win the prestigious FPL title. That is the ultimate achievement and dream of the vast majority, but how do we judge success? Until recently, many regarded a top 10k finish as their ultimate goal. Traditionally, it's been the benchmark to signify an outstanding campaign. If you were fortunate enough to reach those dizzy heights, a top 10k finish was regarded as the pinnacle of many a career. It ensured an iconic badge of honour. With the game's popularity continuing to grow and the competition fierce, you could question whether the new barometer for success should be the top 50k? That figure would be the equivalent of finishing inside the top 10k a decade ago when the number of competitors was just 2-3 million. In today's game, a top 50k rank should be regarded as an outstanding achievement.

With over 11m players, it's reasonable to conclude that the 10k benchmark is outdated. Achieving such a rank has gradually become more difficult year-on-year. You could even argue that a percentage-based model is far more appropriate. For example, if you achieved a top 10k finish in 2002, you were in the top 14% of players. That figure has gradually reduced to 7.69% in 2006, 2.2% in 2016 and 1.22% in 2020. Today, finishing in the top 113k would produce a top 1% finish. With the spiralling number of participants, the advent of content creators and the abundance of FPL information readily available, the game is ultra-competitive. Players are becoming more engaged. Consequently, the gap between ardent and 'casual' players has diminished. Undoubtedly, a higher percentage of players are more knowledgeable, which makes a top finish far more arduous. In all likelihood, retention rates are also on the increase. Whereas there was a tendency for many teams to fall by the wayside as the season progressed, more teams are now completing the season in its entirety.

FPL is continually evolving and at the start of the 2022/23 campaign, the game was given a slot on Sky Sports News. Not only did the slot provide expert guidance from pundits, but it's now common to see FPL data being made readily available on TV screens. The channel has a huge global audience, so such initiatives will continue to drive the game to a new level. Fantasy Premier League has changed significantly since its inception. A game that was once dominated by casual managers playing purely for enjoyment is now an extremely competitive juggernaut with some highly knowledgeable players. Managers who know the tricks of the trade watch the majority of games, study the underlying statistics and absorb as much FPL content as possible. If you are fortunate to achieve a top 10k finish today, it is a remarkable accomplishment. The product on offer, plus extended worldwide coverage, will ensure that the fantasy football phenomenon will continue to thrive for the foreseeable future.

Part 2: Preparing For A New Season

Selecting Your Initial Draft

"If you fail to prepare, you're prepared to fail." – Mark
Spitz

It's mid-June and a new season dawns. Football kicks into life with the release of the new Premier League fixture schedule. Precisely a month has elapsed since the champions were crowned, but for the most committed of FPL players, it's time to go again. We all look forward to the new campaign with refreshed optimism. Selecting your initial draft is one of the most important tasks facing FPL managers. To succeed, it's crucial to make a sound start and build a solid foundation. Within weeks of the fixture schedule being released, the official FPL website springs back into life. A multitude of managers are ready to pounce as soon as the site goes live. Their goal is to obtain a low ID number and there is a benefit to this madness.

In this section, we will discuss topics which will assist you when building your ultimate 15-man squad. The tips can also be read in conjunction with the numerous factors discussed under Transfer Strategy in Part 6 of the book. The advice provided is applicable to your initial squad selection, on activating your Wildcard, or conducting transfer activity. Many managers will have a picture in their mind of the ideal team for Gameweek 1. A team that features players who have been deemed as 'essential' over the summer months. High-scoring attack-minded defenders, standout midfield playmakers, forwards that can consistently score goals or 'Premium' assets who have the potential to deliver major point hauls are all on the wish list. When building your optimum fantasy team, there are many constraints which need to be considered. For example, rules, budget restraints and formation restrictions. With a restricted budget, it's highly likely that you will have to make sacrifices when trying to build your optimum squad.

Low ID

Once a season concludes, it's highly likely that you will share the same number of points as countless other managers. To prioritise rank, FPL considers certain factors when determining a team's finishing position. In addition to their points tally, the total number of transfers made by each team is important. In the event of a points tie, the player who made the fewest transfers, will get the higher rank. If teams are still level, then their ID acts as a tie-break for your final mini-league standing or for prizes. When registering at the start of each season, your team is allocated a unique ID which can be found in the URL at the top of your points page on the FPL website. This number changes each season. Having a low ID is advantageous and improves your chances of winning a mini-league in the event of a tie-break. If multiple managers finish at the top of their mini-league, have an equal number of points and transfers made, then the manager deemed to be the overall winner will be the player with the lower ID.

Rule Changes

Having registered your team, the first thing to consider is rule changes. Familiarise yourself with any changes since the conclusion of the preceding season as they could have an impact on the way you select your initial squad.

Research: O'Brien et al. (2021)

In relevant parts of this book, I will refer to an interesting piece of research conducted by O'Brien et al. (2021). The article considers the amount of skill that is involved in playing FPL. Their researched article is entitled 'Identification of skill in an online game: The case of Fantasy Premier League'. They question whether an individual's performance (FPL managers) is a consequence of skill or luck. They explored this question through the analysis of a large dataset of approximately one million FPL managers. The authors analysed the historical performance of managers in terms of where they had ranked in the competition alongside their points totals in multiple seasons, in some cases over a time interval of up to 13 years. This was their finding:

"We find a consistent level of correlation between managers' performances over seasons, suggesting a persistent level of skill over an extended temporal scale."

The research suggests that the top managers not only outperformed those in other tiers in specific Gameweeks but consistently throughout the season. The top managers performed very strongly, suggesting a high level of preparation in building their squads prior to the start of the season. It is suggested that the top managers have built a well-prepared team in order to take advantage of the underlying fixtures. It is clear from the research that the top managers have demonstrated these skills when preparing and building their squads for the start of the season. Therefore, the research emphasises the importance of pre-season preparation and building your ultimate squad.

Point Magnets

The aim of FPL is to accumulate as many points as possible throughout a challenging season. Points are scored for a player's performance, which includes minutes played, goals, assists, clean sheets, save points plus bonus points. The game revolves around scoring points, so that should be at the forefront of your mind when selecting your initial squad, a group of players to deliver you optimum points. Your goal is to assemble an initial squad that includes players who are point magnets, or those with attacking potential in abundance. Explosive players that have great attacking prowess and are likely to score points regularly. A goalkeeper that will keep clean sheets whilst collecting save and bonus points. Attack-minded defenders who will secure clean sheets whilst chipping in with goals and assists, while your midfield needs to be packed with creative playmakers who will generate attacking returns frequently. In addition, pinpointing the standout forwards who will consistently deliver you goals. Therefore, selecting your initial squad and conducting wise transfers throughout the campaign is a crucial part of the game. Focus on in-form players with favourable fixtures who are likely to produce attacking or defensive returns.

Bonus Points

Bonus points are a key ingredient of the scoring system, yet they are widely overlooked by many FPL managers. They provide a great opportunity for getting an edge over your rivals. Bonus points are devised and allocated post-match according to a Bonus Points System (BPS). The BPS utilises a range of statistics supplied by Opta that capture actions on the pitch to create a performance score for every player. The players with the top three BPS in a given match receive bonus points - three points to the highest-scoring player, two to the second best and one to the third. Bonus points are a factor to consider when you are trying to identify point magnets. For example, during the 2021/22 campaign, Kevin De-Bruyne collected 33 bonus points and Trent Alexander-Arnold 32 points.

Team Structure & Formation

Selecting your first draft is the equivalent of a child going into a candy store. You are spoilt for choice. Hundreds of quality players to choose from and a 100m budget available. You need a team structure in place which will enable you to build a strong, balanced squad to take you forward. A team structure refers to the organisation of a team relative to positions and prices. Maintaining a structured squad throughout the season is an important aspect which should give you long-term stability. The aim is to have a structure which will enable you to easily transition between players. A practical approach is to distribute funds equally throughout your team and to select players at various price points in each position. Adopting this strategy will give you more flexibility, and make your future transfer activity more effective, by enabling you to move easily between different players at similar price points. This tactic should also help to eradicate the need to take any unnecessary hits to facilitate the transfer of your main target.

For example, if you own a 7.5m mid-priced forward like Ollie Watkins, you could easily select a replacement from a wide variety of players with a similar price point in a single transfer. It will also allow you to move quickly for those standout performers during the early weeks. Distributing your funds in each position will also ensure that your team will consistently accumulate points. For example, investing an excessive amount of funds in defence, or in forwards, could backfire spectacularly. If players in those positions are struggling to produce points, it could damage your performance.

No two FPL seasons are the same, so you will need to adapt to the changing circumstances. Traditionally, attacking assets have been the dominant force. However, recently, attack-minded defenders have been prominent. A practical approach is to establish which formation was the most successful during the preceding season. It's a factor to consider when selecting your preferred formation, although your formation can be continually updated as the season evolves. Targeting those players who are producing a significant number of points is essential. Any formation can be chosen, provided your line-up includes one goalkeeper, a minimum of three defenders, two midfielders and one forward. With the game set up to reward attacking assets, it seems logical to target more attack-minded players and either play a 3-4-3 or a 3-5-2 formation. Typically, 3-4-3 has been the favoured formation and it should provide optimal performance. A survey confirmed that a 3-5-2 powerful midfield option was the second preferred formation and playing five in defence was the least favoured formation. However, the recent emergence of attack-minded defenders has provided managers with an alternative option.

During the 2021/22 season, forwards tended to struggle, while attack-minded defenders excelled. A 5-4-1 and 4-5-1 both became prominent formations, although forwards made a resurgence the following season. Generally, attacking defenders are priced more favourably in comparison to midfielders or forwards despite similar points potential. Prioritising in-form, dynamic, attack-minded players from the most productive position will enhance your points potential. Research conducted by Fantasy Football Fix found that the favoured formation during the 2020/21 season was 3-4-3. Of the Top 50 managers, 47.4% preferred this formation. However, that figure decreased to 25.2% the following season. A 4-4-2 formation was a close second, with 23.7%. This percentage was higher though in both the All Time Top 50 (32.2%) and All FPL User groups (39.3%). A 4-5-1 formation accounted for 9.8% in the All Time Top 50 group and a 3-5-2 accounted for 20.2% of team selections.

It's imperative that you start a new campaign strongly. Therefore, selecting many 'template' players is the safest option. Typically, the most popular players will be destined for the template team. Taking a calculated gamble by selecting many differential players early in the season could severely dent your chances of success. It's a time when risks need to be negated. When selecting your initial draft, target explosive impact players with a 'high ceiling'. Players who are likely to accumulate point hauls and a hefty points tally. The addition of several big-hitters will ensure that you're in a strong position to tackle the Gameweeks head on. Another priority is to identify the quality assets who are likely to contribute points consistently. The 2021/22 'Team of Kings', comprising the highest scoring players in each position, with their points tally, is featured below. Alisson was the standout keeper with 176 points, a back four consisting of Alexander-Arnold (208), Cancelo (201), Robertson (186) and Van Dijk (183). The midfield comprised Salah (265), Son (258), Bowen (206), De Bruyne (196) and Mané (183). With five midfielders scoring the bulk of the points, Harry Kane was the solitary forward who made the team with 192 points. It's impossible to manage the perfect team, but if you can accommodate three or four key assets, it will give you a platform to build on.

At the conclusion of the 2020/21 season, 11 out of the top 12 point scorers were either midfielders or forwards. The only exception being Emi Martinez, who had an outstanding season in goal for Aston Villa. In contrast, the following season had an interesting and unexpected outcome. The top 20 points scorers comprised one goalkeeper, six defenders, eleven midfielders and just two forwards. Once again, midfield was the dominant position, with three players exceeding 200 points, five exceeding 170 and a further six surpassing 150 points. A new pattern emerged, as the second-best performing position was defender. Two exceeded 200 points, three accumulated over 170, and a further two exceeded 150 points. The emergence of attack-minded defenders is changing the landscape. Just one keeper exceeded 170 points and two surpassed the 150 mark.

Traditionally, forwards have been reliable, but on this occasion, they were the least effective. Just two featured amongst the top 20 point scorers. Harry Kane finished in 17th place with 192 points, while Cristiano Ronaldo was in 19th position with 159 points. Numerous forwards were either plagued by injuries or misfiring. Consequently, underperforming players were abandoned by many managers who reinvested in other positions. Notably, many flocked to the premium defensive assets; 'big at the back' became very popular and owners were rewarded handsomely. As the season evolves, be flexible and adapt to the optimal formation.

Selection Method

Managers are likely to approach their initial squad selection differently. My first aim would be to include those players who I'm 100% committed to having in my team, barring injuries, etc. Initially, I would aim to include a premium asset in each outfield position. For example, Erling Haaland, Mo Salah and Trent Alexander-Arnold would be the first names included. I would then build the remainder of the squad around its nucleus. You may want to identify long-term holds and those players with short-term potential before their fixtures become challenging. Aim to include several cheap enablers which will release funds for you to invest in more desirable assets, players who will strengthen your team in other areas. An enabler is mainly employed to occupy one of your bench slots, but can be used in an emergency. Therefore, identifying an active player is a bonus.

Having selected your key players and enablers, you can then proceed to finalise your squad by selecting players at different price points in each position. Being flexible allows for easier transition between players. You may find it beneficial to focus on your forwards and then work backwards to your keeper, trying to spread funds evenly in the process. Traditionally, midfielders and forwards have been the top points scorers, hence it's likely that you will invest more in these positions. Your goal is to identify those explosive players who are consistent performers. Furthermore, players that excelled towards the end of the previous season, or during pre-season, offer good value.

Positions

Goalkeepers (GKP)

The majority of managers do not invest heavily in their goalkeepers. Typically, they are the least effective and do not generate the same points per million in comparison to other positions. They have the lowest points ceiling, although Emi Martinez was an exception during the 2020/21 season. Occasionally, cheap gems do emerge and Martinez fell into that category. Generally, they are keepers who are experiencing Premier League football for the first time and are initially valued at 4.5m. Martinez's value had rocketed to 5.3m, plus his ownership had soared to 37.9% by the end of the campaign. He accumulated the seventh highest points tally of all players and he was comfortably the top performing keeper. He amassed 186 points, made 142 saves and collected 27 bonus points in the process. If you owned Martinez from the outset, he was gold.

Utilising one of your valuable free transfers to recruit a GKP is not a popular tactic. Many consider that the transfer could be put to better effect in recruiting a more productive asset. A player who will generate extra points. The odd goal or assist has been registered by Alisson and Sá but attacking returns are rare. The bulk of their points will be generated from keeping clean sheets, save and bonus points. Therefore, the obvious targets are those who are likely to keep plenty of clean sheets while also racking up their fair share of saves. The more saves that a keeper makes, the greater likelihood of bonus points. Managers are also reluctant to take a hit on a keeper. Occasionally, players are confronted with this predicament, their starting GKP becomes unavailable for an unforeseen reason and their backup keeper is a non-starter. Selecting an inactive reserve is always a gamble. Some managers may have already used their free transfer and they suddenly realise that they have no keeper for that GW. However, many do not see replacing a keeper as a viable option and will decide not to incur a points' deduction for a replacement. They would prefer going into the Gameweek with just 10 players. Managers can also get caught

31

out towards the latter end of the season. It has become fashionable for Premier League managers to rest their starting keeper, so it's reassuring to have a playing reserve when your budget allows. Many teams deploy a league and a cup keeper.

The preference is to have a set-and-forget keeper, a player who will be a permanent fixture in your team unless there are unforeseen circumstances, such as a long-term injury. The most common combination is a 4.5m keeper coupled with a 4m non-playing reserve. Selecting two keepers with a combined value of 8.5m will enable you to invest extra funds in quality assets who are likely to be more productive throughout the season. It's fine selecting a 4m budget backup provided your main keeper is a regular starter, injury free and is not prone to rotation. It's unlikely that your 4m reserve keeper will be a regular starter, although Leicester's Danny Ward was an exception during the 2022/23 season. Occasionally, a 5m keeper may be preferred to a 4.5 keeper.

Others prefer to select two cheap/mid-priced playing keepers whom they will alternate throughout the season depending upon fixtures, form and who is playing at home, etc. If you do opt for rotating keepers or defenders, you will generally find two teams with good alternating fixtures by studying the fixture schedule in advance. An investment of between 9-9.5m should be ample funds to provide you with two active keepers who you could rotate. However, there is a downside. Selecting rotating keepers is advantageous, but it can give you a selection headache. Which player do you start and who do you leave on the bench? You will be kicking yourself in those weeks when you don't get your selection spot on.

Although they carry a hefty price tag, a minority of managers will select a premium option like Ederson or Alisson. The stronger defensive teams have a propensity for registering more clean sheets and it's common to see premium keepers finishing amongst the top scoring keepers. However, if they play for a strong defensive side, it's likely that they will produce fewer saves. There is a tendency for several budget keepers from weaker teams to accumulate more save and bonus points. This can offset the clean sheet points registered by the premium keepers. It is not uncommon to see several budget keepers out-score their more expensive counterparts. To enhance their appeal, the price for premium keepers was reduced from 6m to 5.5m at the start of the 2022/23 campaign. Accordingly, they have become an attractive proposition and their ownership has increased. An alternative option is to select a premium and a non-playing budget keeper, which will cost you 9.5m. Selecting a premium keeper in your initial draft is an expensive option. When funds are limited, investing in more productive areas may prove beneficial. As the season evolves and your team value increases, you could then reconsider a premium option.

Alisson had an exceptional 2021/22 season and was the top performing goalkeeper. He accumulated 176 points and finished as the 13th highest points scorer. Hugo Lloris finished in a respectable 21st with 158 points and Ederson in 22nd with 155 points. With limited funds, the most popular and sensible move is to identify a good 4.5m keeper that is likely to keep clean sheets and accumulate save points. Being prudent with your keepers will allow you to invest more wisely in more dynamic players. Combining a 4.5m keeper with a 4m reserve from the same team would be my preferred option. In the event of your first-choice keeper being unavailable, your backup will automatically step in. The unexpected price changes may tempt you to upgrade your starting keeper.

Defenders (DEF)

FPL has evolved and one notable aspect is the emergence of attacking defenders; players who offer a great opportunity to enhance your points total. Instead of their primary objective of stopping the opposing team scoring, many defenders are now given licence to raid forward and join in the attacks. Goals, assists and points hauls have become common for marauding attack-minded defenders. They can combine attacking returns with clean sheet bonus points to make them a potent force. Players like Trent

Alexander-Arnold (TAA) have changed the FPL landscape. They have multiple routes to return and can make a huge impression at both ends of the pitch.

Recently, it has become fashionable to deploy attack-minded defenders. They offer a new dimension and are a welcome addition to the game. They are an attractive proposition and in all likelihood they will outscore the majority of other defenders due to their attacking returns. Some attack-minded defenders may also have a higher ceiling than some similarly priced midfielders and forwards. Seven of the top eight point-scoring defenders for the 2020/21 season were attack-minded. These included Andy Robertson and TAA. The only non-attacking defender was Ruben Dias, who happened to play for the best defensive team in the league. Wing-backs offer multiple routes to return and are a great resource for both defensive and attacking points. Budget allowing, I would recommend targeting players who fulfil this role as they offer attacking potential in abundance and they will maximise your points potential.

The 2021/22 campaign re-emphasised just how many standout attacking defenders currently grace the game. Four of the top 10 highest points scorers for the season were defenders. A feat that wouldn't have been imagined possible in previous campaigns. TAA's remarkable 208 points ensured that he finished in third position overall. His ability to deliver huge point hauls will find him deployed in numerous teams. João Cancelo was fifth with an impressive 201 points, Andrew Robertson eighth on 186 points and Virgil van Dijk ninth on 183 points. Two further defenders were in the top 20. Joel Matip finished in 15th position with 170 points and Aymeric Laporte in 18th with 160 points. Considering that only two forwards featured amongst the list and attack-minded defenders were consistently delivering points, investing in a strong defence was the preferred option for many. This was in complete contrast to the previous season when the list of the top 12 point scorers was devoid of defenders. Similarly, only TAA featured in the top 10 for the 2019/20 season.

Liverpool and Manchester City possessed the best two defences in the Premier League during the 2021/22 campaign and this was reflected in FPL. The top six defenders all came from those clubs. Liverpool players occupied four of the top five places thanks to their returns at both ends of the pitch. The Reds kept an astonishing 21 clean sheets whilst TAA produced eight double-digit hauls. Between them, the four defenders produced 11 goals, 29 assists and an incredible 88 bonus points. Three defenders made the top 10 for the number of assists, TAA contributed 12, whilst Andy Robertson and João Cancelo registered 11 assists. TAA also had the highest number of chances for defenders (90) with Andy Robertson in a distant second with 55 chances.

Recently, the most expensive defender in the game has been TAA at 7.5m. At the other extreme, active defenders like Neco Williams and Nathan Patterson were available at just 4m. A wise approach is to aim for a player from both extremes and fill the other three defensive slots with players priced between 4.5m and 7m. A budget of 25m-27m should be adequate when purchasing your five-man defence. Traditionally, managers invested heavily in midfielders and forwards purely for their attacking returns, but now attack-minded defenders are a viable option. In addition to their potential for keeping clean sheets, their ability to provide attacking returns has heightened their appeal. Being prudent by investing extra funds in those players in the most productive positions is a sensible approach. Hence, the need to be flexible and adapt to the situation.

Midfielders (MID)

Midfielders can be regarded as the *crème de la crème* of FPL, and selecting a premium midfielder is paramount. They have a knack of being the most productive assets and regularly dominate the list of highest points scorers in the game. Attacking midfielders are the playmakers that have the most potential to score major points hauls and a significant points tally. Additionally, many play as part of a front three or as a 'false 9'. Prior to the arrival of Erling Haaland, Manchester City regularly deployed this tactic. The obvious advantage that midfielders have is the fact they score five points per goal, as opposed to four for a forward. Additionally, they are awarded an extra point if their team registers a clean sheet. To demonstrate their dominance, the top points scorers for the past five seasons have all been midfielders.

Season	Player	Points
2017-18	Mo Salah	303
2018-19	Mo Salah	259
2019-20	Kevin De Bruyne	251
2020-21	Bruno Fernandes	244
2021-22	Mo Salah	265

To reinforce their FPL supremacy, three midfielders registered the highest number of double-digit hauls during the 2021/22 season. Heung-Min Son amassed 11 double-digit hauls, Mo Salah 10 and Jarrod Bowen 9. Midfielders also featured heavily in the top 10 for the number of assists. Jarrod Bowen capped an excellent season to finish top with 17 assists, Mo Salah created 14, while Harvey Barnes was joint-third, registering 12. Mason Mount and James Maddison both recorded 11 assists. Unsurprisingly, Mo Salah with 37 and Heung-Min Son with 33 recorded the highest number of goal involvements.

Typically, prices for midfielders vary between 13m for a premium asset like Mo Salah to 4.5m for a cheap enabler like Fulham's Andreas Pereira. Selecting midfielders at various price points will allow you to be more flexible. It's not uncommon to see teams with two premium midfield assets. Spending between 37-39m should be sufficient to field a competitive midfield. Mo Salah is a gifted player and an FPL legend. He consistently produces attacking returns and in the 2021/22 season he boasted the greatest goal threat of any player. His 139 shots, 113 shots in the box, 37 big chances and 55 shots on target were all league-leading totals. Depending upon your preferred option, there are several formations you can deploy to optimise your midfield. My preferred formation is a 3-4-3 or a 3-5-2. They enable you to maximise your points potential by targeting high-scoring, in-form midfield players. Alternatively, you could consider a 4-4-2 formation.

Defensive Midfielders

Selecting a defensive midfielder is a sub-optimal strategy and it should be avoided. Traditionally, they are not point magnets. Defensively minded, they play in a system for a specific purpose and it's unusual to see them marauding forward and creating chances or scoring goals. The very nature of their role generally restricts their effectiveness and the opportunity to generate attacking returns is limited. They are more likely to pick up a bonus point for keeping a clean sheet rather than an attacking return. Unfortunately, they are not rewarded for their defensive ability. For example, by the number of tackles or interceptions made during a game. Therefore, they are not desirable assets, although a regular penalty taker or cheap enabler could be a viable option. However, in all likelihood you, will find better alternatives.

Forwards (FWD)

Owning a proven premium forward is desirable as they are capable of producing a significant points tally. However, the 2021/22 season was an exception to the rule, with the forward position being decimated by a spate of injuries. A mediocre start by Harry Kane was eventually ignited during the second half of the season, when he regained his shooting accuracy and rediscovered his form. His strong finish ensured that he accumulated 192 points to become the top-scoring forward. His nine double-digit hauls were joint third. While his 11 assists ensured he featured as one of the most creative players. The addition of quality players like Erling Haaland, Alexander Isak and Darwin Núñez at the start of the 2022/23 season attracted a lot of interest from FPL players. They became very popular. Premium forwards are usually priced at 11.5m and the cheapest at 4.5m. It's very unlikely that a budget forward will become a regular starter. However, players at this price point do come off the bench to score points. For example, during the 2021/22 season, Joe Gelhardt played 733 minutes for Leeds Utd.

Owning one premium forward provides you with a balanced team. However, it's not uncommon for some to deploy two. An investment of 27-29m should adequately equip you with a fully functional and relatively strong front three. The inclusion of an enabler could save you money and an investment of 24-25m would be sufficient. Those extra funds could be distributed elsewhere. I would aim to include one premium forward, a mid-priced forward and a cheap enabler in my initial draft and reassess as the season evolves. If many of the forwards deliver a significant number of points, then a combination of a premium and two mid-priced forwards would be a great option. The arrival of Erling Haaland provided managers with the opportunity to go with a double premium forward option and a double up of Haaland and Kane became popular.

General Principles

As you strive to build your ultimate 15-man squad to help you succeed, you may find some of the following relevant factors beneficial in helping you to achieve that aim.

Bench

Your substitutes provide cover for unforeseen events, replacing players initially selected in your starting XI who do not feature during the Gameweek. When funds are limited at the start of the season, keeping your bench investment to a minimum is a wise move. This will enable you to field your strongest possible XI. The best bench strategy is discussed extensively in Part 5 of the book.

Balanced Approach

When assessing which players to select in your initial draft or what transfers to make, don't be blinkered. Maintain a balanced approach and consider both the positive and negative aspects of each player under consideration. Review the reasons why they should or should not be included in your squad. Considering both the pros and cons will improve your decision-making process and should lead to quality selections. The player may have a poor disciplinary record, be carrying a niggling injury, have a favourable run of fixtures, or is in good form. All are relevant factors, so weigh up both the positives and negatives before finalising your move.

Rotating Players

One tactic which could bear fruit is rotating a couple of your players. This has become a common practice, particularly for defenders and goalkeepers who have good alternating fixtures. This is a popular approach, which can be an effective way of managing your team by saving you valuable transfers. Studying the fixture schedule will enable you to identify players or teams who have a favourable run of alternating fixtures between them. When deciding which player to start, you can consider their fixture difficulty, home/away fixture and form. Generally, it's more likely for a team to keep a clean sheet at home than on the road. You should seek out value pairings that offer the best potential for both clean sheets and attacking returns. For example, the following scenario would be ideal. Player A has great fixtures in Gameweeks 1, 3, and 6, whilst Player B has favourable fixtures in GWs 2, 4 and 5.

Premium Assets

Due to budget restraints, it's impossible to construct the perfect FPL team. You cannot own all of your preferred targets. The number of big-hitters that you can accommodate in your squad will also be limited. Hence, the need to prioritise. Premium assets are premium for a reason. They consistently deliver a high level of performance, they have a propensity for producing significant hauls and a substantial points tally each season. Initially, the maximum number of premium assets that you will be able to afford in a balanced team is usually two or three. Some are also likely to be on set pieces and penalties for their respective clubs, which is a hugely influential factor. It's advantageous to select a premium asset in each outfield position. For example, TAA in defence, Mo Salah in midfield and Erling Haaland as your forward. This will also allow you greater flexibility when making transfers. Over-investing in premium assets at the start of a campaign will generally mean that you have to make sacrifices in other areas of your team. Consequently, the likelihood is that you will manage an unbalanced team. Building team value is an important strategy. As the season progresses, and your team value increases, your spending power becomes greater. The extra funds will allow you to strengthen your squad and an additional premium asset could be an option.

Regular Starters

An important strategy is to identify those players who are likely to be regular starters for their clubs. Players who are either guaranteed/nailed on to start unless they are injured or suspended. Discovering that several of your squad are struggling for game time is undesirable. A player's lack of minutes could harm your points potential and affect your rank. Unless you have an active bench, the same would apply to those players who are likely to be a rotation risk. Monitoring pre-season games will enable you to pinpoint which players are in or out of favour and likely to be regular starters. Analyse statistics to see who is performing or not performing. In your deliberations, you can also consider the team that they play for, their involvement in cup competitions and whether the player is a rotation risk or not.

Penalty & Set Piece Takers

Penalty and set-piece takers are FPL gold and should definitely be in your thoughts when formulating your first draft. They are point magnets with a huge potential to collect regular hauls. Recently, such players have featured heavily amongst the top FPL point scorers. For example, Bruno Fernandes, Mohamed Salah, Harry Kane and Kevin De Bruyne. By targeting those players on set-pieces and penalties, it's highly likely that your team's points tally will be boosted significantly. Generally, they generate more goals, assists and bonus points than the majority of players and it should be an influential factor in your selection process.

Risk

When selecting multiple players from the same team, consider the element of risk. Occasions do arise where you could be tempted to own several players from the same team. If they have favourable fixtures, that's all well and good. However, if, for example, you own several assets from an underperforming team who are due to face several of the top sides in their forthcoming fixtures, it may prove costly. It is a risky strategy and sharing the risk can be beneficial. There is the option to bench one of the players. However, doubling or tripling up on players could still have an adverse effect on your GW score if it's unsuccessful. The risk is considerably greater if those players are a combination of a keeper and a defender(s) and their opponents are a top performing team. Just a single goal could dent your GW score and rank. If you double up on a top defensive team like Manchester City, then the risk is reduced significantly, although they are still liable to concede goals.

Conversely, there are occasions when selecting multiple players from a club can be profitable. For example, selecting three Manchester City players who are due to face a struggling team who regularly concede and have a poor goal scoring record. Assess each team and fixture on its merits. Ideally, a favourable run of fixtures over a 4-6 period reduces the risk significantly and could be advantageous. Reducing the element of risk, particularly in defence, is likely to significantly lessen the likelihood of a poor Gameweek score and a nosedive in rank.

Out of Position Players (OOP)

One way of optimising your potential returns is to identify those players that are playing out of position (OOP). For example, they may be registered by FPL in one position, but in reality, they are playing for their clubs in a different position. Having 'defenders' who play in midfield is gold. Typically, there is a huge difference between a defender and a midfielder. A midfielder plays in a more advanced position and is more likely to collect attacking returns. Crucially, being classified as a defender will enable them to collect clean sheet points if their team shuts out the opposition. It's a win-win situation. Examples of exceptional OOP players from recent seasons include John Lundstram at Sheffield Utd and Stuart Dallas of Leeds. Both were classified as defenders, nevertheless, both played in midfield.

During the 2019/20 season, John Lundstram amassed 142 points, which included five goals and five assists. A ridiculous number of points, when you consider that he was registered as a 4m defender when, in fact, he was an all-action midfielder. He became such an FPL legend that he was unofficially christened 'Lord Lundstram'.

The following season, another hero emerged. Although Stuart Dallas was registered as a defender, he played every game in midfield. His contribution consisted of eight goals, three assists, 12 clean sheets and he also collected 15 bonus points along the way. Remarkably, he was the top scoring defender in FPL with 171 points and only nine other players bettered his score.

Injury-Prone Players

It's advisable to consider a player's injury record during your decision-making process. Injury-prone players should be avoided as your team's performance will suffer if they are constantly in the treatment room. Their minutes will be limited and it's unlikely that they will deliver the points that you crave. When creating your initial draft, and as the season develops, your player selection should be an in-form player who has no history of injury problems, and is a regular starter. I would recommend following Ben Dinnery (@BenDinnery) on Twitter. Ben is an injury analyst who summarises all the latest injury news, which is invaluable when selecting your team. A great source of vital information to aid you in your decision-making. Such information will enable you to plan effectively. Furthermore, it could also save you an unnecessary transfer.

Discipline

A player's discipline record is equally important and assets who have a habit of collecting cards should be avoided. A yellow card carries a one-point deduction, whilst a red card attracts a deduction of two points. In addition to points deductions, there is a tendency for such players to miss games through suspension. This will add an extra burden to your squad. Points deductions incurred as a result of a poor discipline record soon add up and could make a notable difference to your overall rank over the season.

New Premier League Players

It is tempting to get over-excited about new Premier League players, but occasionally they find it difficult to adapt to their new environment. Even if they have an exceptional record elsewhere, an overseas player, or a player from a lower league, may require time to adapt to the pace of the league, style of football, or even their new surroundings. For example, both Timo Werner and Kai Havertz made the move to Stamford Bridge during the 2020/21 season. Although there were signs of improvement by Havertz towards the latter end of the season, Werner continued to struggle. In contrast, Ollie Watkins, who sealed a move to Aston Villa, was like a duck to water. He adapted in no time and had an excellent season, scoring 14 goals and creating five assists. He amassed 168 FPL points and was the fourth highest scoring forward. Monitoring their progress until such time that they start delivering points regularly may be favourable. When selecting a player from a promoted team, I would still be cautious. Selecting a player with previous Premier League experience, and who performed well, would be reassuring.

New FPL players are not subject to an immediate price change. Player transfers count towards reaching the 'threshold value'. However, a player needs to have been in the league for over eight days before any transfers start to count towards that value. Once that value has been reached, then a player's price rise or decrease is triggered by the amount of purchases or sales of that player. This locking period can be extended to the start of the next GW if the completion of the eight-day period falls within an international break (fplstatistics.co.uk).

Disgruntled Players

Be cautious when considering players who are not totally focused and committed to their club. For example, if a player's new contract negotiations have stalled and there is a stand-off between the player and club. Several factors need to be considered; are they likely to start in the opening fixtures? Will they be committed to the cause? Will their game time be managed? Will the stand-off have an adverse effect on their performances? A similar situation could arise if a player is being actively pursued by a 'top club' but his current club is reluctant to sell. In all likelihood, the player may find it difficult to motivate himself as he seeks a new challenge elsewhere.

FPL Assets

FPL revolves around scoring as many points as possible. Therefore, to optimise your team's points potential, your focus should be on the best FPL assets, irrespective of allegiances. When making transfers, try to distance yourself from your favourite team or players. By all means, pick a player if they are a good FPL asset to own, otherwise identify your players purely based on their performances as an FPL asset. Target in-form players with favourable fixtures. Similarly, keep an open mind and do not discount players who play for the arch rivals of your favourite team. For example, Arsenal and Tottenham. You need to consider each asset based on their FPL potential. Adopting this approach will ensure that you don't ignore an obvious pick purely because of your personal bias. Some are stubborn when it comes to player selection. Occasionally, an in-form player stands out as the obvious transfer target or ideal captain, but for whatever reason, they are overlooked. On most occasions, going with the obvious will reward you.

FDR (Fixture Difficulty Rating) & Fixture Swings

Monitoring FDRs and fixture swings is a crucial part of the game. When selecting your initial draft, analysing the fixture schedule will allow you to effectively plan ahead. You will be able to pinpoint optimal fixture runs. It's a key element when planning your transfers and captaincy options 4-6 weeks in advance. You can then continually monitor optimal fixture swings and rescheduled games for the remainder of the campaign. Team form will also come into the equation. Besides having access to the fixture difficulty ratings (FDR) on the official website, there are also some excellent fixture tickers on several of the third-party websites. Fixture tickers can help you determine which teams have the best fixtures over a given period of time based on how difficult or easy their upcoming opponents are. Targeting favourable fixture swings will enhance your game.

45

Committing to transfers in advance is not wise. However, you can make tentative plans to prioritise in-form players and teams with favourable fixtures over the upcoming Gameweeks. Targeting such players and teams is optimal. It also provides the ideal opportunity to dispose of those players who are underperforming, injured or have a difficult fixture run. When finalising your initial draft, you should be able to pinpoint a suitable time to activate your Wildcard to coincide with a good fixture swing. For example, during the 2021/22 season, GW8 was the most popular time for managers to activate their WC1. A time which coincided with an appealing fixture swing for both Manchester City and Chelsea. Additionally, it was in close proximity to the first international break. A time when gaining team value is viable and injuries on international duty are common. If you experience a major injury crisis, you could always adjust your plans accordingly.

Reserve Fund

At the start of a season, opting to save 0.5m in the bank (ITB) as an emergency fund is a worthwhile tactic. There is a tendency for prices to be volatile at this time. Price increments will also be 0.1m, so missing out on a transfer by the odd sum is frustrating. As the season evolves, maintaining a small reserve fund may prevent you from taking any unnecessary hits. There is a propensity for some managers to take a hit purely to release funds to facilitate the signing of an in-form player that they could not otherwise afford. It's a costly way of conducting your transfer activity, so having a reserve fund is beneficial.

Talisman Theory

Generally, every team has a Talisman, a player who consistently outperforms his team mates. Backing the Talisman can lead to significantly more points over the season. Tom at Who Got The Assist? (@WGTA_FPL) writes a yearly article on the 'Talisman Theory'. The Talisman Theory is the idea that you should make a beeline to the key man in every team - the Talisman - over other players. Most teams in the Premier League will have one key man

- the Talisman - who will score the lion's share of FPL points. If you consider that when a goal is scored by any particular team, you will have a mental image of who it's likely to be before you find out who has actually scored the goal. What is different about the Talisman Theory is that it's a little different from the perennial FPL debates on topics such as fixtures versus form because it's provable.

This is done by analysing FPL data to create a ranking for different teams' top FPL points scorers. This allows you to see which teams are more or less Talismanic and who the Talisman is for each of those teams. Tom at Who Got The Assist? has been reporting on this for the past six seasons. For example, for the 2020/21 season, the top Talisman was Harry Kane, who scored an impressive 28.9% of Tottenham's attacking points. He was closely followed by West Brom's Matheus Pereira with 28.4% of The Baggies' attacking returns, while Bruno Fernandes accounted for 24.7% of Manchester United's attacking returns. The following season, Son Heung-min was the top Talisman with 29.1% of Tottenham's attacking returns. Raphinha was second with 23.6% of Leeds attacking returns and James Ward-Prowse third with 21.9% of Southampton's attacking returns. Retrospectively, it is fascinating to look back on; however, during an ongoing season, it's the theory itself which helps FPL managers to better comprehend which payers they should be prioritising for their team. By identifying a team's Talisman, it allows managers to optimise their transfer decisions to ensure that the player that they are transferring in has the best chance of producing those all-important FPL points for their team.

Monitoring Transfer Activity

Prior to the summer transfer window officially opening, many transfer deals are already in the pipeline. Premier League clubs are eager to tie down players who are on their wish list before they are snapped up by other potential bidders. Once the transfer window officially opens, the transfer activity intensifies and signals the start of a new season. Many clubs would have been active in the transfer market prior to you sitting down to select your initial 15-man draft. It's important to familiarise yourself with all the latest transfer activity throughout the transfer window in order to select your ultimate squad. Monitoring transfer activity is an important part of your pre-season planning and it's a time when a lot can be learnt. Identifying hidden gems and what new Premier League stars are going to grace the game is a useful tactic.

Typically, there is an influx of top players each summer. Erling Haaland's transfer to Manchester City during the summer of 2022 caught everyone's attention. A point magnet who was probably earmarked by many FPL players from the outset. Normally, it's wise to see how a new player adapts to the league, but for a player of his pedigree, signing for the champions with the extra creativity they have at their disposal was appealing. Pinpointing players of interest in various positions is useful, add them to your wish list and then wait for the price reveal. Having identified potential targets, you will be in the best position to select your optimal squad. The beauty is that you can continue to amend your squad up until the Gameweek 1 deadline. The transfer window generally stays open beyond GW1, so continuing to monitor transfer activity beyond that point can still be very rewarding. Particularly, if you identify a hidden gem before a bandwagon gathers momentum. Monitoring transfer activity will also allow you to assess the strength of each team. Whether they are stronger, weaker or of a similar standard to the previous season. A club's transfer dealings will highlight their ambitions for the forthcoming season.

Pre-Season Games

You can gather vital information and clues by monitoring pre-season games, information to assist you in selecting your ultimate squad. You will be able to identify players who are regular starters, which players are in-form, and the positions each player is playing in. There is also the opportunity to spot OOP players. New signings will be getting their first competitive run out for their clubs. You will learn what position they are playing, whether they are fitting into the team and if they look sharp. All important considerations when deciding whether to take a gamble on a new face or not. Some players may have played international games during the summer. You will be able to determine if they look jaded or refreshed and whether they are likely to feature in the opening games. It will also be possible to identify formations, players' game time and, more importantly, any standout performers. Conducting research will assist you in acquiring the best assets to tackle the opening fixtures. Taking stock of all the available information will only have a positive impact as you approach the GW1 deadline.

Play Safe

There is a saying; 'you can't win FPL in the first few Gameweeks but you can lose it'. To succeed you need a steady start, a foundation to build on. Not going too radical at the outset and conforming to the template team will give you the best chance of achieving that goal. Building a solid foundation will put your team in a good position for the remainder of the season. A solid foundation will allow you to be slightly more adventurous with your team selections as the season evolves. You'll have the option to utilise one or two differential players to improve your overall rank. Many teams will look similar at the start of the season and that's because a considerable amount of research has been put into them. Players have conducted thorough research to build their ultimate squads. Many aim for a solid start and then climb to the upper echelons by being consistent and identifying key times to play differential players.

Part 3: Maximising Your Chips

Chip Strategy

The introduction of chips ahead of the 2015/16 season revolutionised the way we play the game. Chips are an effective tool which can enhance your team's performance, helping you to pull away from the pack and propel you up the global rankings. If you wish to succeed and secure a top finish, every point counts, hence the importance of optimising your chips. FPL is a game of strategy. Therefore, having the perfect chip strategy could be the difference between achieving your desired target or not. Managers possess two Wildcards (WC), a Free Hit chip (FH), Bench Boost (BB), plus a Triple Captain chip (TC) to play throughout the campaign. However, only one chip can be played per Gameweek. All offer avenues to significantly boost your score. Deploying your chips wisely during the campaign can dramatically improve your overall rank, but the timing of each chip could be a defining moment in your quest for FPL glory. It's important to recognise that the optimal timing of your chips is team-dependent. The best strategy is the one that fits your team, hence the necessity to play your own game.

Every player will have contrasting opinions as to what is your most effective chip and when is the optimal time to utilise a particular chip. Unquestionably, your two Wildcards are the most powerful chips that you have in your armoury. To gauge the importance put on the FH, BB and TC chips, I asked members of the FPL community which chip out of the three they considered to be the most valuable. Unsurprisingly, 71% of participants considered their Free Hit chip to be the most important, 15% voted Triple Captain and 14% Bench Boost. Each chip will be discussed separately and reference will be made to my research conducted over two seasons. Reference will also be made to research conducted by Fantasy Football Fix for the 2021/22 season. They looked at the usage of each chip by the 'Top 50 Managers', an 'All Time Top 50' group and an 'All FPL' user group. An in-depth analysis of the Top One Hundred Managers chip usage during the 2021/22 season will be discussed in detail in Part 8 of this book. Also included are the salient points of my findings for both the Top One Hundred

Managers and a group of Elite Managers for the 2020/21 season. It provides a fascinating insight into the chip strategies adopted by some of the top managers in the game.

The timing of each chip is key; utilising specific chips in conjunction with a double or blank Gameweek can be hugely rewarding. Typically, there are numerous blank and double Gameweeks each season resulting from fixture postponements caused by inclement weather, illness, or teams participating in cup competitions. Many games are rescheduled to avoid clashes with cup competitions. A typical round of Premier League fixtures comprises 10 games. If, for whatever reason, a team does not have a fixture that week, it becomes a blank Gameweek. A week with nine fixtures or less is regarded as a BGW and recently we have witnessed some weeks with just four games. Navigating a big BGW without utilising your FH chip becomes very challenging and additional transfers could be on the agenda. Therefore, planning for such Gameweeks is essential. A double Gameweek is a week where some teams are in action on more than one occasion. Occasionally, we also benefit from a rare triple Gameweek (TGW). Double and Triple Gameweeks offer FPL managers a great opportunity to capitalise on players with multiple fixtures. Effective planning will enable you to acquire as many DGW players as possible. A tactic which could enable your team to accumulate a substantial score, which ultimately should reward you handsomely. Generally, the best chip strategies are team dependent, so the best strategy is the one that fits your team.

The 'Golden Rule' for playing your FH, BB & TC chips is to try to avoid using them too early in the season and save them for the occasions which offer the best opportunity of maximising your points. Saving the three chips until later in the season offers greater flexibility. If deployed at the right time, they allow you to enhance your team's performance and optimise your points. The FH chip is ideal for tackling a BGW with a limited number of games. Alternatively, the chip can also be used effectively to target a double or triple GW. There is more upside to attacking a DGW. Your Triple Captain and Bench Boost chips are both well suited for attacking a double or triple Gameweek. Although you still need to identify the best DGW to attack. You may find that some DGW teams are struggling for form, while others may have a couple of difficult fixtures.

Wildcard (WC1)

The two Wildcards are regarded as the most powerful chips that you have at your disposal. A successful WC can transform your fortunes and it could be the difference between achieving your goal or not. They are likely to define your season. After devoting some considerable time to constructing your ultimate team to tackle Gameweek 1 and beyond, you will then rely on your two Wildcards for the remainder of the season. One Wildcard is to be utilised in each half of the season. Typically, the divide is GW19, which usually occurs just prior to the New Year. If, for whatever reason, your WC1 isn't activated prior to the deadline, it will be lost. The chip entitles you to make unlimited transfers without incurring any points deductions. Once activated, it will be active until the following Gameweek deadline. You have the capability to completely revamp your squad, hence it's importance. Once activated, there is no going back and, unlike your FH chip, any transfers made are permanent. There are no other rules governing their use.

Wildcards should be regarded as gold and the decision to activate your chip needs to be given serious consideration before proceeding. They should not be used frivolously, hence the importance of avoiding impulsive decisions and being reactionary after a poor Gameweek. In essence, they are a reset button, so identifying the optimal time to activate your WC chip is key.

Additionally, your Wildcards can also act as an insurance policy. A 'get out of jail' card which can be utilised to transform your team in case of an emergency. For example, if you encounter a mini-crisis and are struggling to field a full-strength team due to absentees, the only other solution would be to incur a substantial points deduction for additional transfers. When building your initial draft, studying the fixture schedule is an important aspect of the game. It is common to identify major fixture swings throughout the season. Therefore, earmarking a suitable Gameweek in advance to potentially activate your WC1 is a sensible move. There is the option to amend your plan if the need arises.

Your Wildcards have many advantages, and in particular, WC1 will enable you to reshape your team so that it conforms to the template team. A hypothetical team consisting of the most popular players. Additionally, it provides you with the perfect opportunity to recruit those assets who are regular starters, in-form and those hidden gems that have been uncovered. Simultaneously, your underperforming or injured players can be discarded. Your WC1 is also effective for acquiring players who are soaring in price (to gain team value) and those with a favourable run of fixtures in the foreseeable future. Monitoring players and observing price rises during the early months is important. Many in-form players will see their value increase significantly during this period, a time when price rises are extremely volatile. Building team value is an important strategy, which is discussed in Part 6 of this book. A combination of these factors would be the ideal scenario.

Having observed players' performances over the opening month, many are tempted to activate their Wildcard during the first international break, usually between Gameweeks 8 & 9. Pulling the trigger during an international break is a prime time and has its advantages for a combination of reasons. Besides the reasons highlighted, it will safeguard your team against any injuries that occur during the international matches. Capturing favourable fixture swings which coincide with breaks is also popular and can be advantageous.

Alternatively, you could aim to try to save your WC1 for as long as possible. Another popular time for activating your WC1 is between Gameweeks 15-19. Traditionally, a blank Gameweek features around this period, so activating your Wildcard will help you navigate the BGW, while some teams without their WC may struggle. It will also allow you to prepare for the hectic Christmas schedule, a time when Premier League teams are likely to experience some rotation. Opting to retain your WC for slightly longer does offer some extra reassurance in that it's still available to be used in cases of emergency. Additionally, playing it at this time will also allow you to reset your team for the second half of the season. However, retaining your WC1 for longer does also has its disadvantages. You are likely to find it harder to conform to the template team, and boosting your team value will not be so straightforward.

There was an unexpected twist during the 2022/23 season. With the World Cup being held in Qatar during the winter, FPL afforded managers the opportunity to make unlimited transfers during the six-week Premier League break for the competition. Fundamentally, it was an additional Wildcard which provided managers with the opportunity to reshape their teams between GWs 16-17. Therefore, the season could be cut down into four distinct sections comprising a 9-to-10-week period. Utilising WC1 during the first international break between GW8 and GW9 seemed the optimal time. This break coincided with a favourable fixture swing for some of the stronger teams.

After activating your Wildcard, try to resist the temptation to use your free transfer the following week, as rolling the transfer will benefit you more. Your new squad should be more than capable of holding its own. The only exception being is if you are unfortunate enough to suffer multiple injuries or suspensions, etc.

Wildcard (WC2)

The optimal timing for your second Wildcard is slightly easier to identify. Traditionally, the majority of blank and double Gameweeks feature towards the latter end of the season, a time when your WC2 chip comes into its own. The chip is useful for reconstructing your team in readiness to attack a DGW. Many teams are engaged in cup competitions, both domestically and in Europe. Therefore, it's common to see numerous fixtures rescheduled. Preserving your WC2 until the latter stages of the season is a useful tactic because it allows you to have the optimum squad to navigate the many double and blank Gameweeks. This strategy could prove beneficial. Deploying your Wildcard just prior to a DGW is the optimal strategy. A time when many players will have two games. Rotation allowing, this will give you two bites of the cherry.

The best route to success is to activate WC2 the week preceding a major double Gameweek and then deploy your Bench Boost chip in the DGW. Your Wildcard will enable you to select a 15-man squad full of DGW players in readiness to activate your BB chip to target the double Gameweek. This sets your team up nicely and, theoretically, you could take advantage of 30 separate scores across that DGW. A tactic which could generate a substantial score. Typically. The majority of the highest Gameweek scores achieved in FPL are accumulated by employing this method. It is not uncommon to see weekly scores in excess of 150 points and reaching this mark is extremely realistic. Alternatively, you may prefer to utilise your WC2 after coming out of a DGW to tackle a blank Gameweek or vice versa. Although opting for the first option is optimal. A lot of situations are team dependent.

The only downside of focusing on a DGW is the fact that this strategy may be detrimental to your team's overall performance. For example, during the 2021/22 season, the biggest double Gameweek was GW36. Some teams may have been suffering with a depleted, underperforming squad, yet, they decided to sacrifice their team's long-term performance by holding onto their WC2 to attack DGW36. Activating your WC2, when most needed, enables you to strengthen your team, which will produce a higher weekly score over a period of time. The extra points gained during that time may exceed the number of points accumulated as a result of solely focusing on a DGW. Especially if you owned several injured or underperforming players, or incurred points deductions to strengthen your squad.

Additionally, it could be argued that by activating their WC2 so late, managers weren't able to fully exploit the chip. With just two Gameweeks remaining, managers did not reap the full benefits of the chip. Deciding when to activate your chip is a fine balancing act. Will you see more benefit from strengthening your squad when most needed, or is there more upside from holding onto your WC to attack a huge double Gameweek? If your squad is in good shape, then targeting a DGW is optimal. On most occasions, unless there are severe injury issues, activating your WC2 a week or two prior to a big DGW is optimal. Your BB can then be deployed for the DGW.

An in-depth analysis of the top 10k managers during the 2020/21 season identified a distinct pattern regarding their chip usage. (Statistics courtesy of myfplanalysis.co.ln.) The vast majority of managers activated WC1 between Gameweeks 2 - 6. Presumably, this was aimed at conforming to the template team and building team value. A further 691 managers deployed their Wildcard in BGW9 while 932 managers retained WC1 until the deadline in GW16. Immediately afterwards, there were a number of blank and double Gameweeks. Unsurprisingly, the four most popular weeks for managers to play their WC2 consisted of three double Gameweeks and one blank Gameweek. (BGW18, DGW19, DGW25, DGW26). Many more activated their Wildcard just prior to a DGW.

Free Hit (FH)

Your FH chip is a very powerful chip which can only be played once during the season. It entitles you to make wholesale changes to your team for the week that it is activated. Unlike your Wildcard, once the Gameweek is over, your team will revert back to your original team prior to activation. In the meantime, your original team is still susceptible to price changes. The optimal time to deploy your Free Hit chip is usually in a blank Gameweek with very few games. However, it isn't entirely confined to a BGW and can also be used effectively to attack a DGW. Much will depend upon the strength or weakness of your team at the relevant time.

Typically, my preference is to utilise the FH chip in one of the biggest blank Gameweeks of the season. Using the chip for this purpose is perfect. It enables managers to tailor their squads to a reduced schedule. It also allows you to retain those players who you wish to keep long-term. Deploying the chip to navigate a BGW will enable you to field a full-strength team with the potential to achieve a respectable GW score. It will also alleviate the need to take hits. With a limited number of games in a BGW, it's likely that many teams will be similar. Therefore, you may not see the full benefit of activating your chip at this time. Utilising your FH for a DGW is not so popular as a BGW. However, there could be more upside by targeting a big DGW with the potential to generate a substantial score.

My research identified that during the 2020/21 season, a blank Gameweek was the favoured time for the majority of the top 10k managers to play their FH chip. An incredible 6,204 managers deployed their chip in BGW18, a week with just six games. The second most popular week was BGW29, when 989 managers activated their FH to tackle the four games on offer. Although it was relatively late in the season, just 489 chips were played in TGW35. Notably, 191 of the top 10k managers saved their FH chip until GW38, presumably targeting a strong finish.

Due to the unprecedented number of postponements during the 2021/22 season, managers were provided with a second FH chip (FH2). The chip could not be played in conjunction with any other chip, neither could both of your FH chips be played in consecutive Gameweeks. Undoubtedly, the extra chip contributed to a record points total not only by the eventual winner, but by 2,009 other players who surpassed the previous best total. The season included nine blank Gameweeks with one GW comprising just four games. Many managers without their FH chip struggled to field a full-strength team during those BGWs. It is highly likely that numerous managers had to revert to taking hit(s) during those blank Gameweeks.

The biggest blank Gameweek of the 2021/22 season was GW30 with just four games. Many owned Manchester City and Liverpool assets who both had a BGW due to their participation in the FA Cup. A record number of 838k managers utilised their FH chip to navigate the reduced round of fixtures. Analysis conducted by Fantasy Football Fix found that B/DGW27 was the most popular Gameweek to utilise the FH chip amongst certain groups. A week which included nine games, a blank GW for Liverpool and Chelsea, yet a double GW for others. 56% of the Top 50 and 62% of the All Time Top 50 groups deployed their chip (Likely to be FH1). In comparison, just 10.6% of the All FPL group utilised their chip in B/DGW27. The second most popular Gameweek was DGW37 (12 games) when 64% of the Top 50 group and 50% of the All Time Top 50 group utilised the chip. This was likely to be FH2. It was evident from the findings that the top managers utilised their FH chip in either a blank or double Gameweek, whereas the usage was scattered across many weeks in the All FPL user group.

Triple Captain (TC)

Your Triple Captain chip does what it says on the tin. Instead of doubling your captain's score, it will triple the score. You have one TC chip at your disposal and it cannot be used in conjunction with another chip. Unlike your Wildcard and Free Hit chips, your TC chip can be cancelled after activation. If, for any reason, both your captain and vice-captain do not feature in a specific week, then the chip will be lost. Therefore, it is advisable to select both players from different teams and preferably from different games in case of postponements. The optimum time to use the chip is to target a double Gameweek. It gives you two bites of the cherry rather than one. An excellent strategy is to target an in-form premium asset, with favourable fixtures in a DGW. Although, there is always the possibility that your captain doesn't play the full 90 minutes in both games.

It couldn't have gone any better for those who backed Mo Salah in DGW26 of the 2021/22 campaign. It was literally a defining moment in the season. You either owned the 'Egyptian King' and experienced an exceptional week, or you missed out and suffered a drop in rank. Liverpool faced Norwich and Leeds at Anfield, with both teams struggling at the foot of the table. It was ecstasy for those 1,013,162 managers that had entrusted Salah with their TC chip. Three goals and an assist secured an incredible 84 point-haul. Remarkably, a further 4,057,068 managers captained Salah that Gameweek.

Game time is beyond your control, but even so, your captain should still play sufficient minutes to deliver precious returns. To highlight this point, DGW36 of the 2021/22 season was memorable for one particular team. Rosie FC entrusted Kevin De-Bruyne with their TC chip and were rewarded spectacularly. The Belgian duly obliged with a majestic 90 points. His contribution helped Rosie FC accumulate a magnificent 225 GW points, which stands as the highest Gameweek score in history. Even though a four-point deficit reduced their Gameweek score to 221 points, it was still an outstanding achievement.

During the 2020/21 season, the vast majority of the top 10k managers utilised their Triple Captain chip in a double Gameweek. The most popular being DGW26, a week which consisted of a season's high of 17 games. A total of 4,714 managers played their TC chip while a further 1,598 managers activated their chip in DGW19, which contained 15 games. Analysis by Fantasy Football Fix found that the majority of TC chips during the 2021/22 season were utilised in DGW26, a Gameweek with 14 games. 50% of the Top 50, 62% of the All Time Top 50 and 39% of the All FPL group opted to deploy the chip in this GW. The second most popular Gameweek, was DGW29 which contained 13 games. Some 24% of the Top 50, 34% of the All Time Top 50 and just 10% of the All FPL group utilised their chip. Remarkably, all the All Time Top 50, 94% of the Top 50 and 65.6% of the All FPL group used their TC chip on Mo Salah.

When deploying their Triple Captain chip, there is conclusive evidence that the majority of top managers select a proven premium asset from a top side who is a reliable points scorer. An in-form premium asset with an enticing single fixture is more than capable of generating a substantial score in 90 minutes compared to an average player involved in a DGW. However, selecting an in-form premium asset with favourable fixtures in a double Gameweek is optimal.

Bench Boost (BB)

Many consider the Bench Boost to be the least favoured chip. Although, if used wisely, it can be very lucrative. The chip allows for the points from all four bench players to count towards your Gameweek total, which effectively gives you a 15-man team. Like the TC and FH chips, your BB can only be played once during the season. Once activated, you can cancel the chip prior to the GW deadline if you have a change of heart. Typically, the most popular time to activate the BB is in a double Gameweek immediately following the activation of the Wildcard. The WC provides managers with the opportunity to select their optimal Bench Boost squad. You can prioritise those players who are in-form, with favourable fixtures and likely to feature in both games. Adopting this strategy can be very productive and ensure a significant jump in rank.

However, there is one possible downside. Many retain their chip until the DGWs emerge towards the latter end of the season. Holding onto your chip for so long means that you may have to invest money in building a strong bench, desirable players that could generate big returns. Those players are not likely to be cheap. The argument is that the money invested in strengthening your bench could be better spent on your main playing XI. Investing a significant amount of money in your bench for a prolonged period could prove detrimental to the rest of your team. Some even activate their chip relatively early in the season (including GW1), so that their funds can be channelled into building a strong starting XI.

The optimal time to activate your Bench Boost chip is in a DGW. Rotation allowing, it effectively allows you to rely on the scores of 30 players. Although, it's not uncommon to see players being rotated during a busy spell of games. Hence, rotation is an issue that needs to be considered when playing your BB chip. Trying to avoid those busy periods when there is fixture congestion is helpful. Additionally, targeting those players who seldom miss a game will also help to mitigate against the risk of rotation. The chip is not solely for a DGW and can be effective in a single Gameweek.

Owning a strong bench with favourable fixtures can be a viable option.

The Bench Boost has a high ceiling and the potential to produce significant points totals. The record FPL score was set in DGW34 of the 2015/16 season when 'Savage Strikers' scored a magnificent 226 points after playing their Bench Boost chip. The manager made a bold decision to take five hits to set the team up for a bumper Gameweek. That decision was rewarded handsomely! The bench, comprising David de Gea (12), Matteo Darmian (17), Aaron Cresswell (10) and Phillipe Coutinho (8) generated 47 points.

During the 2020/21 season, the vast majority of the top 10k managers utilised their BB chip to attack a DGW. The most popular week was DGW19 when 2,536 chips were activated, DGW26 attracted 1,700 chips and TGW35 accounted for 1,116 chips. Fantasy Football Fix monitored the use of the BB chip by the Top 50 Managers, the All Time Top 50 group and an All FPL group during the 2021/22 season. The most popular Gameweek to utilise the BB chip was DGW36 when 42% of the Top 50 and 40% of the All Time Top 50 deployed their chip. DGW28 was the second most popular GW to activate the chip, with 26% of the Top 50 and 34% of the All Time Top 50 opting to target the DGW. Of the All FPL user group, 32.8% used their chip in DGW36, followed by 10.9% in GW37. Of the All FPL group, 18.7% did not activate their BB chip. This is indicative of the presence of many inactive teams towards the latter end of the season. There is overwhelming evidence to demonstrate that the preferred time for top managers to utilise their BB chip is to attack a double Gameweek.

Conclusion

My research found that the top managers prefer to utilise their Free Hit chip to navigate a blank GW. While the most popular and optimal time to activate their Triple Captain and Bench Boost chips is to attack a DGW. A piece of interesting research on the impact of decision-making was conducted by O'Brien et al. (2021) My research findings are consistent with the findings from this piece of research. The researchers found the most favourable times for managers to utilise their chips. The following pattern was observed:

"We also observe the difference in point returns as a result of playing the chip, with the distribution for the top managers being centered around considerably higher values, demonstrating that their squads were better prepared to take advantage of this chip (Bench Boost). The fact that managers were also willing to wait until one of the final Gameweeks is also indicative of the long-term planning that separates them from those lower ranked. Similar results can be observed from the other game-chips."

Part 4: The Psychology Of FPL

"I don't want to be at the mercy of my emotions. I want to use them, and to dominate them." – Oscar Wilde

Fantasy Premier League is a game which provokes our emotions. Players experience an array of strong feelings and need to contend with both its peaks and valleys. Moments of euphoria and despair intertwined in a short space of time. The ecstasy of seeing your new signing scoring a hat-trick, while the player that you just discarded collected a 15-point haul. The player who has been on your wish list for weeks has frustratingly just scored another brace for the second consecutive game. Another 'if-only' moment and a tide of negative emotions. We relish the highs but despise the lows. FPL may be an emotional rollercoaster of a game, but annually, millions of players accept the challenge, as the road to the top becomes harder to climb.

In this section, we will discuss relevant topics which are related to our emotional and mental wellbeing. Factors which can influence our ability to play the game effectively, namely: variance, management styles, risk-taking, decision-making, biases and positivity. A study by sports psychologists at Nottingham Trent University found that those who engaged most in fantasy football were more likely to suffer low mood and anxiety, although most players' health was unaffected. A quarter of the 2,000 players who took part in the study reported mild low mood – which can include sadness, anger, frustration, tiredness and low self-esteem – when playing, researching or thinking about the game. That figure increased to 44% for those who were highly engaged with the game.

"Higher levels of engagement appear to increase the likelihood of experiencing issues with mood and anxiety and seem to be having a negative impact on players' lives." – Dr. Luke Wilkins (2021)

Some suggest that there are similarities between FPL and poker, and that the phenomenon of tilting comes into play. 'Tilt' is a poker term for a state of mental – or emotional – confusion, or frustration in which a player adopts a sub-optimal strategy, usually resulting in the player becoming overly aggressive. In poker, it's a relatively frequent occurrence due to frustration, mostly against other players, or simply bad luck. Tilt can also apply to FPL, losing control of our negative emotions, behaving erratically, and thereby suffering adverse consequences. Your long-term plans may be ignored for the sake of chasing points. For example, negative emotions can induce an impulsive transfer. One of your most dependable and consistent performers is abandoned after another fruitless week. They are replaced by the player that is perceived as essential whilst you decide to ignore your non-playing bench. Generally, a well-researched logical transfer will reward you more than an emotionally led transfer. The ability to avoid rash impulsive decisions is important.

Self-discipline is an important aspect of the game, enabling you to cope with both the positive and negative moments. Stay grounded and enjoy the good weeks. Strive to pick yourself up and bounce back after a poor week. Everyone is susceptible to a below-par Gameweek, so it's important not to let the low points make you feel utterly dispirited. There will be occasions when you will benefit from some good fortune or suffer at the hands of some bad luck. We will encounter both the highs and lows. Therefore, acknowledging that the game produces emotions from both ends of the spectrum will help you manage your game. There is a need to embrace both. You won't enjoy the highs without experiencing the lows. It's all a part of the game.

"If you can believe it, the mind can achieve it." – Ronnie Lott

Variance

FPL is an unpredictable high variance game which combines euphoric highs with despairing lows and it's how to react to those swings that's important. Many managers would have heard of the important concept of 'variance', but what is it? Over the short-term, variance is particularly high in sport, partly due to the infinite number of variables which are outside of our control. In FPL, the list is exhaustive. We have to contend with injuries, illness, suspensions, rotation, fixture postponements, inclement weather, poor officiating, player performances, substitutions, etc. Fantasy football can be considered to be a game of chance and, in many ways, it's similar to poker. Skill is undoubtedly the biggest component, but your season can be affected by random events. We also need to acknowledge that the game involves an element of luck. Each week, we place our faith in the FPL Gods and hope that we benefit from those marginal calls, which can be the difference between success or failure. FPL is a prediction game with an infinite number of variables each week, which produces inconsistent outcomes.

The deviation from the predicted probability is called variance. It will not measure how well you play the game, but it shows you how much your results can vary and differ from expectations. How much a situation varies from its average, the distribution of probability by means of random variables. The probability of certain events occurring during a football game can be calculated. For example, the chances of a defence keeping a clean sheet. However, many random events determine the outcome of a game and whether that defence actually manages to keep a clean sheet. Bookmakers are an important source of information, as probabilities can be given in percentage form or odds for many sporting events based on analysis and mathematical models.

Even the best FPL players will experience a prolonged run of poor Gameweeks for no apparent reason. Conversely, they will also benefit from a winning streak. Generally, managers go through their decision-making process and make a sound logical decision, yet, for whatever reason, it yields a negative outcome. There will be instances where your expectations are not met. For example, you could tackle a GW with an exceptionally strong team on paper and a score in excess of 80 seems inevitable. Instead, your team produces a measly 40 points. Random events do occur which could have had an impact on your team's performance. One of your quality players sustains an injury the day before a game while another falls ill. Meanwhile, your star striker and captain is injured and has to be substituted with just five minutes on the clock. All are unforeseen factors that could have had a negative impact on your eventual GW score. Sometimes Lady Luck will be on your side, but on other occasions she will desert you.

An extreme example to illustrate that a whole season can be defined by variance was provided by FPL Review. Team 1 was ranked 270th in the world, having accumulated 2,239 points. They had a strategy rank of 500k, their odds rank was 565,123, and their luck rank 100% (see Glossary). Team 2 was ranked 2,999,884, having amassed 1,744 points. They had a similar odds rank as Team 1 (579,098), but a luck rank of 0.4%. Almost a 500-point swing built from variance. Undoubtedly, it would have left the manager of Team 2 thinking that they had made some poor decisions. If you have played FPL for any length of time, you doubtlessly will have experienced similar situations. A lengthy spell of substandard weeks may be familiar and you are convinced that everything is against you. They are not.

The expectations are that players will get their fair share of good and bad luck and the outcomes will be evenly split. The classic example is a coin flip when you expect to win 50% of the time. However, it doesn't work out like that. If you flip a coin 20 times, you may correctly guess seven of the flips, but 13 guesses will be incorrect. There is a greater chance for outcomes to balance themselves out when the sample size is much larger. For example, it is possible for a League Two side to beat a Premier League side in a one-off match, but if they played each other 100 times in a season, the Premier League team would win the vast majority of matches.

In terms of fantasy football, there will be occasions where you will suffer a poor run of results. In contrast, you will experience a spell of positive outcomes. Over the long-term, it's likely that such occasions will even themselves out. Although a spate of poor weeks can prompt you to make a series of sub-optimal decisions to rectify your perceived mistakes, such decisions can adversely affect your performance. After a substandard week, you instinctively want to address the perceived problems, whether it be by making multiple transfers or activating your Wildcard. That's the time to take a step back, as irrational decisions based on impulse are unnecessary. Actions that could be detrimental to your overall performance. It's far better to reassess the situation once some time has lapsed. In reality, your decision-making was sound. You may have made the right selections, but on this occasion they were unsuccessful. Continue to conduct research and make sensible decisions based on all the information that's available to you. Ultimately, your skill will yield the positive outcomes that you crave.

Luck – or the lack of it – is ever-present in FPL and in the upper echelons it can be the difference between winning or not. Events outside your control will occur frequently, and occasionally you will be on the wrong end of luck. You will experience the downswings as well as upswings, a game of contrasting emotions, so you need to handle the variance. The secret is acknowledging that bad luck does exist. We need to accept that there will be episodes of uncontrollable misfortune, but it's how we react to adversity and cope with emotional swings that's important. It will determine whether you get to enjoy the game or not. Embrace both and enjoy the occasions when Lady Luck is on your side. Such moments should make you more determined to succeed. Some teams will suffer more than others; therefore, scores will take a different path.

The hope is that over an entire campaign such occasions of good and bad fortune will even themselves out. Occasionally, unsuccessful outcomes are not attributed to bad luck but some poor decision-making. It is a question of learning from, and

71

eradicating, those moments. Analyse where it went wrong and what can be done to prevent a reoccurrence. Making consistently sound logical decisions throughout the season will help to reduce variance.

Management Styles

FPL managers are a diverse group of people from all walks of life and from various parts of the world. However, there are a couple of things we all have in common – our passion for football and Fantasy Premier League. We all love the emotional rollercoaster that we put ourselves through over 38 relentless Gameweeks. Nonetheless, there is something that sets us apart; we all possess different playing styles. Our approach to the game varies from player-to-player with different techniques, ideas, goals, and strategies. All players seek enjoyment from the game and to succeed, but the question is; how do we go about it?

Being a successful manager requires certain skills, most notably, dedication, patience, self-discipline, motivation, good decision-making, and a sound temperament. They are all key attributes. Having a good understanding of the best strategies to adopt to help propel you to the top is also advantageous. Selecting your captain, deploying your chips, making transfers, effective planning and conducting thorough research, are all important aspects which contribute to your performance. A variety of FPL information is widely available. Whether it be trawling through realms of data or scouting players by watching live games or a highlights package, you are inundated with information. It could be argued that, for most committed FPL managers, it is a full time job! When managing your team, what is important is how you integrate those skills and knowledge into your management style.

All players have the same aim; to enjoy the game and succeed. The ambition is to score as many FPL points as possible and hopefully finish the season with a memorable overall rank. Goals, assists and clean sheets are at the top of the wish list. How we achieve that aim is where players differ. Firstly, interpreting information. Some managers will watch every live game plus the highlights, whereas others will just watch the highlights package; some will do neither. It's the same with analysing data. Many will spend a great deal of time conducting research; studying statistics, fixture patterns, reading articles, communicating with other FPL managers, subscribing to dedicated FPL websites, watching YouTube videos, or listening to podcasts, etc. They will also seek guidance from fellow players. In contrast, some will do very little. One key element of becoming a successful manager is our ability to seek and utilise information. It is not only about acquiring football knowledge, but how we optimise that information in our decision-making process. Managers will also interpret and apply that information in a different way.

FPL is a game that involves mitigating risk and maximising potential. A factor which is going to have an impact on your decision-making processes is a willingness to take a gamble or calculated risk. Particularly, when it comes to transfers, team and captaincy selections. Some will be risk seeking and take a gamble, while others are risk averse. Players have contrasting opinions. With this in mind, the next factor to consider is what type of manager you are? Do you indulge in a gamble? Are you cautious? Or possibly somewhere in the middle? Some are 'thrill seekers,' and might take risks even when there is no real benefit in doing so. Risk-taking is discussed in-depth later in this section.

FPL continues to evolve and I suspect that some managers are moving from a mindset of playing relatively safe and taking up a more adventurous approach. They are becoming proactive with more risks being taken. For example, there is evidence to suggest that hits are becoming more prevalent. Many are risk averse and play a conservative game, taking as few risks as possible. The question is whether their risk-averse approach is having a detrimental effect on their overall performance, or helping them to succeed at the game? Is adopting a more cautious approach actually holding some back, or has it helped to propel them to the top? The polar opposite are those players who revel in taking a hit or two. They thrive on the challenge of risk and reward. Some even get a 'buzz' out of the odd gamble, others play the game for fun and if that means taking numerous hits, so be it - they are not in it to win it.

During my research, I discovered that there is growing evidence to suggest that many are adapting to change in an effort to take their game to the next level. Managers are finding innovative ways to maximise their points potential. Some strive to improve their knowledge of the game, while others change their playing style. Instead of adopting a safety-first approach, it is now apparent that some are opting to take a more 'aggressive' strategy. For example, in an effort to get the edge over their opponents, they are attacking Gameweeks by utilising hits. Is it a case of some risk-averse managers adapting to keep up with the new wave of aggressive managers? With the advent of social media, it is now common to see the words 'hits' and 'aggressive' linked in the same sentence. Some players are risk-seeking and tolerate risk, they consider it a part of the game. If successful, there are big rewards to be made. Conversely, there are those who view risk as a hindrance. Their preference is to adopt a risk-averse approach and their consistency will ultimately reward them.

FPL managers can be placed into certain categories. There is the ultra-cautious, conservative player who gradually climbs rank with a view to defending it. Their transfers usually involve a 'safe pick', signing a player who is likely to be a regular starter - a Mr. Reliable that can be depended upon. This type of manager is very reluctant to sell any of their regular starters. They conduct their transfer activity after the press conferences, which allows them to be aware of all the relevant, accessible information in order to make a sound transfer. Differential players are not desirable and are seen as a step too far. This type of player is meticulous in their planning with one eye on the Gameweeks ahead. Their captain is likely to be a safe bet, with one of their premium assets being an odds-on favourite. Typically, they have a cautious approach and play very safe.

Then, there is the hybrid manager, not totally risk-averse or gung-ho. They are prepared to take a gamble, but not often. Only when everything adds up. Generally, they select a safe captain but can occasionally be tempted by a differential. This type of manager will aim to complete their transfers as late as possible, but will make early transfers if their funds are running low or the need arises. When making a judgement on transfers or captaincy, their preference is to make a decision based on the 'eye test', what they see during games, although they may quickly browse through data. They will generally stick with a template team but can be tempted by an in-form differential. A manager who will take a hit if the circumstances are right.

Finally, there is the manager who thrives on risk. They are likely to make their transfer(s) early in the week to save on funds. A player who constructs an adventurous team built with the sole aim of attacking rank: a team littered with differentials. They are also prone to a 'one week punt', a concerted effort to be rewarded with a points haul from a player with a great fixture and low ownership. They are willing to gamble on a relatively unknown 'hidden gem' and are partial to a hit, even if the odds are against a haul. A manager who is happy to discard their most reliable players if a better option comes into focus. Their planning is sparse and rarely relied upon. They are not accustomed to rolling a transfer and prefer to tackle problems as they arise. Perhaps you can relate to some of these traits and identify which category you fall into?

You could question whether being too rigid is having a negative impact on some managers. As the game evolves, there is a necessity to adapt to the changing circumstances, but some players are reluctant to do so. They may reach a certain milestone, but because of their risk-averse nature, their progress is being thwarted. Some are not fulfilling their full potential by being reluctant to change. Perhaps a more ambitious and adventurous approach may help them achieve their milestone. A manager who consistently attains a certain rank but then doesn't proceed to capitalise on that due to their cautious strategy. Conversely, some will argue that they only achieved the rank they did because of their risk-averse approach.

My research uncovered a prime example of a lack of ambition. Halfway through the 2020/21 campaign, Team A was cruising at the top of the overall rankings. Eventually, their rank plummeted and their challenge fizzled out. As the season evolved, rival managers adopted a proactive approach; they opted to attack by taking hits. Presumably, hoping for a late surge to win the coveted title. In contrast, Team A opted to sit back and rest on their laurels. Their risk-averse approach ultimately cost them. They took just two hits in the second half of the season, one hit in two blank Gameweeks. They declined to attack the five double and one triple Gameweeks that were on offer, while others took advantage of the situation.

This coincided with just two green arrows in the final nine Gameweeks. They slipped out of contention while the risk-seeking teams around them prospered. Their rivals grasped the opportunity and went on the offensive. They took hits, which ultimately rewarded them with net gains and an improved rank. Did the risk-averse manager become so engrossed in trying to avoid a hit, regardless of the circumstances, that it had a detrimental effect on their rank? The eventual winner, Michael Coone, accumulated 24 in points deductions between Gameweeks 31-38. His bold move to attack delivered the coveted title. This example highlights that each manager adopts different ideas, strategies, risk thresholds, and reacts to situations in different ways.

I believe that players are adapting to the ever-changing game. In the past, many were risk-averse, but now there is evidence of change. For example, during the 2021/22 campaign, every Top One Hundred Manager made at least one additional transfer. Amongst them, the average number of points deductions was 46.40, with the eventual winner making 10 additional transfers throughout the season. We regularly encounter risk in our decision-making, and numerous decisions need to be made weekly. Taking a hit is just one example. Instead of being risk-averse and totally focused on avoiding hits at all costs, keeping an open mind may be advantageous. Don't discount a gamble in moderation if a good opportunity to maximise points presents itself.

With increased competition and the widespread availability of FPL material, you could question whether there is now a new type of player: a manager who is enhancing their skills by soaking up the wealth of information on offer and finding innovative ways to optimise their points potential. My research suggests that many are becoming more adventurous and are taking hits in their quest for glory. It may well be that many are now prepared to take a calculated risk to succeed. Players are seeking more knowledge, adopting the right strategies, and making sound decisions. The steps taken will be reflected in their rank. FPL continues to evolve, so there is a necessity to adapt to the constantly changing game. Having a flexible approach and adapting to change may prove beneficial. There is no right or wrong way to play the game, and we all approach the game differently. Only by improvising and experimenting will you learn what works and doesn't work for you. You will identify the best strategies to adopt, improve your decision-making and learn from any mistakes. Eventually, you will find the right chemistry which will deliver both success and enjoyment of the game.

"Enjoying success requires the ability to adapt. Only by being open to change will you have a true opportunity to get the most from your talent." – Nolan Ryan

Decision-Making

"The more familiar with a situation you become, the quicker, the better your decision will be." – Lionel Messi

In Fantasy Premier League, numerous factors are totally outside the control of a manager. For example, Premier League team selections, match officials, weather conditions and the dreaded VAR decisions, to name but a few. We are also unable to influence luck, an element of the game which undoubtedly can be both beneficial and damaging. However, what you can control is one of the key components of the game, namely your decision-making. It is an integral part of FPL and the quality of your decisions will define your season. Effective decision-making will propel your team up the rankings and help you to stay one step ahead of your mini-league rivals. Therefore, you need to consider how you can optimise your decision-making processes to make you an effective manager. Undoubtedly, many players make ineffective decisions and mistakes which they ultimately regret.

The aim is to make solid logical decisions throughout a prolonged season to ensure a successful outcome. As a manager, you're responsible for making hundreds of important decisions during a typical campaign. After selecting your initial draft, you will deliberate on decisions for hours each week over selection issues. As the Gameweek deadline approaches, some agonising decisions need to be made. What's my best XI? Which player do I sign, if any? Do I take a hit? Who do I leave on the bench and in what order? How many active players do I need on the bench? Who will get the armband? A countless number of major decisions have to be made regularly. We also encounter 50/50 decisions frequently, a straight choice between two players of similar abilities, statistics and fixtures. Which one do you select? You also need to identify the optimal time to deploy your two Wildcards and three chips you have at your disposal. In the context of FPL, each element where you are required to make decisions regularly is vitally important. Hence, sound decision-making is crucial. To aid you in your decision-making process, information is key. Therefore, gathering as much information as possible to assist you in that process is necessary.

Decision-making is regarded as the cognitive process resulting in the selection of a belief or a course of action among several possible alternative options. It could be either rational or irrational. The goal is to have sufficient information to make the best possible decisions. Conducting research by analysing fixtures, form, player points projections, injuries and rotation patterns is an integral part of that process. Some will also seek press conference updates and read many articles with player recommendations. Managers may spend a substantial amount of time conducting research and watching games but it's pointless unless that knowledge is best put to good effect. There's a need to make the most of our newfound knowledge and that can be done by making sound logical decisions.

Many 50/50 decisions will be unsuccessful, so that is the time to ask yourself specific questions to learn from the experience. They are all relevant questions: Did I consider everything during my decision-making process? Was I under stress? Did I have decision-fatigue? Was I pushed for time? Did I overthink the situation? How do you currently approach your decision-making? I suspect that many bypass specific stages of the process and instead make impromptu, damaging decisions. Emotionally led decisions rather than logical decisions based on all the information available. Improving your decision-making by having a sound process should reduce the number of bad decisions being made and enhance your game. Decision-making is the process of making choices by identifying a decision, gathering information, and assessing alternative resolutions. Bechara and Damasio (2005), highlight the importance of emotions in decision making. How many of the following seven steps do you take in your decision-making process?

1. Identify the decision
2. Gather relevant information
3. Identify the alternatives
4. Weigh the evidence

5. Choose among the alternatives
6. Take action
7. Review your decision

There is also a strong likelihood that many managers bypass much of the decision-making process due to cognitive and personal biases: biases usually affect decision-making processes. They appear more when a decision task has time pressure, is done under high stress and/or a task is highly complex. Approaching an FPL deadline could certainly fall into this bracket. There are numerous common biases affecting your decision-making: Survivorship Bias, Confirmation Bias, The IKEA Effect, Anchoring Bias, Overconfidence Biases, Planning Fallacy, Availability Heuristic and Progress Bias. These will be discussed later in the section.

An important factor in your decision-making process is decision fatigue, which refers to the deteriorating quality of the decisions you take after a long session of decision-making. There is a tendency for peoples' decision-making to be impaired as a result of having recently taken multiple decisions. By the end of a session involving multiple decisions, you may be talked into making random choices. Decision fatigue can actually lead to people avoiding decisions entirely and it can also increase reliance on mental shortcuts and biases. A further issue is decisional conflict and regret. Individuals experiencing decision fatigue may experience a greater degree of decisional conflict. An individual becomes uncertain about which course of action to take when deciding between various options involves regret, risk or challenge to their values. LeBlanc et al. (2009)

Various measures can be taken to help avoid decision fatigue. Firstly, follow a set routine. For example, the first thing you do pre-deadline on a Saturday morning is to finalise your key FPL decisions, captaincy, starting XI and bench order. Additionally, decrease your options to reduce the number of choices you have to make and try to be more consistent. For example, when determining which transfer to make, try to reduce the number of serious options. Focus on one or two players who have excellent underlying statistics, form and favourable fixtures and avoid having to make a decision between numerous players. Another example is the strength of your bench. Arguably, investing your budget equally amongst your 15-man squad creates a selection dilemma and increases the number of options available. Selecting a relatively strong XI and opting for a weaker bench removes some of those difficult decisions. Likewise, having a pair of rotating keepers or defenders provides another selection headache. Eliminating options can improve your decision-making process.

It is also beneficial to set yourself a time constraint. Once the time has elapsed, then finalise your decision. Probably the most important factor in decision-making is to make your decisions in the morning when your brain is fully functioning and you're clear of decision fatigue. Do the most important thing first. Having a good night's sleep recharges your body and your decision-making will be more effective. The same could be said about food consumption. Avoid decision-making when hungry or tired. Low glucose levels have been scientifically linked to poor decision-making. Eliminate rehashing decisions – once you've made your choice, then stick with it. Further useful considerations to overcome decision fatigue include planning daily decisions the night before. If you do have to make good decisions later in the day, then eat something first.

There is a tendency for some to make late, impromptu transfers where little or no research has been conducted. Instead of dealing with injury or suspension issues in their team, they focus on a player who has been deemed essential by fellow managers in the confines of the Twitter 'bubble'. A rash decision may trigger a catalogue of unwanted events that could have a negative impact on your team. Accuracy of information on which to act is key. Seek accurate information on which to judge your best decision. It's also advisable to eliminate information overload so your decision-making process isn't clouded.

During a typical Gameweek, emotions run high and, undoubtedly, that influences many players. Many make emotionally led decisions fuelled by frustration or anger, resulting in knee jerk or rage transfers. Decisions made on impulse can be detrimental. Emotions need to be managed so that logical decisions are made based on the best information available. There is also a tendency for some to be too reactive, which also leads to bad decisions. For example, replacing a reliable asset with a player who has just scored a brace, even though they have shown little form. Many will have more pressing issues but instead they focus on removing the player that missed a penalty, an open goal or hasn't scored for several games. Ideally, instead of making a rash decision, the best course of action would be to give it time and reassess. You can re-evaluate and make the best decision to address the most pressing issues in your team. Some managers also succumb to transfers through a fear of missing out. Generally, such transfers will not only be unsuccessful but a distraction from the more pressing issues. It's critical not to let fear rule your decision-making.

The preference should be to consider the relevant steps of decision-making before committing to your final decision. Having a thorough decision-making process can help you make more deliberate, thoughtful decisions by organising relevant information and defining alternatives. You should also take ownership of your own decision-making and not rely on the army of experts in the fantasy football family. Weigh up both the positives and negatives for each possible solution.

Having considered all the relevant information, you will then be in a better position to make a well-informed decision and identify the solution best for your team in the long-term. Seeking a second opinion can be beneficial, ideally, someone that you have confidence in to provide sound advice. Listening to too many people can cloud your judgement and confuse you even more. You will be bombarded with contradicting information and who is to say what information is useful and what is a distraction? Playing your own game is paramount.

There is a need to acknowledge that not all bad outcomes are as a result of sub-optimal decision-making. There's a distinction between a bad decision and a bad outcome. Understanding how to tell the difference between these two concepts is key. Perhaps you went through all the steps in your decision-making process, but for whatever reason, the outcome wasn't positive. The player that you recruited for a hit didn't get their expected haul, while the player replaced was fortunate to score a hat-trick. A classic case of outcome bias, the tendency to evaluate the quality of a decision based on the eventual outcome rather than the thought process. Those who register an exceptional Gameweek are assumed to have made better decisions than those who struggled, but that isn't the case. Look at the quality of your decisions rather than the eventual outcome.

For example, in GW1 of the 2022/23 season, I decided to play safe and I selected an in-form Harry Kane in preference to Erling Haaland. At some point, both players had been in the final draft as the Gameweek deadline approached. My instinct was to go with Harry Kane, an established Premier League player who had scored numerous goals in an excellent pre-season. Spurs were facing a very obliging Southampton defence in their opening game. Alternatively, Erling Haaland, who is a fantastic footballer, was due to face West Ham. However, he had never played in the Premier League. Do you go with the tried and tested option who has a better fixture, or the new player who faces more difficult opposition? Many managers would have faced the same predicament. The rest is history. Although Spurs scored four goals in their demolition of The Saints, remarkably, Kane collected just two points. In contrast, Haaland scored a brace and collected the three bonus points as he registered a 13-point haul in a 2-0 City victory. An 11-point swing from one decision.

At no time did I question my decision to select Kane ahead of Haaland. I was completely happy with my thought process and decision-making. It was just an unfortunate outcome. FPL is a game of fine margins, your decision-making and the logic may all have been sound, but on occasions there will be both successful and unsuccessful outcomes. You may have worked your way through your decision-making process and made the optimal decision based on all the known facts. Having a reliable decision-making process will ultimately reward you and lead to success over the long-term.

An example of a positive outcome comes from GW14 of the 2022/23 campaign. I had a 50/50 transfer decision to make, either Callum Wilson to Gabriel Jesus or Vladimir Coufal to Ben White. Jesus was the more attractive option because you would expect a mid-priced forward to outscore a budget defender. However, Coufal didn't start regularly and was redundant on my bench. I considered the pros and cons of each transfer, including fixtures and form. Wilson, Jesus & White all had two good fixtures before the extended World Cup break. Jesus and White had a favourable fixture against struggling Nottingham Forest, while Callum Wilson faced Aston Villa. Jesus was not on penalty duty and he was also sitting on four yellow cards, one away from a suspension. In contrast, Wilson was on penalty duty and had scored in his previous game.

The aim should always be to put any fires out and resolve the main weaknesses in your team. Therefore, I opted to replace Coufal with White. Besides hitting the bar, Wilson scored two goals, provided two assists, and collected a 19-point haul. Meanwhile, Jesus collected nine points by creating two assists. Coufal didn't feature for West Ham and scored no points, while White recorded six points for Arsenal's clean sheet. Overall, I was 16 points better off as a result of that transfer decision. Referring back to the research conducted by O'Brien et al. (2021) previously referred to, the authors demonstrate the following:

"Managers' ranks over multiple seasons are correlated and we analyse the actions taken by managers to increase their likelihood of success. The prime factors in determining a manager's success is found to be long-term planning and consistently good decision-making in the face of noisy contests, that upon which the game is based on."

The research highlighted the importance of your decision-making in FPL. It is a key factor in your success. O'Brien et al. discovered that a majority of teams feature a core group of players, which results in a large proportion of teams having a similar make-up. This phenomenon is called the 'template team', which emerges at different points throughout the season.

"Similarities between managers' decisions over time that result in the emergence of a 'template' team, suggesting a form of herding dynamics taking place within the game are also observed. Taken together, these findings indicate common strategic considerations, and consensus among successful managers on crucial decision points over an extended temporal period."

The article discusses a manager's decision-making in relation to their transfers, captaincy selections and building team value. There is also an in-depth look at the use of chips and the emergence of a template team. The main observations from the research suggest the following:

"We divided the managers into tiers based upon their final position in the game and observed that the managers in the upper echelons consistently outperformed those in lower ones, suggesting that their skill levels are present throughout the season and their corresponding rank is not dependent on just a small number of events. The skill-based decisions were apparent in all facets of the game, including making good use of transfers, strong financial awareness, and taking advantage of short- and long-term strategic opportunities, such as their choice of captaincy and use of the chips mechanic.

"Arguably the most remarkable observation presented in this article, however, is the emergence of what we coin: a template team that suggests a form of common collective behaviour occurring between managers. We show that most teams feature a common core group of constituent players, at multiple time points in the season. This occurs despite the wide range of possible options for each decision, suggesting that the managers are

acting similarly, and particularly so for the top-tier managers, as evident by their higher similarity metrics."

I would highly recommend reading the full article, which you will find fascinating. The findings are consistent with my research and what I have observed as an FPL manager. Ultimately, we are responsible for making our own decisions. Therefore, we need to own our decisions and take responsibility for the outcome. FPL is an emotionally charged game. Hence, it is important to evaluate your decision-making process rationally rather than emotionally. Ensure your decisions are driven by knowledge and logic rather than frustration or anger. The emphasis should be on focusing on your decision-making process and not the outcome. Having a reliable process in place will reward you over the long-term.

"Making good decisions is a crucial skill at every level." – Peter Drucker

Taking Risks in FPL

"He who is not courageous enough to take risks will accomplish nothing in life." – Muhammad Ali

Risk-taking is an integral part of the game and managing an FPL team carries an element of risk. Risk will play a significant part in your overall performance. Players frequently encounter situations involving risk. Hundreds of decisions need to be made throughout a season. Managers deliberate over important decisions weekly and many will face the same dilemma; shall I pick several differential players to chase rank? Sign Player A who has a set of favourable fixtures even though he hasn't scored in several games? Is it worth a hit to recruit an in-form forward? Should I forget the obvious standout captaincy candidate with a mammoth EO and instead pick a differential captain? The question is; do you take a risk or play cautiously? The other question; when is the best time to take a gamble? Risk should be at the forefront of your mind and a sound method should be in place to ensure that disastrous weeks are avoided. A poor Gameweek can be demotivating and adversely affect your enthusiasm for game.

The term risk is given different definitions depending on the field and context. The common themes include loss, injury, or in a situation where something unpleasant may happen. The *Oxford English Dictionary 3rd Edition* defines risk as;

"(Exposure to) the possibility of loss, injury or other adverse or welcome circumstance; a chance or situation involving such a possibility."

A suitable definition which could correspond to FPL is the following:

"The likelihood of variation in the occurrence of an event, which may have either positive or negative consequences." – Risk Assessment and Management Panels

For example, there will be occasions where a player's expectations are not met. You may estimate your final points tally for the season or predict what you will score in an upcoming double Gameweek. Your expectations are based on the number of points that you have scored in recent seasons or recent DGWs. Your estimates will have an upper and lower range, and your total points are expected to be somewhere in between. However, it's possible that your score could drop short of your lower expectation, or exceed your top expectation.

The probabilities of those two unexpected events occurring can be estimated using data from previous seasons. The source of the risk can cause a deviation from the points you are expecting to score. The deviation can be either positive or negative, i.e., you score less or more than expected. The aim is to try to reduce the chances of a negative deviation by risk management. Brand et al. (2007), suggest risk-taking is a component of the decision-making process in situations that involve uncertainty and in which the probability of all outcomes rewards and/or negative consequences.

Managers have different playing styles and will come to different conclusions based on certain factors. This includes their own personal risk appetite, tolerance, or threshold. Risk appetite is a tendency towards risks; risk tolerance is an acceptance of variance; and risk threshold is a quantified limit, beyond which you will not accept the risk. It is necessary to control risk, therefore risk management is an essential part of the game. Players are either risk-averse, risk-seeking or risk-neutral. FPL is a strategy-based game and to outscore millions of other competitors, risk-taking is pivotal. High risk equals high reward. However, the circumstances and timing of those risks is key.

Sizeable FPL communities now exist on social media and groupthink has become common. A safety in numbers mentality, which quickly leads to a template team forming relatively early and evolving as the season progresses. Some players will be tempted to select differential players just to be different and break free from the crowd. It's a risky strategy that could either reward you handsomely or obliterate your ambitions. Selecting numerous differential players simultaneously can backfire spectacularly, as the template team is often based on sound judgement by many players. Managers who have done their homework and identified the best players to sign. Hence the importance of finding ways to differentiate your team from the pack.

Certain measures can be taken to reduce the element of risk in FPL. For example, many managers will either 'double' or 'triple-up' on players from a specific team. This tactic could work wonders. Conversely, it could be a recipe for disaster, particularly if they are defensive assets. A solitary goal will wipe out clean sheet points and also damage your chances of collecting any bonus points. However, selecting multiple players from a very strong team with a great fixture could produce a significant points haul and contribute greatly towards an impressive GW score. The safest approach is to distribute the risk by selecting defenders from several strongly performing defensive teams, rather than concentrating just on one team.

Beware of the 'Twitter Bubble'. The FPL community on Twitter is only a small section of players and trends are not representative of FPL in its entirety. There is a tendency for many to follow the crowd and the fear of missing out, groupthink, or herd mentality all come into play. Consequently, simply by listening to and following others, many will incur unnecessary points deductions by making additional transfers. Something they wouldn't have done had they played their own game.

Ideally, the aim should be identifying the optimal team to accumulate the most points regardless of a player's effective ownership. However, EO has to be considered. For example, when selecting your captain, do you mitigate risk by selecting the player with a substantial EO or do you gamble by selecting a differential player to gain rank? Taking the safe route will protect your rank, while a successful differential pick will improve your rank significantly. Conversely, an unsuccessful differential selection can be catastrophic. In this situation a lot will depend on your risk appetite or whether you are content with your current position or want to take a risk to gain rank. Being prudent and avoiding risk is the safest approach.

Making wise player selections can reduce the negative consequences of risk. Simply by avoiding those players who are injury prone, have discipline issues, are one yellow card away from a suspension, new to the league, or a rotation risk. They all carry a high level of risk and, besides reducing risk, you will also save yourself a wasted transfer. You can also negate risk by replacing an injured or suspended player with a definite starter. Adopting these tactics is a sensible approach.

Another example is managing your bench. If you have no active players on your bench, it carries a significant amount of risk. Conversely, if you have a fully functional playing bench, your risk is minimal. The less bench cover you have, the more likely it is that you will have to incur a points deduction, in the event of injury. Therefore, having at least one playing substitute is essential and preferably two or three. Throughout this book, you will see references to flexibility. Having a flexible team structure with players at different price points in each position and rolling transfers can prevent unnecessary transfers.

Many FPL managers focus on winning their mini-league in preference to achieving a better overall rank. Consequently, there is a tendency for some to have one eye on their rivals, which may influence their decision-making and risk appetite. Besides EO, you may react to what is occurring with your rival teams. Many have an in-form player that you don't own. If you don't respond and sign that player, there is a possibility that your chances of winning the league are over. You could either back your own judgement and focus on your team, or sign the player to negate the threat from your rivals. Take a gamble and go without the in-form player or manage the risk by playing safe.

It is worth monitoring your risk-taking and not being driven by emotionally led risks. Identify the best time to take a risk. I would suggest that doing everything in moderation is the sensible approach to take. For example, selecting differential players. There will be occasions when you will need to attack to improve your rank, or defend to maintain your rank. When you do go on the offensive, then do so in moderation. Allow yourself one or two differential players, but going to the other extreme and selecting numerous differential picks could prove very costly. Similarly, the same could apply to your transfer activity. Taking a hit and incurring a four-point deduction is not going to have dire consequences if it's unsuccessful. However, taking three or four hits in a GW, could drastically damage your overall rank if unsuccessful. The greater the risk, the greater the consequences. Conversely, the greater the risk, the greater the reward. Risk takers tend to make decisions with both high potential benefits and high potential adverse outcomes, rather than choosing more cautious alternatives (Slovic, 1987).

The Psychological Game

"Our greatest battles are that with our own minds." –
Jameson Fran

Cognitive bias is a systematic thought process caused by the tendency of the human brain to simplify information processing through a filter of personal experiences and preferences. Also known as psychological bias, it's the tendency to make decisions or to take action in an unknowingly irrational way. For example, you might subconsciously make selective use of data, or you might feel pressurised to make a decision by strong colleagues. Decision-making in FPL is full of cognitive biases, different biases which continually influence the way some play the game. It is highly likely that many managers are affected by biases when playing the game. There are some that we are acutely aware of, yet fail to respond to. There are others that we unwittingly succumb to regularly.

In this section we will discuss some of the most common biases that could impact players in their pursuit of glory. Biases that could potentially result in sub-optimal reasoning and decision-making. The aim is to overcome any cognitive biases to make rational decisions. Being aware of, and recognizing, the various biases at play will enable you to understand how they can affect your decision-making. Responding to, and controlling, any biases will lead to logical decisions and enhance your game.

Action Bias

The thought that we should be doing something, whereas, in fact, things should be left alone. A tendency to act as opposed to restraint. For example, a goalkeeper who dives to the left or right during a penalty kick, even though statistically they would be better off just staying in the middle of the goal (Bar-Eli et al., 2007). Some may be too reactive and act immediately after one event. Sometimes, doing nothing and monitoring a situation before taking action is more beneficial. This may lead to better decision-making.

Many FPL players are too reactive and succumb to poor decisions. For example, knee-jerk rage transfers. Action bias may also be more likely in overconfident individuals or if a person has experienced prior negative outcomes where subsequent inaction led to failure (Zeelenberg et al., 2002).

Ambiguity Effect

The ambiguity effect is a bias where a lack of information influences decision-making. The effect implies that people tend to select options for which the probability of a favourable outcome is known, over an option for which the probability of a favourable outcome is unknown. For example, you are deciding which FPL striker to sign. Do you choose a striker who has just had an average season but their statistics are available, or do you select a relatively unknown striker who is new to the league and you don't have any data to compare the two? It's likely that the unknown player will be of a lower value, and have a lower ownership, purely because they are unknown. In this situation, you are more likely to select the player that you know something about, rather than the player who is relatively unknown, although they could be equivalent, or even better.

Anchoring

Anchoring bias causes us to rely too heavily on initial information, using it to make subsequent decisions. There is a tendency to favour the first piece of information that we learn about a particular topic. Once your opinion is formed, it can be difficult to consider other options. This is common when you are acting under pressure or have to make a snap decision. For example, when comparing your captaincy options, you may read several articles in relation to several standout candidates. After reading the first article featuring Mo Salah, you are more likely to select him as your captain, even though there may be better alternatives. Regardless of the accuracy of that information, people use it as a reference point, or anchor, to make subsequent judgments. You can avoid the anchoring effect by asking yourself questions which may reveal anchoring behaviour and recognise whether your decisions are emotionally driven. When deciding to buy, sell, or hold a player, think about whether you are giving enough consideration to all the available information and options. Actively challenge your assumptions and expectations by considering alternative scenarios and potential outcomes.

Availability Heuristic

The availability heuristic is a bias in which you make a decision based on an example, information, or a recent experience, that is readily available to you, even though it may not be the best example to inform your decision (Tversky & Kahneman, 1973). It is similar to the anchoring effect. The availability heuristic causes us to place a higher value on ideas that come to mind first. We are likely to "trust our gut" and go with the first instinctual solution we come up with. A tendency to utilise information that is widely covered and discussed in order to make our decisions. For example, it's become common knowledge amongst FPL players that Player A has become the regular penalty taker for his team. This dominates the discussion on social media. Regardless of the fact that they have contributed very little to the team or accumulated very few FPL points, you select them for your team based on that new information. In FPL, we also tend to rely on a player's recent performance in our decision-making process rather than a long-term trend. You may omit other possible solutions purely because you place more emphasis on the first idea, which you are convinced is the right one. It's a bias that is closely associated with transfers and, in particular, knee-jerk transfers.

Bandwagon Effect

The bandwagon effect is probably the most common and best known of all FPL biases. Many are aware of it, but it's still easy to be susceptible to it. It is likely that the vast majority of FPL players have jumped on a bandwagon during their FPL career. Social media is very influential and there is a propensity for people to adopt certain behaviours, styles, or attitudes simply because others are doing so. Once a belief gathers momentum, there is a tendency for people to adopt that belief. A bandwagon may emerge even though there is no data or evidence to support the theory that a specific player is a good FPL option. It is also common to see many flock to players who are gaining value early in the season to gain team value. Many don't want to miss out on such players and want a piece of the action. Some decide to ignore their personal misgivings and instead decide to follow the behaviour of others.

Belief Bias

Belief bias comes into effect when a person tends to judge the strength of arguments based on the plausibility of their conclusion rather than how strongly they support that conclusion. A person is more likely to accept an argument that supports a conclusion that aligns with their values, beliefs, and prior knowledge, while rejecting counter arguments to the conclusion. For example, in an effort to identify the best player to sign, you analyse data. You discover that the player with the best overall statistics is a player you dislike or underrate. Even though they appear to be the best option, you will be less willing to acknowledge the data and will be reluctant to sign the player.

Blind Spot

The blind spot is the cognitive bias of recognising the impact of biases on the judgement of others, while failing to see the impact of biases on one's own judgement. We believe that we are less susceptible to the very biases that we highlight in other individuals.

Choice-Supportive Bias

Choice-supportive bias is a propensity to retroactively ascribe positive attributes to an option one has selected and/or demote the forgone options. This occurs once a decision has been made. For example, if a manager chooses Player A over Player B, they are likely to ignore the faults of Player A while highlighting the negative faults of Player B. They are also likely to notice the advantages of Player A but ignore or de-emphasise the advantages of Player B.

Clustering Illusion

Clustering illusion bias is particularly applicable to FPL, a bias that arises from seeing a trend in random events that occur in clusters that are actually random events. The bias is often called the "hot hand fallacy", a phenomenon where a person who experiences a successful outcome has a greater chance of success in further attempts. For example, player A has scored in two consecutive games, so some will assume that their scoring streak is likely to continue because they are full of confidence or are benefiting from better finishing. In reality, streaks occur naturally in a small sample size, even if they appear to be non-random.

Some are inclined to overthink and try to attribute meaning to that trend or streak to try to justify the selection of a specific player. There are a couple of ways to avoid the clustering illusion. Firstly, instead of relying on data from the past week or two, expand that to include a 4-6 GW period. Random patterns seem more apparent when you have a small set of data. Therefore, a longer period will provide a more accurate picture of a player's performance. Secondly, seek information from a variety of different sources. When you make a decision/prediction based on a small amount of data, the chances of a mistake are high.

Confirmation Bias

A propensity to search for, interpret and utilise information in a fashion that confirms, supports and reinforces one's already established beliefs and preferences. There is also a tendency to disregard any evidence which doesn't support the belief. A bias which is common amongst FPL managers. We have sewn the seed in our minds of the player we would like to sign, or to select as our captain, for that Gameweek, but we look for a seal of approval. For example, running a poll amongst the FPL Community on Twitter. Typically, we look for fellow managers to support and reinforce our already established beliefs. You may still sign a player that you liked from the outset, despite your research indicating that the player isn't a particularly good option.

Conservatism Bias

Conservatism bias is a resistance to change your opinion about something, even when presented with new information. A bias that is related to anchoring. This is a common FPL bias and is relevant to your decision-making. One's unwillingness to effectively utilise new information to update a plan. It is always wise to consider the new knowledge that becomes available in order to make the optimal decision. For example, new data is made available to suggest that an alternative player would be a better signing. That data, along with all relevant information, should be considered as a part of your decision-making process and your plans adjusted accordingly.

Endowment Effect

The endowment effect is where we place a higher value on something that we own. For example, in FPL there could be a propensity for some managers to retain certain players irrespective of them being an underperforming FPL asset. The effect often leads to stubborn behaviour. The displeasure of losing a player outweighs the pleasure we would get by signing an alternative. Some managers are inclined to focus their transfers on moves that won't lose points, rather than those that might gain points. For example, one of your strikers hasn't scored for several games, but instead of replacing them with an in-form striker your preference is to retain that out-of-form player. You decide to keep the underperforming player purely because their next fixture is favourable and you don't want to miss out on a potential points haul. Sometimes, managers become attached to specific players because they have done well for them in the past. Avoiding sentiment and distancing yourself from that player is a sensible approach to adopt.

Mere-Exposure Effect

The mere-exposure effect is a psychological phenomenon by which people tend to develop a misguided preference for things that they are familiar with over unfamiliar alternatives. For example, if you are a Manchester Utd fan and watch the majority of their games, you may be more inclined to pick Utd players when selecting your FPL squad.

Gambler's Fallacy

The gambler's fallacy is a mistaken belief about sequences of random events. In FPL we often see the term 'Player A is due a goal'. There is an assumption that because a particular event hasn't occurred as frequently as expected in a given period of time, it is likely to happen more frequently in the future or vice-versa. Therefore, we regularly make the assumption that Player A is due a goal because he hasn't scored a goal in his last four appearances, even though the statistics paint a different picture. However, the fact that they haven't scored in their most recent performances should be disregarded as it doesn't make them more likely to score in the next game. A combination of statistics and eye test from the previous games can be considered, but the upcoming fixtures should be looked at in isolation.

Framing Effect

The framing effect is a cognitive bias where people decide on options based on whether the options are presented with positive or negative connotations. People tend to avoid risk when a positive frame is presented but seek risks when a negative frame is presented. In terms of FPL, the way that data is presented can lead you to making a sub-optimal decision. Occasionally, data is presented to support a particular narrative. Hence, collecting data for a particular player from a number of different sources will be beneficial.

Groupthink

Otherwise known as herd mentality, a topic that is discussed in Part 7. The practice of making decisions as a group, typically resulting in unchallenged poor-quality decision-making. This is very prevalent amongst the FPL communities on social media.

Hindsight Bias

Hindsight bias is also known as the knew-it-all-along phenomenon or creeping determination. It's the tendency for people to perceive past events as having been more predictable than they actually were. For example, if a player collects a major points haul, it can be easy to be annoyed by the fact that you didn't select that player even if their performance was totally unexpected. People act like an outcome was more predictable after the event than it was prior to the event.

Omission Bias

Omission bias is the phenomenon in which people prefer omission (inaction) over commission (action). People tend to judge harm as a result of commission more negatively than harm as a result of omission. For example, you select Mo Salah as your captain early in the week and he collects 2 points in his game. In contrast, Harry Kane, your vice-captain registered a 15-point haul. You will feel better about the outcome if you had stuck with your original captaincy selection than if you had changed the captaincy from Kane to Salah just prior to the deadline.

Outcome Bias

Outcome bias is the tendency to evaluate our decisions based on the eventual outcome, as opposed to the decision-making process (Baron & Hershey, 1988). It's impossible for all of our decisions to be successful. Occasionally, people will make a poor decision. However, on many occasions, you may have come to the correct and justified decision, but for a number of reasons it was unsuccessful. It's assumed that those who had a good Gameweek made better decisions than those that didn't, but that's not necessarily the case. Instead of questioning whether you made the best decision, you should be asking yourself if you are happy with the decision-making process you adopted and the decision you made. Avoid outcome bias by evaluating decisions based on the decision-making process rather than the eventual outcome. Focusing on the process should lead to a more effective and accurate decision-making process.

Optimism & Pessimism Bias

Optimism bias leads people to believe that they are more likely to experience good over bad events. It can also cause people to overestimate their own success in comparison to others. In contrast, pessimism bias causes people to overestimate the likelihood of negative things and underestimate the likelihood of positive outcomes. This goes hand in hand with outcome bias. The easiest way to avoid optimism bias is to have a balanced approach. In FPL, instead of just focusing on one Gameweek it is worthwhile looking at the bigger picture.

Plan Continuation Bias

Plan continuation bias is the inclination for an individual to continue with an original course of action that is no longer viable, or once better alternatives have become available. For example, you sign a quality player for a forthcoming DGW and the long-term. They fail to deliver a goal or an assist in four weeks and look below par. Their team is also struggling on the pitch. Meanwhile, several players have exploded onto the scene with some major point-hauls. They become viable options. Instead of considering alternatives, you persist in your original plan to hold on to the player even though they are consistently underperforming. There is a need to continually reassess your plans and adapt to a changing game.

Primacy-Recency Effect

The primacy/recency effect is the observation that information presented at the beginning (primacy) and end (recency) of a topic tends to be retained more than information presented in the middle. We may place high importance on the first piece of information that we receive, followed closely by the most recent information. This could easily apply to several FPL situations. For example, when selecting your initial team or activating your Wildcard. There will be a tendency to select players from your first and last number of drafts and very few from the middle drafts. One way to avoid this is to consider all of your options. For example, when selecting your 15-man squad, you could screenshot every draft so you have a complete picture of your thought process throughout your planning stage. They can be referred to prior to finalising your selection.

Pseudocertainty Effect

The pseudocertainty effect refers to people's propensity to make risk-averse choices if the expected outcome is positive, but make risk-seeking choices to avoid negative outcomes. A classic example of this in FPL is those managers who are having a successful season and play safe to protect their rank. While those that are chasing rank are tempted to take more risks to make up ground on those above them.

Recency Bias

Recency bias is a cognitive bias that favours recent events over historical ones; a memory bias. Recency bias gives greater importance to the most recent event. A bias that can often lead to a manager chasing points and can produce knee-jerk decisions. A player scores a points-haul and suddenly they are highly desirable. More emphasis is placed on their most recent performance rather than the fact that they have been underperforming for a period of time.

Scarcity Heuristic

The scarcity heuristic is where people tend to place a higher value on items that are perceived as scarce and a lower value on things that are seen to be abundant. Gold is a good example because we value it entirely for its rarity. In fantasy football, this can be observed when we over-value premium players and under-value budget options. You may be inclined to play out of form premium assets because of their value, while ignoring in-form budget players who are accumulating points consistently.

Selection Bias

Selection bias is a distortion in a measure of association due to a sample selection that does not accurately reflect the target population. It is sometimes referred to as the selection effect. For example, you conducted a poll amongst Manchester Utd supporters about who would be the best FPL captain in a particular Gameweek; Bruno Fernandes, Kevin De Bruyne or Harry Kane. It's highly likely that Fernandes will be the popular choice. If you asked the same question with a wider audience, it is likely to produce a different outcome.

Sunk Cost Fallacy

The phenomenon whereby a person is reluctant to abandon a strategy or course of action because they have invested heavily in it, even when it is clear that abandonment would be more beneficial. A typical FPL example is our reluctance to sell a valuable asset, even though the player hasn't been producing significant points. Their value may have increased considerably since you first purchased them. Although you should sell them, you don't because you're overly influenced by the money invested in them. You can avoid the sunk cost fallacy by rationally assessing whether the strategy/outcome is successful.

Survivorship Bias

Survivorship Bias is a cognitive fallacy in which, when looking at a given group, you only focus on the successful individuals rather than the group as a whole. The bias can lead to people becoming overly optimistic because multiple failures are overlooked. For example, the bias is a logical error that occurs because we assume that success provides a clear picture of a player's ability without factoring in any failures. For example, you watch the highlights of a particular game and note the two big chances that a midfielder created for a colleague. However, what you did not see was the countless times that the same player lost possession of the ball through some poor passing. You conclude that the player had an excellent game and is a desirable FPL asset, even though they gave the ball away numerous times.

A good way of making sound logical decisions, that also minimises the impact of biases, is to adopt a data-driven approach. Statistics are relevant and do not take into account our feelings towards players in our decision-making process. Being aware of the various biases at play and avoiding them will lead to a more effective decision-making process.

Remaining Positive

"If you quit once it becomes a habit. NEVER QUIT." –
Michael Jordan

FPL is an emotional rollercoaster and we are all susceptible to the emotional stress caused by the highs and lows of the game. This can have an impact on our mental health. It's now common to see members of the FPL community sharing their experiences of the negative impact the game is having on their mental well-being. Many are likely to go through a bad spell at some point.

The important thing is knowing how to cope with those occasions. Acknowledging that we will experience both ends of the spectrum will help us manage our emotional feelings and elevate our game. Studies suggest that there is a tendency for more experienced players to be able to cope better with the emotional aspects of the game. Players enjoy the highs when their team produces an exceptional week beyond all expectations, and they can't wait to reset and go again. In contrast, many will suffer a horrendous week and cannot be bothered to look at their team. The negativity has taken its toll.

At the start of a new season, many managers will adopt a strategy to help them navigate through an arduous campaign: a long-term plan to help them achieve their overall aim. Whether that be winning a mini-league or achieving an outstanding global ranking. The primary aim of playing FPL is to seek enjoyment. However, having aspirations and setting yourself a milestone at the outset will keep you motivated throughout a demanding season and enhance your game. Each time you hit a new milestone, it's an achievement. It revitalises one's passion for the game, whether it be breaking through the one million barrier for the first time, the top 500k or the top 10k. The milestone has been conquered. It's something that turbo charges a manager's enthusiasm for playing the game. Prioritising and setting yourself goals will keep you motivated during the highs and lows, but it will also inspire you to achieve that target.

Unsurprisingly, many players who have an impressive GW will share their success on social media. Conversely, many who have experienced a disappointing week will be reluctant to share their team's performance. This creates a false perception. Social media will give the impression that the vast majority of players had an exceptional week and you are one of a minority who had a discouraging week. It's something that doesn't help to lift your spirits. In reality, this couldn't be further from the truth. You are being fed a distorted picture because, generally, many will only highlight the positives. There is a tendency for many to discuss their favourable outcomes, but not their poor performances. Hence, social media is building a false impression. Some players who suffer a sub-standard Gameweek will be negatively affected by the positivity amongst other players. In addition, an extremely poor week will see your rank and standings in your mini-leagues plummet. This has the potential to dent one's confidence, particularly if you are an active member of the FPL community, or based in leagues with your work colleagues or friends. Bragging rights are on offer. If you are a 'committed' player, it's likely that the negative effects are going to be more significant.

The important thing is how you cope with the moments of despair. No player is immune from a shocking Gameweek; acknowledging that it's inevitable will help control your emotions. The ideal response to a setback is to bounce back with an outstanding week. Every player will experience the highs and the lows. It should make you more determined to succeed. Accepting that you will experience those low moments may help you to keep a positive mindset. It's just one week in a long season and you can guarantee that many will be in a similar situation. Embracing the lows will allow you to enjoy the highs even more.

Many players are totally focused on FPL and frantically follow the action at every conceivable moment, periodically checking their score and live rank as the GW develops. If it starts to get too much, then that is the time to take a step back and have a cooling-off period. If you are becoming emotionally drained, then you may find a short break beneficial. Some players now commit to the 'Match of The Day Challenge', avoiding all the football news and catching up with all the day's action on a highlights programme later in the day. Instead of having a long fix of peaks and troughs throughout a typical match day, you get to experience the highlights without the stresses and strains of following the real-time action.

Several steps can be taken which could prove beneficial to your mental well-being. Having a set routine is a good idea. For example, focusing on your decision-making in the mornings when you are fresh. Wait for the conclusion of all the press conferences before you confirm any transfers. Setting up your bus team (see Glossary) at the start of the week just in case you won't have the opportunity to update it later in the week. Identify the websites, podcasts, content creators which can provide you with the best FPL information. Avoid match updates, live scores and rank when matches are in progress. Taking a step back when things get overwhelming is a sensible move. If you are regularly active on social media, it may be the ideal time to take a short break. Alternatively, if you are struggling, there will be members of the FPL community on social media in a similar situation. Many people will be more than happy to listen to what you have to say. Don't be afraid to talk. Find someone that you trust or enjoy talking to, and ask them if they can give you some time to talk things through.

If you do encounter a bad spell, never throw in the towel. FPL is a marathon and not a sprint and you will have sufficient time to turn your fortunes around. The appropriate word is perseverance. Having a positive mindset will help. Take the poor Gameweeks on the chin, dust yourself down and be ready to go even stronger the following week. As a part of my research, I examined the performance of some of the top players towards the business end of the 2020/21 season. A crunch time, whether you are still looking to improve your rank, consolidate a top 10k finish or win your mini-league. Undoubtedly, by now, many teams would have thrown in the towel and become inactive as their enthusiasm for the game has diminished. However, there is still a lot to play for; pride, bragging rights, to name just a few. Never give up.

> **"Success is not final, failure is not fatal:**
> **it is the courage to continue that counts."** –
> Winston Churchill

The next time that you experience a spate of red arrows, then consider the followings findings. Below, you will find five examples of teams that achieved a top 1k, 10k and 100k after heroic performances in the final eight GWs of the 2020/21 season. The statistics are provided courtesy of myfplanalysis.co.in.

Team	Rank after GW30	Rank after GW38
A	32,029	896
B	28,759	957
C	26,442	807
D	24,465	898
E	23,399	475
Team	Rank after GW30	Rank after GW38
A	174,693	6,424
B	152,801	8,587
C	149,279	9,694
D	127,724	4,963
E	121,562	9,992
Team	Rank after GW30	Rank after GW38
A	747,818	90,078
B	702,849	87,791
C	687,044	81,530
D	676,463	82,224
E	664,544	75,747

Notably, each team made remarkable progress during those final eight Gameweeks. It is common to see significant jumps in rank at the start of the season when the majority of teams are grouped together. However, to make such progress towards the end of the season highlights what can be achieved in a short space of time. This should offer you plenty of encouragement, so the next time that you see your rank plummet, do not concede defeat.

Irrespective of a couple of disappointing Gameweeks and a drop in rank, it is possible to turn your season around and achieve an excellent rank. Keep the faith.

"Inspiration comes from within yourself. One has to be POSITIVE. When you're positive, good things happen." –
Deep Roy

Part 5: Strategies To Succeed

"Our goals can only be reached through the vehicle of a plan. There is no other route to success." – Pablo Picasso

FPL is a game of strategy and has been compared to chess. You need to plan your moves well in advance. A good strategy requires a forward-looking manager who is willing to adapt and find innovative ways to accumulate FPL points. To succeed, the strategies you adopt are key factors that can make or break your season. In this section, we will discuss three key aspects of the game, including captaincy, your bench strategy, and planning. Strategies that will help you out-manoeuvre your rivals and gain an advantage.

Captaincy: Selecting The Right Captain

Important decisions need to be made regularly throughout the season, from your initial draft to your Gameweek 38 team selection. Arguably, selecting your captain is the most important decision that you will make each week. The importance of your captaincy selection cannot be over-emphasised as it can account for up to 30% of your total points tally over the gruelling campaign. The outcome of your Gameweek can be defined by the number of points scored by your captain. Additionally, the success of your captaincy selections will have a huge bearing on your final rank. It can be the difference between achieving your desired target or not, or whether you finish with an average or elite rank. Therefore, selecting your optimal captain for each GW should be given top priority.

Your aim is to select the player in your starting XI who you believe will deliver the most FPL points that week. As opposed to choosing a leader on the pitch, or a player you particularly like. It's likely that your captain will be an expensive asset who is fundamental to your team's success. A proven premium player who is capable of delivering significant point hauls consistently to bolster your points total. Occasionally, premium assets do suffer an off day, but reliability is one of their classic traits. They have a propensity to deliver FPL points. A prime example of selecting your best captain is that of Mo Salah in DGW26 of the 2021/22 season. Title-chasing Liverpool faced Norwich City and Leeds Utd at Anfield, two teams that at the time were struggling at the foot of the Premier League table. Salah performed heroics and accumulated 28 points. For those managers who had activated their Triple Captain chip, that amounted to a handsome 84 points. The decision whether or not to Triple Captain Salah for that DGW made a huge difference not only to your Gameweek score but to your final overall rank at the conclusion of the season.

There are several valid reasons for taking a hit. I suggest that signing a player who you intend to captain in the next fixture and in the foreseeable future is a viable option. This becomes a far more attractive proposition if the player is in-form and their next set of fixtures is favourable. Typically, the points deficit incurred will be erased immediately or soon afterwards. Additionally, they will continue to reward you for the remaining period that you own them. That is a factor to consider in your decision-making process.

Another factor which invariably plays a part in that process is a player's ownership (TSB%) and the likely effects of their effective ownership upon your rank if you decide to captain them or not. If you are trying to chase rank, you may want to consider a differential captain. It is a risky strategy, particularly if many of the premium assets with a high EO have favourable fixtures. If your differential captain fails whilst the highly owned premium assets thrive, you will see your rank plummet. Conversely, if your differential captain produces a masterclass and most of the premium assets fail, it could be hugely rewarding. Typically, you would benefit from a substantial climb in rank. Protecting or attacking rank is discussed in the Sword and Shield strategy.

Generally, the safest route to success, and to protect your rank, is to play safe and select a captain who is a reliable premium asset. There is a group of proven premium players who consistently deliver outstanding performances and FPL points. Ideally, an in-form premium asset with a favourable fixture. Traditionally, come the business end of the season, they feature amongst the highest FPL points scorers. For example, Mo Salah, Harry Kane and Kevin De Bruyne all fall into this category. It's no coincidence that they are all quality players, are on set pieces, and a couple of them are on penalty duty. The FPL landscape changed during the 2022/23 season with the arrival of Erling Haaland. He immediately demonstrated his class and registered double-digit hauls frequently. After a blistering start to the season, Haaland was in high demand, culminating in him setting a new captaincy record in GW10. He not only featured in 84% of teams, but no fewer than 7,105,791 managers gave him the armband that week. That equated to 67% of all players.

A useful tactic is to draft a captaincy matrix and identify a captaincy option six to eight weeks in advance. Despite forward planning, you can always reassess and adjust your selections as the season evolves, or if the need arises. Fixtures, form, injury and the possibility of rotation, etc. should also be considered as a part of your decision-making process. Occasionally, we experience instances when a player comes into red-hot form, attracts our attention and demands the armband. A prime example of this was Ilkay Gundogan during the 2020/21 campaign, when he had had a blistering spell for Manchester City. A combination of favourable fixtures, impressive form and substantial points is too good to ignore. Gundogan certainly fell into that category.

Gundogan exploded into life in GW13 with a 10-point haul against West Brom. Over the next 14 weeks, the City maestro was irresistible. During his purple patch (see Glossary), Gundogan was simply sensational and he took the league by storm. He was the top FPL points scorer during that spell after accumulating 130 points. That comprised 12 goals and 3 assists. Gundogan's popularity soared and, like many others, I captained him in DGW24 when he was due to face Spurs and Everton. Unfortunately, he sustained an injury during the Spurs game, which ruled him out of the Everton game. However, he still had sufficient time to score 38 points in City's 3-0 victory.

Another example of targeting an in-form player is Heung-Min Son, who went on an exceptional run towards the latter end of the 2021/22 season. Between GWs 24-38 he scored a staggering 150 points. If you were fortunate enough to have captained him regularly during this red-hot spell, it could have been game changing. Son was a points magnet. He was ably assisted by his team mate Harry Kane, who scored 126 points, to be the second highest scorer in that profitable period.

An excellent website for monitoring your captaincy statistics is premierfantasytools.com. The site provides you with details of your captaincy selections and success rate. Many FPL websites produce weekly captaincy articles which will aid you in your decision-making process. Typically, the main captaincy candidates and their GW fixtures will be discussed. Digesting information from such articles can be very beneficial.

My captaincy picks for the 2021/22 season were a tale of two halves. The first half of the season had a 78.95% success rate, whilst that figure dipped to 63.16% during the second half. Mo Salah's dip in form after his return from AFCON may have contributed to a disappointing finale. My team registered 27 successful selections, an overall success rate of 72%. All 27 selections produced double-digit hauls with five of those exceeding 30 points. I amassed 630 points, with the most successful week being DGW26, when I captained Mo Salah. The 'Egyptian King' gave me 56 valuable points. In contrast, the epic failure during the season came from Watford's Emmanuel Dennis in DGW23. Dennis had shown glimpses of form so, like many, I entrusted him with the armband. The DGW included an enticing fixture against bottom of the table Norwich City. Some petulance by Dennis saw him shown a red card in the Norwich game. Not only did he score minus two, but he was also ruled out of the second game through suspension. My 630 captaincy points accounted for 26% of my total points, which was significantly down on the previous season.

To highlight the importance of your selections, below you will find a summary of the average number of captaincy points achieved by managers at various ranks from one to 6m during the 2021/22 season. The data displays the rank parameters plus the average number of points accumulated (statistics are courtesy of www.livefpl.net). As a comparison, the statistics for the previous season have also been included.

Overall Rank	Average Captain Points 2020/21	Average Captain Points 2021/22
Top 100	619.24	783.38
Top 1k	611.23	754.70
Top 10k	601.25	731.15
Top 100k	578.58	697.11
100k-200k	559.31	672.31
200k-300k	546.80	653.93
300k-400k	541.94	642.37
400k-500k	528.85	628.63
500k-600k	526.98	625.57
600k-700k	519.44	619.45
700k-800k	517.15	614.44
800k-900k	511.06	598.31
900k-1m	508.82	601.77
1m-1.5m	501.56	582.14
1.5m-2m	483.73	546.40
2m-3m	469.69	525.48
3m-6m	421.89	462.42

It is noteworthy that there is a significant increase in the average number of points in 2021/22 in comparison to the previous season. This is applicable to players at all ranks up to 6m. Undoubtedly, the record number of double Gameweeks combined with an extra FH chip contributed to the rise in average points. The statistics confirm that there is a very strong correlation between captaincy points and overall rank. It is interesting to note that the average number of points decreases gradually as your rank worsens. The statistics will enable you to determine how successful your captaincy selections were for both seasons. In all likelihood, the average number of points achieved by teams with a rank exceeding 1m is reduced as a result of the inclusion of many inactive 'ghost' teams. However, there is still overwhelming evidence to demonstrate that a higher number of captaincy points contributed to a team's improved performance and rank. It's also highly likely that the owners of the top teams are more engaged in the game.

Remarkably, there was a significant increase in the number of captaincy points (164.14) for the Top One Hundred Managers between both seasons. It's reasonable to assume that the increased number of DGWs, plus Salah's magnificent 84 triple captaincy points in DGW26 were influential factors. The top captaincy score for 2020/21 was 732 points, a figure that is overshadowed by the incredible 908 points achieved in the following season. Typically, captaincy points account for approximately 30% of a top team's total score. However, for the 2021/22 season, that figure rose to a staggering 36.77% of their entire score. A statistic that reaffirms the value of your captaincy selections.

Unbelievably, 12 of the 13 teams responsible for the highest number of captaincy points managed to clinch a top 7k finish. The only team not to do so, achieved an overall rank of 51k. Of the top 20 teams for captaincy points, two recorded a top 100 finish, three teams finished between 100-500, four 500-1k, five 1k-5k, two 5k-10k and two between 10k-20k. Listed below are the number of teams with the highest captaincy points who finished at various ranks below the 10k barrier.

Overall Rank	No of Teams
Top 100	5
200-500	4
500-1k	5
1k-2k	3
2k-5k	9
5k-10k	5

Successful captaincy selections can build you a strong foundation for an exceptional season. Listed below are the teams who finished inside the top 10k during the 2020/21 campaign with the highest number of captaincy points. Highlighted are their overall rank, captaincy points, FPL points and captaincy points as a percentage of their total points (statistics courtesy of myfplanalysis.co.in.)

Overall Rank	Captain Points	Total Points	Captain Points as a Percentage
5,638	732	2510	29.2
5,178	730	2512	29.1
5,461	728	2510	29
4,021	726	2519	28.8
967	724	2557	28.3
6,923	722	2503	28.8
2,139	720	2537	28.4
6,469	718	2506	28.7
5,366	715	2511	28.5
9,155	707	2494	28.3

The top manager accumulated 732 points, which accounted for 29.2% of their total score. The majority of top managers made excellent captaincy choices, which accounted for 28% - 30% of their entire score. A percentage which enabled them to finish the season with an impressive rank. I analysed the captaincy selections made by the top 10k managers during the 2020/21 season to ascertain which players were the most popular. It also identified which position those players played in. Below is a summary of the findings. The data highlights the number of times that a player was the most popular captaincy choice during the season with their highest GW ownership (TSB%).

	Times as Top Captain Pick	Highest Percentage
Salah	12	93.83
Kane	7	94.44
De-Bruyne	6	79.63
Fernandes	6	95.06
Gundogan	3	75.93
Aubameyang	1	93.21
Bamford	1	85.80
Vardy	1	42.59
Son	1	36.42

Just nine players featured as the most popular captaincy options amongst the top 10k managers. Unsurprisingly, six of the players were midfielders and three were forwards. Four of the players only featured once, while the four most popular selections were premium assets. It's evident from the data that the top 10k managers were targeting a premium asset with good fixtures for the majority of the season. For example, Liverpool had a favourable run of fixtures to close the season, hence it was no surprise to find that Mo Salah was the favoured choice for the final three weeks. Some of the selections are self-explanatory. After putting Southampton to the sword in GW2, Son was the standout choice in GW5 as Spurs entertained West Ham. Ilkay Gundogan featured regularly during his purple patch between GWs 13-27.

The captaincy statistics for the Top 50 managers from the 2020/21 season, along with an Elite group of All Time Top 50 players, were analysed (statistics courtesy of Fantasy Football Fix). Mo Salah was the most popular option amongst the top 50 managers with 29.4%, followed by Harry Kane with 22.2%. Salah and Kane were also the preferred choice for the All Time Top 50 group, with 33.4% and 16.9% respectively. The data revealed that the top managers preferred a premium asset as their captain, particularly those on penalties. As a comparison, I looked at an All FPL User group, which comprised the remaining FPL managers. A different approach was adopted by this group. Harry Kane was their preferred captaincy choice with 17.3%, followed by Bruno Fernandes with 17.2%. Surprisingly, Mo Salah was only third with 14.8%. There was a distinct difference between the All FPL User group in comparison to the other two groups. One possible explanation for this is the fact that the All User group included many inactive teams.

A similar analysis was conducted for the 2021/22 season. Due to the increased number of double Gameweeks, it was evident that the choice of captaincy was far more widespread, with players like Emmanuel Dennis and Wout Weghorst becoming popular options. Mo Salah was again the preferred captaincy choice for both the Top 50 (47.1%) and the All Time Top 50 groups (50.6%). It was evident that both groups had selected 70% of their captains from the 'big six' teams. In comparison, the All FPL user group captained Salah just 39.3% of the time. Although they did target players from the top six teams. The analysis showed that merely attacking a fixture is not enough, picking an in-form player is just as important.

There is a tendency for some to overthink their choice of captain; keeping it simple is the safest route. Generally, there are very few standout candidates per GW, so it's unusual to be confronted with a selection headache. For the majority of the time, your decision is straightforward and the most obvious captaincy candidate is evident. Therefore, try not to overcomplicate a straightforward decision. However, on occasions, you will encounter weeks whereby you will have several standout options. That's when it becomes really difficult. Owning at least two premium assets is recommended as it provides you with a minimum of two strong options to choose from. With the uncertainty surrounding fixture postponements, it is always advisable to pick your captain and vice-captain from different teams. Ideally, both are not involved in the same fixture either. This is a sensible precaution because being deprived of both will cost you dearly.

Your captaincy selection is crucial therefore, it's advisable that you give your decision-making serious consideration. Thorough research needs to be conducted, and fixtures and form are two important elements of your decision-making process that need to come into the equation. As with your team selection, selecting a differential player as your captain can be very rewarding. However, it is a very risky strategy. If your captaincy choice fails and the most popular captains thrive, you will experience a significant drop in rank. To set yourself apart from the pack, it's a case of picking a differential captain at the appropriate time. Personally, I wouldn't make a habit of it, otherwise it will ultimately cost you. Unless you are desperately trying to climb rank or win your mini-league, the safest route to success is selecting a proven in-form premium player with a favourable fixture to fulfil that role. Double Gameweeks provide the ideal opportunity to achieve a substantial captaincy score. Therefore, targeting an in-form DGW premium player with two good fixtures is optimal. The pure jubilation of a captaincy haul is what we play the game for.

Bench Strategy

When building your 15-man squad, you will have a substitute keeper and three outfield players. Your substitutes provide cover for any unforeseen events and will automatically replace a selected player who doesn't play any minutes that Gameweek. If your goalkeeper doesn't feature, they will be replaced by your sub-keeper provided they play. An outfield player will be substituted by the highest priority outfield substitute who played that GW and doesn't break formation rules. For example, if your starting XI only has three defenders, a defender can only be replaced by another defender. Your preferred XI will determine which outfield players are left on your bench. Therefore, your bench order is important. You need to consider the pros and cons of each player before prioritising your bench order. The strongest sub needs to be your first sub and the weakest your third sub.

Adopting an effective bench strategy is important as it's another key aspect of FPL which will contribute towards your success. There are two schools of thought. Firstly, leaving an excessive number of points on your bench is indicative of poor team selection. Conversely, owning a strong squad with high-scoring quality players stranded on your bench highlights the strength within the squad. Attitudes towards the bench vary considerably amongst managers. Some regard the Bench Boost chip as the least valuable chip and consider it to be a hindrance. Many argue that a fair chunk of your budget is swallowed up by strengthening your bench in readiness for activating your chip. Money that could be better spent on strengthening your main playing XI. Leaving a sizeable number of points on your bench and not on the pitch is frustrating and undesirable.

Recently, the demands on the bench have changed considerably. The Covid pandemic caused a record number of fixture postponements and highlighted just how important your bench can be. Consequently, we have become accustomed to relying on our benches more often. The 2022/23 season heralded a change in rules for the Premier League. Ultimately, the changes could have an impact on the way we utilise our bench. Due to the demands on players, clubs are now allowed to make up to five substitutions per game, which will undoubtedly have a knock-on effect for FPL managers. Clubs will exploit the new rules and game time management will be a major issue. In all likelihood, bench players will be called upon frequently and rotation will be a common theme. Some players will either start a game and be substituted early, while others will appear off the bench and play a limited number of minutes. Trying to identify which players are likely to start is important and the dynamics of your bench will change. Therefore, the impact of the rule change needs to be monitored. Selecting your optimal team and bench order weekly is challenging, but luck allowing it rewards the stronger managers.

Preferably, the aim is to leave as many points as possible on the pitch and not on our bench. Although, the game is fraught with 'what-ifs' and 'if-only' moments, plus there are those 50/50 team selection decisions we often encounter. Trying to minimise the number of bench points could make a considerable difference to your final rank. The more points stranded on your bench, the lower your rank. Conversely, the higher the points accumulated by your starting XI, the higher your rank will be. The question is: how do you minimise the number of bench points and maximise your weekly score?

Traditionally, when completing their initial draft, the majority of managers opt to invest more funds in their starting XI to the detriment of their bench. They leave their bench threadbare and rely upon 'enablers' or 'bench fodder'; terms used to describe cheap players who usually fulfil a role as a substitute, normally second or third sub. Players who have little chance of being regular starters. The benefit, of course, is that their low price enables managers to invest the extra funds to strengthen their main starting XI. That could be the difference between owning a mid-priced or premium asset. However, as the season evolves and team value increases, managers will have extra funds to invest in their bench if they so wish.

When tackling their bench, managers opt for several different tactics. Risk-averse managers will build a well-balanced squad with a fully functioning bench that boasts three active players. Owning a bench comprising regular starters will almost guarantee a full-strength team every week. This offers some reassurance during unprecedented times. However, spreading your budget across the entire squad is the only downside. Regular starters are likely to cost you more than backup players, which will have a knock-on effect. Investing more in your bench will reduce your buying power and the number of premium assets may be limited. The only question is; is it worth having quality players marooned on your bench weekly?

Some argue that owning a stronger bench is an effective way of increasing team value, while others will maintain that doing so will have a detrimental effect on your points tally. There are alternative means to gain team value. For example, using your free transfers or Wildcard to target not only the best signings, but those that are increasing in price. Distributing money across your entire squad creates a new dilemma - who starts and who remains on your bench? Suddenly, with increased competition, you're likely to have a weekly selection headache. Investing extra funds on your bench not only takes value from your playing XI, but selecting your optimal team each week becomes more challenging. In today's climate, it is desirable to have sufficient playing coverage on your bench in the event of unforeseen circumstances. However, investing in your bench to gain team value may not be a viable option.

Another group of managers will play relatively safe by owning a minimum of two playing outfield substitutes. This will provide adequate coverage in the event of absentees. Generally, their third sub-spot is occupied by an enabler, usually a 4m defender. This tactic allows them to invest the extra funds in their starting XI. The chances of this type of team incurring hits to cover injuries and suspensions increases slightly. The third type of manager is more daring - a manager who will seek to invest heavily in the starting XI to maximise output. Typically, they show no desire to invest in their bench and opt to take a gamble by owning just one active substitute who is usually an enabler. The other two spots are taken up by 'super-subs' who either get the odd minute, or no game time at all. Such teams may be fortunate at the beginning of the season, but as the season progresses and injuries become more prevalent, they may struggle to field a full-strength team. Owning just one playing substitute is a risky strategy and the chances of this type of team incurring hits to cover absentees increases significantly.

Occasionally, some rare hidden gems are uncovered. Typically, they are cheap players with no playing history who were initially expected to fulfil a backup role. An injury crisis could see them catapulted into the team, they perform well and go onto become regular starters. Many look for a bargain, so once a budget player becomes a regular starter and shows some form, they become an attractive proposition amongst the FPL fraternity. Their price will soon rise, so the sooner you spot them and jump on the bandwagon the greater reward. Two good examples from the 2021/22 campaign include Jacob Ramsey and Anthony Gordon. The one time that you will require a fully functional bench is when you play your Bench Boost chip.

It is common to see FPL managers posting images of their teams amongst the FPL community on Twitter. Typically, they relate to their starting XI or a summary of their weekly performance. However, it's now routine to see some post images of their bench performance, a bench which proudly boasts 30-50 points. Occasionally, their bench will outscore the rest of their team. For example, FPL Psycho (@PsychoFpl) left 55 points on his bench in GW28 of the 2021/22 season (Martinez 12, Targett 4, Kane 13 & Cash 26). Having an excessive number of points stranded on your bench is disheartening and is one of those low points in FPL. A classic 'if-only' moment. Undoubtedly, the majority of players have experienced similar moments at some point during their FPL careers. It's inevitable that eventually all managers will be guilty of leaving too many points on their bench, a frustrating experience which can have an adverse effect on your rank. At the conclusion of the 2018/19 season, I left an incredible 371 points on my bench.

That figure has gradually been reduced and during the 2021/22 season I accumulated 216 bench points. That included eight double-digit hauls, the highest being 23 points in GW29. Making a concerted effort to reduce your bench points by selecting your optimal XI, and the best bench order, will prove beneficial.

Recently, there has been an unprecedented number of fixture postponements, with several of those occurring after the Gameweek deadline. Consequently, managers have had to rely on their bench more often than they normally would. If you were on the wrong side of those post-deadline postponements, clearly your luck was out. For example, in GW13 of the 2021/22 season, Burnley vs Tottenham was postponed within an hour of the scheduled kick-off. The culprit on this occasion was not Covid, but heavy snow at Turf Moor. Frequently, we encounter 50/50 calls which could go either way. For example, choosing between two players who have similar underlying statistics and fixtures. The stronger your squad, the tougher the decisions.

During the pandemic, it was remarkable to see a considerable number of managers being caught out by having insufficient playing cover on their bench. In addition to Covid infections, managers had to contend with the usual injuries and suspensions. Consequently, many suffered, although some success stories did emerge from the disruption. For example, Stuart Dallas with his unexpected 17-point haul at Manchester City in GW31 of the 2020/21 season. It seemed that the entire FPL community benefited from the Leeds defender being automatically subbed off their bench with his haul. Many were delighted with the outcome and, for once, fortune was on their side.

Bizarrely, during the 2021/22 campaign, there was a spate of injuries amongst the forwards. Consequently, many incurred points deductions purely because they didn't have adequate bench coverage and couldn't field a full-strength team. Non-disclosure of injuries at press conferences or late training injuries is unfortunate, but the lack of planning can also contribute to unnecessary hits being taken. Managing your bench is a fine balancing act. You do not want your bench to account for a significant amount of your 100m budget when that money could be better spent elsewhere. However, neither do you want a bench full of enablers with no playing coverage whatsoever. Neglecting your bench is perilous because it can cost you points deductions.

Every season, some bargain defenders offer great value. There are the odd 4m gems and plenty of 4.5m players who not only start regularly but have the potential to accrue clean sheets points and the odd attacking return. For example, Ben White at Arsenal. If you are looking to save 0.5m to invest elsewhere, selecting a 4m defender as your third sub is wise. Owning a non-starter who gets an unexpected transfer and manages to acquire some minutes at their new club is an added bonus. For example, Neco Williams who went on loan from Liverpool to Fulham during the 2021/22 season. The primary function of a 4.5 million midfielder is to fulfil a standby role on your bench, but be available in an emergency. It's unusual to see a midfielder at this price point start for their respective team. Although, occasionally, a few go against the grain. My preference would be to select a 4.5m defender ahead of a midfielder at the same price point because they have the potential to score more points. Upgrading a 4.5m midfielder to a 5 - 5.5m player may be beneficial if your intention is to utilise them as your first sub.

The majority of playing forwards cost in excess of 6m. However, on occasions, viable budget strikers do become available. Normally, they play for a newly promoted team. A couple of examples who offered good value during the 2021/22 season were Emmanuel Dennis and Josh King of Watford. Dennis was initially listed at 5m and King 5.5m. They both registered attacking returns and their prices rose frequently. Occasionally, a 4.5m forward will get the odd few minutes off the bench, but it's not a regular occurrence. For example, Joe Gelhardt of Leeds who managed to play 733 minutes during the 2021/22 season. He collected 43 FPL points in the process. As part of my research, I ascertained the average number of bench points for managers of all ranks up to 6m during the 2021/22 season. For a comparison, the bench points for the previous season are also included in the table below (courtesy of fpllivenet.com). If you managed to restrict the number of bench points to below the average at your rank, then you did well.

Overall Rank	Average Bench Points 2020/21	Average Bench Points 2021/22
Top 100	239.39	224.62
Top 1k	242.53	224.56
Top 10k	237.37	218.90
Top 100k	232.71	217.34
100k - 200k	225.74	211.46
200k - 300k	240.62	207.78
300k - 400k	223.79	209.70
400k - 500k	229.54	209.69
500k - 600k	224.38	204.42
600k - 700k	214.12	201.10
700k - 800k	216.31	215.11
800k - 900k	216.02	209.02
900k - 1m	227.45	199.51
1m - 1.5m	209.10	198.90
1.5m - 2m	206.92	209.53
2m - 3m	191.88	182.34
3m - 6m	153.28	165.32

It's noteworthy that 15 of the 17 groups recorded a drop in the average number of bench points in comparison to the previous season. Only those ranked between 1.5m-2m and 3m-6m left slightly more points on their bench. It's highly likely that many of those teams would have been inactive for a part of the season, hence the unusual pattern. The data suggests that the number of fixture postponements and absentees had a huge impact on team benches. In all likelihood, due to the Covid pandemic and a spate of injuries, substitutes were called upon more frequently. Players were not only dependent upon their first sub, but had to rely upon their second and third subs often. That's if teams had sufficient coverage, of course. My team incurred 17 auto-subs during the season and I routinely found that neither of my first two subs were playing, so my third sub was relied upon. Undoubtedly, at some stage during the season, many made additional transfer(s) or fielded an under-strength team due to inactive bench players.

It's notable that the teams ranked in the top 1k accumulated more bench points than any other rank. It's highly likely that this is due to the fact that managers at this level are very engaged, invested their funds wisely, and owned strong squads. The average number of points decreases with rank and those with a rank exceeding 2m left the fewest points on their bench. It's reasonable to assume that the number of inactive teams at this level could be responsible for this. There is a tendency for many teams to become inactive as the season evolves. I compared the number of bench points accumulated by the top 10 teams in the world during the 2020/21 and 2021/22 seasons. My analysis produced one incredible statistic. The team that finished fourth in the world in 2020/21 didn't take a hit during the entire campaign. However, they left a staggering 333 points on their bench. To finish so high and to leave so many points on their bench is indicative of a strong squad. A summary of my findings is detailed below.

Top Ten Teams	Bench Points 2020/21	Bench Points 2021/22
1	235	211
2	240	258
3	216	234
4	333	260
5	240	218
6	212	207
7	216	193
8	265	244
9	272	216
10	216	215
Average	244.50	225.60

It was noticeable that there was a marked reduction in the average number of bench points amongst the top 10 teams between the 2020/21 and 2021/22 seasons. The highest number of bench points in 2021/22 was 333, and the lowest was 212. A huge variation. The following season, the highest was 260 and the lowest 193. If you own a strong squad and are fortunate with player absentees, then the need to utilise hits is reduced. A strong performing squad also negates the need to take a hit. The only time you may consider a hit in these circumstances is to target a double Gameweek unless you are blessed with many DGW players.

Having no bench cover is a fire which needs to be extinguished as a matter of urgency. Ideally, your FT needs to be utilised to recruit a playing sub at the earliest opportunity. It's always comforting to have at least one playing outfield sub to provide cover for those unexpected moments, even if it's only a player who is likely to score two points. A minimum of two active subs is advisable, but owning three can be regarded as a luxury. However, it does provide you with excellent coverage, plus you should also own a well-balanced squad. When planning ahead, it is beneficial to target a playing defender to cover the back line and a cheap midfielder/forward to cover the front eight. Owning a second keeper is also an option which will allow you to rotate players depending upon their fixture difficulty. When finalising your bench, it's imperative to consider the optimal order. Each Gameweek, try to identify your strongest XI based on form and fixtures and prioritise your bench accordingly, with your first substitute being your strongest reserve player. The new five sub rule could influence the way you approach your bench selection in the future.

Planning

"Before anything else, preparation is the key to success." –
Alexander Graham Bell

Fantasy Premier League is a marathon and not a sprint, so there needs to be some careful and meticulous planning for the 38 gruelling Gameweeks ahead. Planning is a fundamental part of the game and the foundation of your success. It's no coincidence that FPL has been compared to the game of chess; you need to be one step ahead and plan your next moves well in advance, since chess is a classic game that requires strategy. The same applies to FPL. Better planning will ensure a stronger team performance. Prioritising favourable fixture runs, teams to target, potential transfers and preparing for a blank or double Gameweek in advance will enhance your game. Careful planning will also improve the quality of your transfer activity and help reduce the necessity of taking a hit.

FPL is a fast-moving, unpredictable game and circumstances can change quickly. For example, the Covid pandemic caused chaos, with many games being postponed and rescheduled at short notice. In fact, the 2020/21 and 2021/22 seasons produced a record number of blank and double Gameweeks. Furthermore, injuries and suspensions are inevitable, whilst inclement weather can also cause postponements during the winter months. Therefore, planning ahead in the current climate is key. The most talented and organised managers will plan meticulously ahead, especially for any upcoming double or blank Gameweeks. They will be aware of optimal fixture swings and have their forthcoming transfers mapped out for many weeks ahead. Having a clear plan in place will allow you to conduct some fine tuning and tweak your team and transfer targets if and when the need arises. It's important to continually update your plans and address issues as they arise.

Prioritising your transfers will enable you to manage your team effectively by dealing with the most pressing issues first and then methodically working through them. Addressing your main weaknesses is a sensible strategy. Those players who have sustained a long-term injury, are underperforming, or lacking game time need to be replaced. Identifying in-form players with a favourable run of fixtures will allow you to prioritise your transfers and remove those weak links. This should enable you to avoid any unnecessary hits.

Each summer the players' price reveals are awaited with great anticipation as it signals the start of another FPL season. Once the official FPL website goes live, your planning can commence. At this point, you will be able to build your initial 15-man squad and then tinker merrily away until the GW1 deadline. Your planning will intensify once clubs start to play their pre-season friendlies. Not only are players' performances important, but also team selections. Monitoring pre-season friendlies will enable you to identify in-form players, those who are likely to be regular starters, or those who may be bench warmers. As Gameweek 1 approaches, the number of friendly games and intensity increases. There are plenty of clues on offer and there's a lot to be learnt. Team selections, formations and injuries can be monitored, while potential hidden gems and in-form players can be identified.

When finalising your initial draft, it's always advantageous to try to identify the teams that have a favourable run of fixtures over the first four to six Gameweeks. Additionally, pinpointing teams that have the best fixtures commencing around GW6, could prove beneficial. You could then transition to those teams with good fixtures once your initial fixtures start to turn. It's common to see big fixture swings throughout the season. At certain times, the 'big six' or in-form teams will have a difficult or favourable run of fixtures when they play several of the newly promoted teams or struggling teams. Identifying those fixture swings and selecting players from those clubs during their optimal fixture runs can help you to stay one step ahead of your rivals. The fixture difficulty ratings (FDR) on the official FPL site are a good place to start, but there are informative fixture planners on various FPL websites. Fixture tickers are really useful tools for assisting you with your long-term planning. They can help you determine which teams have the best fixtures over a given period of time based on how difficult or easy their upcoming opponents are.

Once the season is up and running, then the serious work begins. Many will look at the optimum transfer for the following week, but focusing further ahead is optimal. Frequently, an in-form player with a great fixture will stand out as the obvious transfer with a potential points haul. Such a player is very tempting. However, it's worth focusing on your long-term plan. The Scout on the official FPL site wrote an interesting article entitled 'FPL champions tips - Plan ahead with transfers'. The article describes the transfer strategy adopted by Michael Coone which led to his success in 2020/21. Forward planning was a big factor in his success, staying one step ahead of his rivals and winning the coveted title. By pinpointing teams with favourable schedules and the best players to target, he identified differentials well in advance.

"I focus a lot of my strategy around fixtures but get the form player in that team for that fixture. It's definitely a mixture of both. You can't ignore either. The key to getting ahead is getting them two weeks or three weeks before they become a well-owned asset. When the stats are up and the stats are looking brilliant, everyone in the game will get that player". – Fantasy Premier League (2021)

The signing of Ilkay Gundogan in DGW19 proved decisive. Between GWs 19-24, the midfield maestro produced an incredible 94 points for the eventual winner. Gundogan was also given the captaincy against Spurs in GW24. His planning produced further success when he focused his free transfers on Ben White, Joel Veltman, and Jesse Lingard. His planning proved key with the three players combining for 28 points in GW29. Michael stated:

"I think a lot of people may go into Gameweeks and say, 'Maybe next week I want all these players because they're playing great fixtures, and they're playing well.' They might take two or three hits to make their team perfect for that particular week. But the key to getting ahead is to avoid hits and to plan your transfers out for two, three, four, five Gameweeks".

Effective planning allowed Michael to restrict his points deductions to 12 in the first 30 Gameweeks. However, he did then go on the offensive and his team incurred 24 points deductions over the final eight GWs, as he targeted the title.

The other major consideration is focusing on the forthcoming blank and double Gameweeks. Careful planning for such GWs is essential. The optimal strategy is to sign as many players as possible who will feature during those Gameweeks. Prioritising your transfers will enable you to sign your preferred targets over a period of time. Signing blank or double Gameweek players gradually will reduce the need to take unnecessary hits. The same would apply when you are planning to activate your Bench Boost chip. The FPL Community is hugely grateful for the outstanding work conducted by Ben Crellin (@BenCrellin). Ben analyses fixture postponements and predicts when the rescheduled fixtures are likely to feature in the future. His work is invaluable. Having an idea when blank and double Gameweeks are likely to occur will enable you to plan ahead. Ben is also renowned for his stunning spreadsheets, which can assist greatly with your planning. Several FPL websites offer planner tools and spreadsheets to assist you with your planning. You can also optimise your planning by using cutting-edge prediction models. Managers are now armed with players' projected points and fixture difficulty ratings.

A fascinating piece of research on the impact of decision-making was conducted by O'Brien et al., (2021). The article considers the amount of skill that is involved in playing FPL. The research highlights the importance of your planning when playing the game. Their researched article is entitled 'Identification of skill in an online game: The case of Fantasy Premier League'. The authors analysed the historical performance of managers in terms of where they had ranked in the competition alongside their points totals in multiple seasons, in some cases over a time interval of up to 13 years. It was found that the stronger managers' planning was far more thorough than those with a lower rank:

"We find a consistent level of correlation between managers' performances over seasons, suggesting a persistent level of skill over an extended temporal scale. The fact that managers were also willing to wait until one of the final Gameweeks, is also indicative of the long-term planning that separates them from those lower ranked. Similar results can be observed from the other game-chips."

Many previous title winners have highlighted the importance of planning. The most successful managers are well organised and plan ahead meticulously. For me, a six-week period is ideal. The more preparation that goes into your game, the better manager you will become. Effective planning will allow you to focus on in-form players, teams, and optimal fixture runs. Additionally, it will improve the quality of your transfer activity and enable you to avoid any unnecessary hits. Some good traits for effective planning are being flexible and open-minded. This will enable you to stay one step ahead of the 'curve' and beat your rivals to those in-form gems. Never forget:

"By failing to prepare, you are preparing to fail." –
Benjamin Franklin

Part 6: Transfer Strategy

Covid Pandemic

The Covid pandemic transformed the way managers played FPL. Successive seasons of Covid infections produced major disruption to fixture postponements and player absences wreaked havoc throughout the Premier League. If the 2020/21 season wasn't challenging enough for FPL managers, then the following season took it to a new level. The chaos ensured that managers had to adapt to the challenges of untold surprises being relentlessly presented to them. It was a case of expect the unexpected.

A typical FPL season entails meticulous planning along with thorough research for the most committed players. Normally, your invested time rewards you with a better overall rank. However, trying to navigate through the global Covid pandemic instigated new obstacles for not only the 'casual' player but also the most talented and hardened FPL fanatic.

The chaotic 2021/22 campaign will go down on record as the toughest season to date, with the previous season not far behind. There was an unprecedented number of fixture postponements and re-scheduled games. Consequently, the season included eight blank and seven double Gameweeks. There were also six Gameweeks, which were both a double and a blank Gameweek. In those weeks, some teams had two fixtures while others had none. The pandemic caused chaos, not only for the Football Association and Premier League teams, but also for FPL players. Managers not only had to contend with injuries and rotation, but there was the additional burden of trying to cope with the increasing number of Covid infections and rescheduled games. Consequently, some tough decisions had to be made. With so many fixture changes, the fixture schedule was literally torn up and re-written again.

To pacify the television companies, and the worldwide football audience, managers endured a continuous run of extended Gameweeks. The games started on a Friday evening and continued through to the following Thursday before the reset button was pressed and the cycle started over again. The quick turnaround and back-to-back deadlines kept managers on their toes, with some completely missing deadlines. Many failed to set their team, conduct transfers, or select their preferred captain. They were all overlooked. The turbulent times tested the managerial skills of players of all abilities, even the most committed. Undoubtedly, the additional DGWs contributed to the record score registered by the eventual winner. The irony is, the first fixture postponement of the season was not as a result of Covid, but inclement weather.

Thankfully, after the introduction of a Covid vaccine programme, the reported number of positive cases amongst players and staff at Premier League clubs dropped significantly. Consequently, there was a marked drop in Covid related match postponements, and the 2022/23 season has returned to normality. FPL is an unpredictable game; we never know what is around the corner. Hopefully, there will be no recurrence of the pandemic in the future and we can all continue to enjoy the game without distractions.

Transfer Strategy (GWs 2 - 38)

"Strategy without tactics is the slowest route to victory. Tactics without strategy is the noise before defeat." – Sun Tzu

Making transfers is a fundamental part of FPL and the importance of your transfer strategy cannot be over-emphasised. Apart from completing your team and bench selection each Gameweek, making transfers accounts for the majority of the FPL decisions you will make. Transfers are a precious commodity and each transfer should be valued. It's vital that you use them wisely across the season and not make frivolous transfers. Incredibly, official figures show that during the 2021/22 season, a total of 434,390,761 transfers were made. That equates to 47.38 transfers per manager, not forgetting that many teams became inactive as the season unfolded. Therefore, the average number of transfers for active players will have comfortably exceeded that number.

If you can master the art of executing good quality transfers, you will become a successful manager. After finalising your initial draft and navigating Gameweek 1, your focus will turn to managing your squad for the remainder of the season. You have total control of your transfer dealings and you are the sole person responsible for steering your team through 38 gruelling weeks of fantasy football.

Adopting some key transfer strategies can help you achieve your season goal, boost your rank and also give you an advantage over your mini-league rivals. How you manage your transfer activity will have a huge bearing on your eventual outcome. An efficient transfer strategy will ensure a successful season. The main aim should be to conduct effective transfers and minimise unnecessary hits. FPL is played for enjoyment and signing in-form quality players lifts our spirits. Nevertheless, it's easy to get carried away on a tide of emotion and allow your discipline to slip. Suddenly, you accrue needless points deductions. Fighting the urge to tinker with your team too much is paramount.

To emphasise the importance of your transfer strategy, had I retained my GW1 team throughout the 2020/21 season, I would have been 684 points worse off on the final day of the season. Therefore, to succeed, your transfer activity is crucial. It's not only about identifying the best players to sign, but knowing when to hop on and off a specific player. The timings of your transfers are key and could make a significant difference to your score and rank. For example, trying to stay one step ahead of your rivals is an important tactic. Therefore, identifying the in-form players and hidden gems before they become highly owned will be hugely rewarding.

If your team has just delivered a stunning score and looks in good shape for the next round of games, it will provide you with the opportunity to carry over your free transfer to the following week. Hence the expression, to "roll" a transfer. Using your transfers sparingly and carrying a transfer over to the following GW is an excellent tactic. Besides giving you greater flexibility, it will also minimise the chances of you taking unnecessary hits. However, you are only allowed to hold two free transfers at any one time. If, for whatever reason, you do not use at least one of your free transfers, then one of those transfers will be lost. Many of the tips discussed when making your initial squad selection will equally apply to your transfer activity and when activating your two Wildcards. We will now focus on topics which you may find beneficial when conducting your transfer activity.

Free Transfer (FT)

Managers have one free transfer per Gameweek. Taking into account your initial squad selection, chips and Wildcards, that leaves you with 34 valuable FTs to help you navigate through the campaign. Transfers provide you with the ideal opportunity to acquire those players who are in-form, will feature in a double or blank Gameweeks or have a fantastic run of fixtures. Simultaneously, your transfers give you the opportunity to dispense with the services of your underperforming players, those who have sustained long-term injuries/a period of suspension, or those lacking game time. Each free transfer should be viewed as four points. Therefore, every transfer is valuable and each one should be optimal. Targeting top quality players with a high ceiling – those who are likely to be prolific and produce a substantial number of points – should be prioritised.

Perfect Team

In an ideal world, every manager would love to own the perfect team. A team that has quality, in-form explosive players, or players who are the highest point scorers in their positions. Assets who are likely to contribute points consistently. Whether it be goals, assists or clean sheets, they all translate into big FPL points, green arrows and an improved rank. Unfortunately, due to budget restraints, it's impossible to build the perfect team. There will be desirable assets that you cannot accommodate in your team. As it's impossible to create the perfect FPL team, it's wise not to over-manage your team in pursuit of perfection. There is a tendency for many to take unnecessary hits when trying to build the perfect team. During that process, some questionable transfers are made. A reliable points scorer may be discarded to make way for an 'essential' asset purely because that player has just secured a brace. Having patience and confidence in the players that you own is paramount. Ultimately, your patience will reward you. The players that need replacing are those that are injured, lacking game time, or underperforming.

Mini-Wildcard

Rolling a transfer is a great tactic to deploy, enabling you to have the benefit of two free transfers at your disposal for the following Gameweek. Utilising both of your free transfers will enable you to release funds in order to facilitate the acquisition of a more expensive option that you were previously unable to afford. Alternatively, there is a further option which could be advantageous. You could utilise your two free transfers in conjunction with a hit and play a 'mini-wildcard'. This provides the opportunity to refresh your squad. Three transfers can make a significant difference to an underperforming team if you wish to make key changes. A mini-wildcard provides greater flexibility with the option to target in-form players with favourable fixtures, or those with a double or blank Gameweek in the foreseeable future. This strategy has been adopted by several previous FPL winners, including 2016/17 champion Ben Crabtree, and 2017/18 champion Yusuf Sheikh. Yusuf Sheikh saved his FT on 10 occasions and he went on to play a mini-wildcard on four separate occasions. Ben Crabtree saved his FT on nine occasions and played seven mini-wildcards across the season.

Patience

One of the key attributes of becoming a top manager is patience. My impatience has cost me a considerable number of points over recent seasons. I learnt the hard way that patience is a virtue. I am sure that I'm not the only manager who has a frustrating player who repeatedly finds their way into your team. My nemesis is Jamie Vardy, who has tormented me regularly. Such a talented footballer but a very frustrating FPL asset to own. There was a distinct pattern. He continually 'blanked' when he was in my team and then went berserk as soon as he was sold. Additionally, you can also add rotation and his persistent injuries to the list of frustrating factors. Periods in and out of my team throughout the season coincided with his unpredictable form. The Jamie Vardy experience has certainly taught me a lesson.

Patience is key and getting the timing of your transfers right can prove crucial. The term 'one-week punt' is used frequently, but transfers should be regarded as a long-term project and not purely to chase points. There is a tendency for some to jump the gun and prematurely replace reliable players solely because they haven't delivered points in recent games. They may have a difficult fixture ahead, but their subsequent fixtures may be against several of the struggling teams. The urge to sell without serious consideration could result in another unnecessary and wasted transfer.

A misfiring attacking asset should be given every opportunity to make amends. Players are initially signed for a valid reason; you believe in them and have confidence in their ability to produce FPL points. Hence, they deserve a reasonable amount of time to repay your faith. If they continue to underperform after being given an extended opportunity, you can then reassess and act. Impending fixtures, form, and team form are relevant. An attacking asset will experience a barren spell and also hit a purple patch at some point. Therefore, showing a degree of patience will facilitate a more effective use of your free transfers. Eradicating needless transfers will provide you with the opportunity to concentrate on addressing more pressing issues by replacing the weakest link in your squad.

Self-discipline is an important element of your game, and adopting a degree of patience is essential. Groupthink and bandwagons are prevalent amongst the FPL community, and it's easy to be drawn into signing the next essential player. Rushing to sign a player that has just scored a brace and collected a 15-point haul is tempting. However, they may have a difficult run of fixtures on the horizon. Neither is there a guarantee that they will repeat the feat in the foreseeable future. Managing your team can be a stern test of your resolve when the wider FPL community is moving en masse to sign the next playing sensation. Do you move to hop on the bandwagon or do you trust your judgement and bide your time? In addition, given the fact that you can make an unlimited number of transfers, the temptation to make multiple transfers at a cost is overwhelming. Be patient and play your own game.

Mistakes

Everyone is prone to making mistakes. To become a successful FPL manager, it is good to acknowledge and reflect on one's mistakes. Errors are inevitable, therefore it's key to learn from them in order to prevent a reoccurrence. Identifying mistakes will allow managers to address their weaknesses, which will eventually enhance their game. Stubbornness isn't a good FPL trait. Some may be reluctant to learn from a mistake. It's worth analysing the mistake, where you went wrong, and what can be done next time to prevent a repetition. Otherwise, the failure to learn from a mistake could prove costly in the long-term. If a transfer is unsuccessful, it doesn't necessarily mean that you made the wrong decision. If you analyse your decision-making process, it's possible that you made the right decision based on all the relevant information available, but the decision just didn't reward you on that occasion.

Knee-jerk/Rage Transfers

Regardless of a player's performance or lack of returns, try to avoid making impulsive transfers during – or shortly after – a game when your emotions are running high. Let the dust settle and consider your transfer options later in the week once you have had time to reflect. An early transfer may be totally unnecessary and regretted later. Additionally, avoid conducting your transfer activity when you are not in the right frame of mind. For example, intoxicated or emotionally charged. Planning for and conducting research are key factors in a successful transfer. It's unlikely that an unplanned impromptu transfer, which hasn't been thoroughly researched or thought through, will be successful. Try not to be too reactive and respond to a player who has just scored a brace while discarding one of your most reliable players in the process. Hasty decisions can cost you.

Speculative Transfers

Making transfers which haven't been fully researched is a huge gamble and should be avoided. Each free transfer is valuable, so it's essential to make the best use of the FT by signing a quality player to improve your squad. If you do consider a one week 'punt', the optimum time is the week prior to activating your WC. Your Wildcard will provide you with the opportunity to replace the player without wasting a free transfer or, even worse, a hit.

Upside Chasing

Recently, some managers have adopted a new approach by 'Upside Chasing'. This strategy revolves around targeting high-impact players with a high ceiling. Players who have the potential to produce a substantial points-haul and significantly improve your rank quickly. It's high-risk management and involves selling popular players to target other big-hitters with better fixtures. However, constantly switching between one big-hitter to another to target prime fixtures is a risky strategy because EO will come into the equation. It involves selling players who may be highly owned. In addition, you are using your valuable free transfers.

Adaptable

FPL is unpredictable and a typical season produces many unexpected twists and turns. Circumstances change frequently and unexpected occurrences do occur. For example, fixture postponements, hidden gems emerging, injuries, suspensions, managerial changes, players and teams finding (or losing) form. Be flexible and adapt to an ever-changing game. Having a flexible approach will enable you to maximise your team's points potential. The secret is to keep an open mind, don't succumb to any biases, don't be stubborn, and adjust your game according to the circumstances. For example, logic says that you should target in-form players but do not totally discount players who are perceived as failures. Such players may be given an opportunity and become a revelation. For example, both Jesse Lingard and Kelechi Iheanacho were written off prior to their excellent form during the 2020/21 season.

Deadlines

The Covid pandemic caused chaos and fixture postponements. The rescheduling of games became commonplace. Consequently, fixtures were staggered and Gameweek deadlines changed frequently. Surprisingly, many managers missed those deadlines. We still encounter rescheduled fixtures for a number of reasons, hence the importance of making yourself aware of the next Gameweek deadline. A sensible move is to get in the habit of selecting your team, captain, and bench order for the upcoming Gameweek as soon as the current GW goes live on the website/app. In the FPL community, it is affectionately known as setting up your 'bus team' - a team you'd be happy playing if, for whatever reason, you couldn't update your team. You still have the option to continually amend your team right up until the deadline if the need arises. For example, reacting to any injury news or relevant information disclosed during press conferences. If you miss a deadline for whatever reason, then at least your team will be set. A simple mistake of missing a deadline and failing to select your optimal team or captain could have a detrimental effect on your weekly score and rank. Ultimately, it could prove costly at the end of the season. Hence, the importance of setting yourself a reminder and setting up your team at the earliest opportunity.

Sword and Shield Strategy

Relatively early in the season, there is a tendency for a 'template' team to form - a hypothetical team comprising the most popular players. This team includes players with a high effective ownership (EO) and evolves as the season progresses. Generally, as soon as a template team emerges, many managers will target those players to safeguard their rank. Adhering to the template team during the early months will be beneficial. This will ensure that your team makes a steady start and builds a solid foundation for the remainder of the season. This will prevent your chances of success from evaporating early. Conforming to the template will also help to build your team value as the price of the most popular players rapidly increases.

Knowing when to use the sword and when to use the shield is an important strategy, which can enhance your game. An aggressive approach intended to climb rank can be regarded as the sword, while a more cautious approach to protecting your rank can be regarded as the shield. The timing of knowing when to attack and when to defend is key. A lot depends on whether you wish to attack to gain rank or defend to protect your overall rank. If you wish to be aggressive and attack rank, then you play more differentials. If your premium assets have tough fixtures, you may entrust the armband with an alternative in-form player. Attacking a DGW, or those weeks where you are deploying a chip, can also be beneficial. In contrast, if you are happy with your progress and you wish to protect your rank, it's worth considering aligning your team with that of the template team. Less risk means a better chance of maintaining or improving on your current rank. Adopting a risk-averse defensive approach may also be beneficial when you are struggling to field a strong team in a BGW or when you do not own the most popular captaincy choice. Throughout the season, managers will adopt one or the other, depending upon what they wish to achieve in that Gameweek.

Differential Players

A differential player is a player with a low effective ownership, generally regarded as a player who is owned by fewer than 5% of managers (TSB). However, it's not uncommon to see a figure of 10% also being discussed. Generally, a player who has low ownership is not expected to deliver the same level of returns as the more popular players. Players have become popular for a reason: their points projection is higher. They may have a good points record, be in-form, have a favourable run of fixtures, or a combination of those factors. Identifying the optimum time to select and play a differential player is pivotal. Generally, a favourable fixture where a points haul could potentially propel your team up the overall standings. Conversely, selecting differential players could prove very costly if the player(s) fails and the template players deliver returns. You are likely to experience a significant drop in rank. The question is, how many differentials are managers prepared to include in their team at the same time? You may be able to survive a Gameweek reasonably well if you just select one or two differential players, but owning multiple differentials could be a different story.

To be successful, it's not imperative that you continually pick differential players. It is identifying the best time to play those players, be patient and opportunities will arise. There is no need to chase differential players, as on occasions you will encounter weeks where there will be a 50/50 decision to be made. That may be a suitable time to deploy a differential. Successful selections can reward you handsomely, particularly if they experience an outstanding GW and many of the highly owned assets fail. It's one way of vastly improving your rank and pulling away from the pack. At some stage, you may take a calculated gamble and select a captain with a low EO who is not an obvious choice. A sensible approach is to set yourself a solid foundation before starting to play many differential players. You may find that selecting differential players is more effective towards the latter end of the season as you seek to climb rank. Some select differential players simply because they are bored with owning a team of template players and wish to be different. However, players are template for a reason. They have a tendency to deliver points regularly. Selecting many differentials is a risky strategy. However, the rewards can be significant if your selections are successful.

Early Transfers

One of the golden rules of FPL. Refrain from making any early transfers unless it is absolutely necessary. Doing so could ultimately cost you. The timing of your transfer is important and it could save you from taking an unnecessary hit. Many managers make early transfers for a number of reasons. Some make 'rage' transfers, while others try to avoid price changes. However, there are several factors which could have a negative impact on your performance if you were to complete an early transfer. Various events could occur in-between Gameweeks, including injuries, suspensions, ill health, etc. Therefore, making early transfers is a gamble which could backfire. The majority of managers opt to leave their transfer activity until after the relevant press conferences later in the week. Following this routine will allow you to be better informed on any possible issues. For example, injury updates or the possibility of rotation. It's noteworthy that recently, several managers have withheld significant injury news in their press conferences, which has caused mayhem.

One time, you could consider an early transfer is due to an imminent price increase. By delaying a transfer, you will have insufficient funds to recruit your preferred target. If you have the exact funds needed to complete the transfer and the player's price is due to rise overnight, an early transfer is feasible. However, it shouldn't become a habit as it is a calculated risk. Leaving your transfer(s) as late as possible will allow you to benefit from any press conference updates and eradicate a wasted transfer. Occasionally, photographs of players become available on social media, which could be useful in determining a player's fitness. Particularly players who have previously sustained an injury. Discovering that your newly acquired asset is injured is not a pleasant experience and can be damaging.

Effective Ownership (EO)

Effective ownership does play a part in FPL and it is something to consider when selecting your team and captain. If you don't own and select a highly owned player with a very high EO and they go on to record a points haul, there could be severe repercussions. A significant drop in rank is likely. Generally, it's premium assets that have the highest EO. The EO will fluctuate depending on a number of factors. Form, fixtures, ownership and captaincy are all influential factors. The more popular the player is for ownership and captaincy, the greater effective ownership becomes.

Many will sign a player who is perceived as essential simply because they are growing in popularity and don't want to miss out. Another group of managers will consider the implications of not owning a player who is likely to have a high EO. They will sign the highly owned player purely to safeguard their rank. EO equals the percentage of managers who started the player, plus percentage captained, plus percentage triple captained. This summed percentage gives you an indication of the effect this player has on the average. For example, if a player has an EO of 150%, it means that every point that the player scores raises the average by 1.5 points. This metric can help you determine the impact that various players will have on your rank should they collect returns. Depending on your rank, it is common to see some premium assets attract an EO in the region of 150-200%. However, on occasions, effective ownership has exceeded 200%. If a player with an exceptionally high EO delivers a return, it can be very damaging to your rank, unless you have captained them or triple-captained them yourself.

In theory, having a player with an EO above 100% in your XI will not protect your rank unless you have captained them. Occasionally, I have suffered an immediate 5k rank drop in rank purely because Harry Kane scored a goal. Kane, with an EO above 100%, was in my team. However, I hadn't given him the captaincy that week.

As the season evolves, there is a tendency for numerous teams to fall by the wayside. They become 'ghost ship teams'. For whatever reason, managers stop playing the game and their teams become inactive. This can cause problems. For example, ownership and EO. Many inactive teams could have had a very popular asset as their captain on the last occasion that they were active. Consequently, the captaincy will stay with that player for the remainder of the season. This has a knock-on effect on every other team. It's highly likely that this scenario is creating a false EO and data. For example, towards the end of the 2020/21 season, Spurs had a BGW, but it did not stop Harry Kane being captained by over a million managers. You can monitor EO on www.fpllive.net, an informative website which can assist you in managing your team effectively. You are able to discover your team's template rating, the EO for each of your players, plus the EO for those teams around you, and those ranked in the top 10k.

Alternating (Yo-Yo) Transfers

Some needlessly waste valuable transfers by making 'yo-yo' signings, flip-flopping between players, a tactic deployed when chasing points. There is a tendency for managers to be attracted by a bandwagon even if it's only a short-term fix. Others decide to take a one week 'punt' and on occasions they revert to the player that they had just sold. While others will jump from one premium asset to another or back to their original premium asset. For example, Harry Kane is due to face Liverpool and Arsenal in his next two fixtures. In contrast, an in-form Erling Haaland faces struggling teams in his next two fixtures. Teams that have recently conceded a hatful of goals. Many will be seriously tempted to cash-in on Haaland's fixtures at the expense of Kane before reverting back to Kane for three enticing fixtures against sides battling relegation. The upside being, that a manager could benefit from both moves and accumulate a significant number of points.

You could be rewarded handsomely, but it will be at a cost. Firstly, you are using two of your crucial transfers. More importantly, you may have other fires to put out within your team. More pressing needs, such as a spate of injuries while having no bench coverage. Ideally, these issues need resolving as a priority. The choice is to either sign Haaland at the expense of Kane or replace an injured player with a guaranteed starter. The Haaland transfer could be to the detriment of the rest of your team and there is no guarantee that he will outscore Kane. In these circumstances, some may even consider taking a hit if they have utilised their FT elsewhere. If possible, it's wise to try to avoid short-term alternating transfers which could be better utilised elsewhere.

Play Your Own Game

There are numerous playing styles and, with so many participants, your decision-making could easily be influenced by others – particularly on social media. Be aware of FOMO (fear of missing out) and herd mentality. If you are seeking advice from others, who is to say that the advice you receive is sound advice? There is a tendency for many to get drawn into the hype surrounding bandwagons which regularly circulate amongst the FPL communities on social media. Don't be driven by bandwagons and play your own game. Many FPL decisions that have to be made are team-dependent. Therefore, what suits one team may not necessarily suit another. Therefore, do what's best for your team.

If you have any doubt about your proposed transfer(s), then seeking a second opinion is advantageous. However, instead of being swayed by countless managers, try to identify a 'buddy'. Someone that you can approach for that second opinion. Ideally, a player that you have confidence in and who will give you sound advice. Additionally, it's important to ignore your mini-league rivals and solely focus on your own game. Let them do the worrying as you climb rank. Focusing on your mini-league rivals could distract you from the bigger picture. The fun of FPL is that it's your team. Conduct your research and play your game. It's pleasing to know that when you succeed, it's as a result of your skill and no one else's.

Rotation

With numerous competitions and larger squads, rotation is becoming an ever-increasing problem. It's inevitable that rotation will be an issue, particularly when you own players from the 'big' clubs. Rotation is also an issue at other clubs, but to a lesser extent. Rotation is more prevalent in the second half of the season once the cup and European competitions are in full swing. Generally, rotation applies more to the clubs that are fighting in several competitions simultaneously. Premier League managers need to prioritise competitions. Therefore, rotation at clubs involved in European or cup competitions is common. It is a factor to consider during your planning and decision-making process. The risk of rotation can be partly mitigated by conducting thorough research to establish if a player that you intend to sign has a history of rotation at his current club.

Undoubtedly, the new five substitutes rule will have an impact and game time management will be prominent. It's likely that there will be a greater number of substitutions and many players will experience a dip in game time. Some may even struggle to play for 60 minutes, creating a knock-on effect for FPL managers. The additional 60-minute appearance point may be lost and even more concerning would be the loss of clean sheet bonus points by a defender safeguarding a clean sheet. There are several examples from the 2022/23 season. Like many, it has already cost me. The Everton vs Liverpool game in GW6 ended in a 0-0 stalemate. However, TAA, who was owned by 40% of managers at the time, was substituted in the 59th minute to miss out on his clean sheet. The loss of four points for just a single minute of game time. Another prime example was Ben White being substituted at Brighton in GW18. He was 20 seconds short of the 60-minute mark and his potential clean sheet bonus points. How close can you get? In GW30, Antony was subbed off at 59:59 during Manchester Utd's 2-0 victory over Everton.

Sideways Transfers

Each of your 34 free transfers is precious. Therefore, 'sideways' transfers could be regarded as a wasted opportunity. Transfers need to be used sparingly and quality players need to be prioritised. Those who can improve your team and are likely to deliver you more FPL points. Therefore, try to avoid making sideways transfers. For example, you already own one defender from Team A, but you are considering replacing that defender with another Team A defender. If Team A kept a clean sheet, then both defenders would benefit. It's questionable whether it's worth using a valuable transfer on two similar players, playing as defenders for the same team. Are they likely to score a significant number of points more than the player you already own? For example, swapping Creswell and Kehrer at West Ham. One may be slightly more attacking, but utilising a transfer for this purpose is probably not worth it. Transfers could be better used on more pressing needs or to target players with a higher ceiling who are likely to score more points.

Fixtures or Form

A regular debate that exists amongst the FPL community is fixtures or form. Many will have differing opinions on which should take priority. Do you select in-form players, or those who have favourable fixtures in the foreseeable future? However, both factors need consideration in your decision-making process. Do you select the in-form Player A, who has registered returns in the last three games, or Player B, who hasn't delivered a return in the last three games? Player A faces Manchester City, whilst player B faces a struggling team who haven't scored a goal or kept a clean sheet in recent games. It's advisable to consider both a player's form and underlying statistics, while also taking into account their forthcoming fixtures. Planning 4-6 weeks in advance is far more beneficial than solely focusing on the forthcoming GW.

It's always desirable to select an in-form player, but neither can you beat a favourable run of fixtures. For example, signing Harry Kane when three out of his next four opponents are struggling teams. A scenario which is both appealing and could be very profitable. There is the old adage, that a premium asset is fixture proof: if you own a quality player, they will deliver returns regardless of the opposition, particularly if they are in-form. Premium assets are premium for a reason: they are proven reliable assets that consistently deliver points. Hence the price tag.

Managers need to be flexible and adapt to changing circumstances. For example, when conducting transfers, a change to fixtures or form can influence your decision-making. Form needs to be continually monitored and those underperforming need to be replaced by in-form players with favourable fixtures. Ideally, a combination of both. You may own several players from an underperforming team who are in the middle of a winless run. It doesn't make them bad players. Nevertheless, it may affect their potential points. The arrival of a new manager can also influence transfer market moves. For example, suddenly you find that one of your players has fallen out of favour and they have been demoted down the pecking order. Conversely, you may benefit from a new manager 'bounce'. Players not playing regularly need to be addressed at the earliest opportunity, otherwise it could prove costly.

You can gleam a lot of information by studying forthcoming fixtures, their FDR (fixture difficulty rating) and underlying statistics of the player you are planning to sign. Analysing data and pinpointing favourable fixture runs is optimal. We are inundated with every imaginable statistic and you could literally spend days trawling through the realms of data. There are numerous websites which offer valuable information to aid you in your decision-making process. Every conceivable football statistic for every player and team is available, including their current form. My personal preference is fixtures over form, but ideally, a combination of both is preferable when contemplating your next transfer. Both are equally important, so both factors should be considered in your decision-making process. A player with both form and fixtures is better than a player with just one or the other. Each are essential ingredients in producing a quality transfer. An in-form player facing a struggling team is the best-case scenario.

Statistics & Eye Test

Metrics play an important part in FPL. There are several ways in which statistics are analysed to evaluate a player's performance. Sports analytics company Opta has created a set of performance metrics including xG, xA, xGI, xGC, xCS. They provide a crucial insight into how a player or team is performing. For example, xG (Expected Goals) measures the quality of a shot based on several variables such as assist type, shot angle and distance from goal, whether it was a headed shot and whether it was defined as a big chance. Adding up a team or player's xG can give an indication of how many goals a team or player should have scored on average, given the shots that they have taken. I am not going to go into the intricacies of each metric, but suffice to say that they are an invaluable tool and an essential part of your research.

In addition, numerous other performance measurements are available from various football websites. Data can be used as a reference point, but recent performances should also be considered in your deliberations. Statistics don't tell you everything, so watching live games or extended highlights compliments the data that is available. Invaluable information can be gleaned by conducting an 'eye test'. Did the player look sharp or sluggish? Were they involved in the game? Did they present a goal threat? Did they create any chances? All relevant factors that you can consider with the available data.

There is no right or wrong way to play FPL and there are various playing styles. Some may prefer to rely purely on statistics, whilst others may prefer to rely entirely on the eye test; a combination of both seems a logical way forward. Certain factors will be missed by the eye test and some by statistics, therefore combining both factors will complement each other. Analysing underlying statistics alongside the eye test is advisable if you wish to identify your optimal transfer. The more information that you have at your disposal, the greater the likelihood of reaching the optimal transfer. Analysing statistics, studying form, and considering fixture difficulty objectively can enhance your game. I would advocate a policy of conducting thorough research, combining both data and conducting an eye test. A combination of both is invaluable and will undoubtedly improve your decision-making process when contemplating transfers.

Bookmakers

Bookmakers are a useful source of information. It's not very often they get it wrong. They provide various odds for upcoming games and monitoring such information can aid you in your decision-making process. A useful website is Drafthound. They work very closely with bookmakers' odds, so you can obtain the most accurate predicted probabilities for many factors before each Gameweek. These include odds for goals, clean sheets and predicted points.

Podcasts

Podcasts are another great source of useful information. They are well-informed and can enhance your game. The market is flooded with podcasts, so identifying your preferred material is worthwhile.

There are too many to mention, but a simple Google search will provide a list of quality FPL Podcasts.

Hidden Gems & In-form Players

One profitable avenue for points is to identify hidden gems that are relatively unknown. They can be a game changer. Traditionally, each season, some hidden gems emerge. Players who come from nowhere and embark on a fantastic run of form. Generally, they are players who have never been in the spotlight, but they will be good FPL assets. When given an opportunity, they impress in those appearances and go on to have an outstanding season. Identifying hidden gems early is an added bonus, a signing which will enable you to stay one step ahead of the game. Hidden gems are likely to be available at a knock-down price and will have low ownership. An excellent differential player who has the potential to catapult your team up the global rankings. Undoubtedly, their form and competitive price will attract many managers. Consequently, their ownership and value will soar.

Similarly, it's important to spot those players that are finding form, and to strike before their popularity grows. Being one step ahead of the game is a huge bonus as low ownership means there are more gains to be made. A player who hits a purple patch will be much sought after and not owning them could be costly, with your rivals stealing a march on you. Ultimately, quality transfers are down to good decision-making and timing. Getting the timing right could reward you with some significant points. The moment a player displays some form, it won't take long for managers to acknowledge their points potential. Suddenly, they are in great demand. Many like to jump on a bandwagon, so it's beneficial to jump aboard early enough to take advantage of that player's form. There is a tendency for the stronger managers to stay one step ahead of the 'curve'. The key is identifying in-form players before your rivals in order to capitalise on it.

A classic example of in-form players occurred at the start of the 2020/21 campaign. Harry Kane and Son Heung-min terrorised defences and both accumulated several big hauls, most notably, when Spurs thumped Southampton 5-2 in GW2. After falling behind, Spurs hit back and blew the Saints away. Kane scored a goal and created four assists as he collected an impressive 21-point haul. Meanwhile, Son went one better by scoring four goals and accumulating 24 points. If you happened to own them, it was ecstasy. If not, you soon knew about it because your rank plummeted. Over the following 10 Gameweeks, both Kane and Son maintained their blistering form and continued to deliver amazing scores. Kane accumulated 84 points while Son amassed 77 points. At the time, they were the league's standout performers. Many of the top managers benefited from at least owning one of the players during this period. However, the happiest – who were really smiling – were those who owned both players. Son also hit a purple patch at the latter end of the following season. Between Gameweeks 20-38, Son scored an incredible 162 points to boost his points tally to 258 points. A total which ensured that he concluded the season as the second highest points scorer, just seven points behind Mo Salah. His form also bagged him 23 goals to share the Golden Boot with the Liverpool maestro. Missing out on an in-form player could ultimately prove very costly and, consequently, your rank will suffer.

Bandwagons

Managers jumping on and off a bandwagon is a regular theme throughout a typical season; players that are fashionable and popular whilst gathering increasing support. There is a tendency for some to hop from one player to another, depending upon their appeal. In most cases, it's a player who is perceived as essential after scoring a brace. There is nothing to suggest that they have turned into a goal machine or will be a sound pick for the future. Chasing last week's points isn't always a good option. It's fine recruiting such a player, provided it's a long-term signing and not merely a short-term fix. The other factor to consider is that not every player that becomes fashionable is going to be a resounding success.

On occasions, FOMO or groupthink comes into play. Some are tempted to complete a transfer purely because their perception has been influenced by others. The disadvantage of hopping from one bandwagon to another is that there is no long-term planning; it's purely a case of chasing short-term points. Several other factors need consideration. Firstly, such moves are eating into your valuable free transfers. Secondly, the rest of your team is being ignored. You may have more pressing issues that need resolving, but instead of putting the fires out, you focus on chasing points. Players who are underperforming, injured or lacking game time need replacing.

Putting Fires Out

'Putting fires out' is a common FPL expression. Typically, the majority of teams will experience situations where their squad isn't in a particularly good shape during the season. For example, you may own players who are underperforming, suspended, missing out on game time, while the number of injuries continues to grow. Instead of targeting a player who has just collected a 15-point haul, it may be time to focus on putting the fires out. If you don't address your problems, they could escalate and, in all likelihood, it will cost you dearly. Prioritising your weaknesses is good housekeeping and resolving problems at the earliest opportunity is an essential part of FPL. Simply, by implementing this strategy, you will build a stronger and more productive squad. Replacing such players with in-form regular starters with a favourable run of fixtures is a wise move. Chasing points for short-term gains is not a particularly good tactic to deploy. If a player collects a 15-point haul one week, there's no guarantee that they will immediately repeat the feat. Ordinarily, it turns out to be an isolated case. Jumping from player to player, chasing points also eats into your free transfers. If the plan is to sign the player as a long-term investment or to captain them, that may be a different proposition.

Press Conferences

Monitoring press conferences is an essential part of your GW planning. News is eagerly anticipated and any snippets of valuable information will assist you in your transfer decision-making process and team selection. An excellent source of information is FPL News (@ColmVHayes). Colm provides in-depth coverage of the latest news from each press conference. Leaving your transfers as late as possible is recommended as this enables you to be aware of all the main talking points from each Premier League club. You may discover some crucial injury/rotation/team news that will assist you.

Team Value and Price Changes

Gaining squad value is an important strategy adopted by many, particularly at the start of the season. A strategy which can help you gain more points. The most volatile period for price increases is Gameweeks 2-12, hence the importance of being vigilant in this period. Every team is active at the start of the season, so many will target in-form players or those who form a part of the template team. In all likelihood, their value will increase. The advantage of building team value is that it allows you greater spending power as the season evolves. The extra funds will enable you to strengthen your squad, assembling a team sprinkled with quality players and premium assets. Players that you would otherwise have been unable to afford. Simultaneously, you could dispose of the enablers that you have been dependent upon, or those players who are injured, underperforming, losing value or have a difficult run of fixtures.

Premium assets are usually a safe bet for price increases, but there is also scope to accumulate value elsewhere. In-form players, those with an optimal run of fixtures, or have just collected a major points haul, will see their popularity grow. A price rise is almost inevitable. Monitoring potential price changes is an important aspect of the game, as it can help you pinpoint sound investments. There are several websites/apps which provide information on price changes. Two such sites are www.fplstatistics.co.uk and www.fantasyfootballfix.com. Timing your transfers is essential. If you get your timing right, there is the potential to make significant gains in team value. It's worth noting that price changes generally take place overnight (1-2am UK time).

The player with the largest increase in value over the course of the 2021/22 season was João Cancelo, who saw his value increase from 6m to 7.2m. Heung-Min Son's value increased by 1.1m and TAA by 0.9m. Some teams can gain up to a staggering 10m in value over an entire season. My team, Bluebirds Flying High, finished the 2020/21 season with a team value in excess of 109m. In comparison, the highest team value amongst the top ten teams was 108.3m, and the lowest was 104.7m. Some players place great emphasis on team value, so it's not uncommon to see some take hits to build that value. Personally, I do not believe making additional transfers to gain team value is a viable option. However, building team value by using your free transfers or activating your WC early can be a profitable strategy. If your players consistently collect points, their value will increase. Points will improve team value, but not necessarily the other way around.

Player prices change regularly depending on the popularity of the player in the transfer market. The price shown on your transfer page is a player's selling price. This selling price may be less than the player's current purchase price. When selling a player, you will never receive their current market value. You will receive 50% of the profit accrued whilst you own that player. A sell-on fee of 50% (rounded up to the nearest 0.1m) will be applied on any profits made on that player. For example, if you own Harry Kane and his price has risen from 12m to 12.4m since you signed him, you will have benefited by 0.2m. 50% of his actual price rise during that time. You only benefit when there are increments of two. For example, if you purchased James Maddison for 8m and his current price is 8.3m, his selling price for you will be 8.1m. A player's price can rise or fall by up to 0.3m in a Gameweek.

Another factor to consider is price 'locks'. These generally occur when a player has a red flag for an injury or suspension. Consequently, they become ineligible for price changes. Their price will remain locked for a period of three days once the red flag has been removed. Any new player added to FPL will not be the subject of an immediate price change. A player needs to have been in the league for over eight days before any transfers count towards the threshold value. Once that value has been achieved, then a price change is triggered by the number of purchases or sales of that player. The locking period can be extended to the start of the next GW if the completion of the eight-day period falls within an international break. (fplstatistics.co.uk). FPL award no prizes for achieving the highest team value. Undoubtedly, team value does help, but your team should be your priority rather than solely focusing on team value.

Websites and Third-Party Apps

Numerous websites offer FPL material or football data. The information available can enhance your game. The likes of premierleague.com, fbref.com, soccerstats.com and understat.com are all free to use and provide excellent statistics. You can also subscribe to several other FPL websites which provide underlying statistics, fixture tickers, player projections, price changes, team planners and some great articles. Many are mentioned throughout this book.

Part 7: Additional Transfers

The Minus Two Debate

A hot topic which is regularly discussed amongst the FPL community is the 'minus two' debate. We are talking about the situations where you are unable to field a full-strength team unless you make additional transfers. Managers weigh up the pros and cons of making an additional transfer and contemplate whether it's worth taking a hit or not. It's a subject that frequently crops up when teams try to negotiate a blank Gameweek or when a team suffers multiple absences and there is insufficient bench cover. Some will advise you to avoid a hit under these circumstances, whilst others will encourage you to do the opposite, "go for it as it's only a minus two". Let me explain...

If you plan to tackle a Gameweek with an under-strength team, it's likely that your team will not perform so well as a full-strength side. Logic says that in all probability, your team will be expected to score more points if you have more players on the pitch. However, the question is this: if you can field a team of 10, is it worth incurring a four-point deduction to recruit a definite starter for that GW? You may be considering an in-form forward who is due to face a struggling team. Very tempting, especially if the opposition has conceded numerous goals over recent weeks. Neither has the opposition scored in recent games, so an attacking defender from the same team may also be on your radar. Both scenarios provide a great opportunity to score a substantial number of points. Do you gamble and take a hit or play safe and just field 10 players? Undoubtedly, countless managers face this dilemma regularly. It's a situation that we are all familiar with.

Each player is awarded two points for completing a 60-minute appearance. Let's consider what we need to be asking ourselves. Firstly, is the player that we are targeting a definite starter and, if so, are they likely to play the full 90 minutes? If yes, then great. However, there is one possible downside. The manager may unexpectedly decide to freshen up the team and there is rotation. You discover that your new acquisition is on the bench. Alternatively, your player does start, but they sustain an early injury and have to be replaced. There is also the possibility of them being subbed-off prior to the 60-minute mark. They are all conceivable. If they play the 60 minutes, then the points are in the bag, unless, of course, there's a twist. Let's assume that a player manages to complete 60 minutes. In this situation, a four-point deduction is theoretically only a two-point deficit. That's before taking into account any possible goals, assists, or a clean sheet. To counteract that, there is the possibility that a player is either rotated or doesn't complete the 60 minutes. The next consideration in the equation is the possibility of that player collecting a one or two-point deduction for a yellow or red card. Possible outcomes which could reduce or even wipe out those two points.

Firstly, let's consider a defender. Ideally, we would like them to keep a clean sheet. If they play 60 minutes but concede a goal, that's fine. They will still collect two appearance points. Therefore, two of the four-point deficit is recovered, and it becomes a minus two transfer. However, if they concede two goals, they will lose one of those points. Now consider the other side of the argument: the defender plays at least 60 minutes and the team keeps a clean sheet. The player will collect six points, a net gain of two points, and everyone is happy. Additionally, they could register an attacking return or collect bonus points (BPS) for their performance. Is it worth the gamble? Managers have differing opinions. You can either play safe, and field an under-strength team, or supplement your team by taking a hit. If you opt for the second option, you have a realistic chance of collecting two points, which would ensure it's a minus two transfer. Registering a clean sheet, an attacking return, bonus points, or a combination of the three, would be an added bonus. Multiple returns would not only repay the hit, but produce a handsome reward for the manager.

Many vow not to take a hit on a goalkeeper, but let's just consider the pros and cons of such a move. A goalkeeper is very similar to a defender, with one slight difference. The chances of them scoring a goal or creating an assist are slim. However, as a defender, they will be awarded two points for a 60-minute appearance plus four additional points for preserving a clean sheet. Additionally, they have the potential to collect bonus points (BPS), plus valuable save points that are on offer. For example, in recent seasons, Sam Johnstone made 166 saves and Aaron Ramsdale 146 saves. For every three saves, keepers are awarded an extra bonus point. They can also collect five bonus points for a penalty save. These are influential factors that need to be considered.

Midfielders will collect two points on completion of 60 minutes. In addition, they will receive an extra point if their team records a clean sheet. Suddenly, a four-point deficit has become a one-point deficit. Given the position they play, a midfielder has the potential to generate multiple attacking returns. Signing a midfielder in these circumstances can be rewarding. They are more likely to produce an immediate net gain by registering attacking returns. Similarly, for forwards, playing in an advanced role offers the potential to score goals and create assists. With those come bonus points. An ideal opportunity to eradicate a points deficit. Clearly, losing points for conceding a goal doesn't come into the equation. Do you take a gamble and incur a four-point deduction, or be risk averse and tackle the Gameweek with an under-strength team? The prospect of an in-form forward, on penalties, and facing a poor defensive team for only a two-point deduction is very appealing.

Many risk-averse managers opt to play safe in these circumstances. Conversely, many players will decide to take a hit when in a similar position. It's all down to risk appetite. A hit doesn't guarantee a net gain. However, fielding that extra player could be very rewarding if you pinpoint a good option. The long-term benefits of an additional transfer should also be considered. A hit in these circumstances is not only to bolster your team for that week, but it's also a permanent transfer to strengthen your squad. That player may be retained for the remainder of the season. Signing a quality asset for a two-point deficit raises the question, stick or twist? A classic risk and reward situation.

For example, during the 2020/21 season, I found myself struggling to field XI players in blank Gameweek 36, after attacking TGW35.

Hence, BGW36 was a case of damage limitation. Potentially, I was looking to start the fixture with just six players. I opted to take two hits, which enabled me to tackle the Gameweek with nine instead of six players. Leicester city had a BGW followed by two difficult fixtures to finish the season, so I sold my three Foxes assets. Replacing them were Harry Kane and the Leeds duo, Patrick Bamford and Stuart Dallas. Of my new signings, Bamford collected just one point after he was subbed off on 75 minutes. Nevertheless, both of my other players delivered. Stuart Dallas kept a clean sheet and secured six points in Leeds' 4-0 victory at Burnley. Meanwhile, Harry Kane scored a goal and collected two bonus points in Spurs' 2-0 victory over Wolves. My three new signings collectively accumulated 15 points.

Another example comes from the 2021/22 season. In BGW19, I replaced Emmanuel Dennis and Mo Salah with Cristiano Ronaldo and Jarrod Bowen. Both of their respective clubs were without a fixture that week and both were due to travel to the Africa Cup of Nations (AFCON) competition shortly afterwards. Ronaldo and Bowen only produced a combined six points, generating a two-point net gain. However, I suggest that transfers should be considered as a long-term project. When determining the success of a transfer, a minimum five-week period should be considered. This timescale will provide a true reflection of a transfer's success or failure. Dennis and Salah collectively scored 16 points over the following five-week period, while Ronaldo and Bowen scored a combined 64 points. The transfers generated a net gain of 44 points, which I considered to be a triumphant hit.

A combined double and blank Gameweek is now becoming common. Some teams have two fixtures while others have no game. If you are struggling to field a full XI because you own numerous BGW players, replacing them with DGW players could theoretically work out to be a costless transfer. Provided your new acquisition completes 60 minutes in both games, the minimum of four points collected across the two games will cover the cost of the hit. The only downside is if they lose points through conceding several goals for a defensive asset or collecting a card. There is always the possibility that the player collects an attacking return, a clean sheet, save points or bonus points. This is an influential factor to consider if you encounter these circumstances.

Every transfer needs to be given serious consideration and thoroughly researched. It's also important to monitor the outcome of each transfer to establish if they are successful or not. Taking a hit to bolster team numbers is a viable option. This tactic can be extremely beneficial if the player(s) that you are seeking to sign are guaranteed starters, in-form and have favourable fixtures.

Additional Transfers

We have all faced the same dilemma. The question is: do we take a hit or play safe? FPL is continually evolving, so I ask the burning question that probably divides the FPL community - is taking a hit worth it? There are two schools of thought. Some managers love taking hits, while others loathe them. A good analogy is 'Marmite'. You either love them or hate them. I hope to shed some light on a subject which is probably debated annually by players of all abilities. Besides the five chips that managers have at their disposal, you could question whether hits should be regarded as a sixth chip. Chips and hits both provide you with the opportunity to optimise your potential points. The only difference being that, whereas all the current chips carry no penalty, with a hit you incur a four-point deduction for the privilege. The deficit is called a 'hit', hence the term 'taking a hit'. Unlimited additional transfers can be made and points incurred are automatically deducted when the Gameweek commences.

Taking a hit is a complex subject with many variables. For example, formation, player absentees, officiating, type of Gameweek and fixtures, etc. It's not as simple as asking yourself if the player that you sign is likely to outscore the player that you are replacing by more than four points in the first game immediately following the transfer. At the moment, that seems to be the consensus on measuring the success of a hit or not. Numerous other factors should be considered. For example, is the player going to be your captain? Are they in-form, a regular starter, a season keeper, likely to rise in value, have a favourable run of fixtures or double or blank Gameweeks on the horizon? These are all relevant questions that should be considered during your decision-making process.

Depending on your risk appetite, some managers proactively look for opportunities to collect extra points and are prepared to take a gamble. Conversely, there are those who are risk-averse. The emergence of a new breed of manager who is motivated by additional points may be changing the way we approach the game and the FPL landscape. They are exploring new avenues to search for those extra points. When the topic of hits is being discussed amongst the FPL community, it's now common to see players refer to their 'aggressive' approach. A competitive strategy, attacking Gameweeks at every opportunity. To keep one step ahead of your rivals, you need to seek innovative ways to enhance your game. Tactics that will give you the edge. Whether it be analysing more data, watching more games, viewing more FPL channels, listening to podcasts, taking more risks, maximising your chips or taking hits. They all have the potential to deliver points.

If used wisely, additional transfers can be an effective tool which could give you that edge over your rivals. We will discuss the reasons why players take hits, and the negative perception associated with them. Furthermore, we will identify those occasions when they can be effective and those occasions when they are not viable. The possible reasons as to why hits appear to be becoming more acceptable within the game will also be explored. Instead of merely using hits as a necessity in cases of emergency, there is a new incentive. There is a tendency for some to take a hit in order to optimise their potential points. My comprehensive study of hits over recent seasons has allowed me to obtain a better understanding of their use, efficiency, and value. Several steps can be taken to eradicate any unnecessary hits. For example; being flexible, demonstrating patience, and with effective planning. Pinpointing those occasions which offer the best opportunity for a successful outcome is key.

There are occasions when you desperately want to sign an in-form player at short notice. They may have just hit a hat-trick, or delivered a couple of assists, and their next fixture is against a struggling team. A tantalising scenario; such occasions arise frequently. Suddenly, the player is a very desirable asset and you view them as an integral part of your team for the foreseeable future. It seems that every man and his dog within the FPL fraternity is targeting this player, and the bandwagon is in full swing. If you don't move now, you may find that you've been left behind. If you have sufficient funds to complete a free transfer, there is no issue. However, a problem arises when you lack the funds to finance the deal. Undoubtedly, we have all faced this dilemma at some point. What to do next is the big question. Having two free transfers to release funds from elsewhere in your team is ideal. If not, there are only two options open to you. Firstly, you can disregard the player who is in red-hot form. Alternatively, you can take a hit in order to release funds to complete the purchase. Selling a player to facilitate the purchase of another is a common occurrence in FPL. Notwithstanding, it can become a costly practice. For many, the temptation to tinker is irresistible, particularly when the fear of missing out (FOMO) comes into play.

Suffice to say, if used wisely, a successful hit can reward you with a sense of accomplishment. Equally, the reverse could happen and it's a complete disaster. Hits are not only convenient in the event of an emergency, but they are a useful weapon to have in your armoury to attack specific occasions. Making an additional transfer has three possible outcomes. Firstly, the transfer is unsuccessful and you lose a number of points. Secondly, your transfer is successful, but having removed the four-point deficit, there is no net gain. Thirdly, your hit has been a success, resulting in an immediate net gain and a jump in rank.

The important question is: how often does the gamble pay off? Taking a hit carries an element of risk and has the potential to fail regardless of the amount of research conducted. You are not solely relying upon your skill to succeed, but to a lesser extent, you're dependent upon some good fortune. You may well have logically thought through a transfer and made the optimal move. However, the transfer was unsuccessful. Conducting research and pinpointing in-form players with favourable fixtures reduces the element of risk. Consequently, the transfer is more likely to produce a positive outcome. Rotation and injuries are factors that also need to be considered.

Generally, taking a hit will cause your rank to plummet even before a ball is kicked. In contrast, if you don't indulge in an additional transfer, you will have the pleasure of seeing your rank improve prior to the Gameweek commencing. The increase in rank will depend upon the total number of hits taken that week. Prior to kick-off, you are able to view the instant fluctuation in rank at www.livefpl.net Additionally, you will be able to obtain the average number of points deductions incurred by both the top 10k managers and managers as a whole. Carrying a hefty points deduction into a GW is a daunting burden. Particularly when you consider that your team needs to score those hard-earned points even before you break into credit. What happens if all your players 'blank'? Is your calculated gamble going to pay off? The pressure is really on. The term 'blank' refers to the occasions when one of your players doesn't register a return; i.e., a goal, an assist or clean sheet. Taking multiple hits in a Gameweek is a scary moment, yet one major haul and the deficit is wiped out. A calculated gamble that managers indulge in frequently.

Typically, the vast majority of managers take hits. However, there are some players who possess the will power to resist temptation and navigate through the entire season unscathed. For those that achieve their goal, it's the equivalent of receiving a badge of honour. Undoubtedly, those players who complete the task and avoid incurring points deductions across the season feel a sense of accomplishment. Nonetheless, there is one obvious question: did their risk-averse approach benefit them or hamper their performance? One would assume that avoiding hits is beneficial: but is it?

Many managers do not monitor the effectiveness of their hits. Therefore, they are not in a position to confirm whether their transfer activity had been a success or not. Maintaining an effective record of your transfer dealings is beneficial. Did the transfer(s) produce a net gain, loss or break even? Monitoring the effectiveness of your transfers will help you ascertain whether your transfer activity is being productive. Additionally, you will also be able to identify those occasions when your transfers are optimal. Many may be pleasantly surprised by the outcome of their transfer dealings. Especially if they adopt a sensible approach and carefully choose the appropriate times to take a hit.

Negative Perception

Generally, hits are portrayed in a negative light and frowned upon. The overwhelming perception of additional transfers is that taking a hit is really damaging. Even to the extent that after confirming the transfer(s), you reflect on your 'moment of madness'. Undoubtedly, some will contemplate exactly why they took the hit or, even worse, multiple hits. The alarm bells start to ring as you ponder an enormous drop in rank. There appears to be a lot of guilt attached to positive action taken to enhance your overall game. Action taken to generate extra points and strengthen your team at the same time. The sole aim is to improve one's overall rank. The question is: why is there a negative perception associated with taking a hit? I guess that the guilt aspect comes from the fact that you are doing something against the norm. Something that is despised by many.

Negative comments are rife, yet positive comments are scarce. It would be interesting to know the origins of the negative perception associated with hits. The obvious question is: why are hits perceived in such a negative light and is it justified? Is it as a result of overwhelming evidence through one's personal experience, or has it just escalated without any foundation? One of the choices you have when faced with a problem is to change your perception of the problem. People sometimes resist altering their perceptions, believing they are right in what they see, hear, and remember. The truth is, your perceptions are often inaccurate, particularly in emotionally charged situations. FPL certainly creates emotionally charged moments.

One way of being more open to changing your perceptions is to consider the ways in which your perceptions may be inaccurate. How you focus your attention affects your perceptions. When you have an idea in your mind, you tend to look for evidence that supports that idea and not pay attention to evidence that says the idea isn't accurate. This is confirmation bias. One way of checking your perception is to check the evidence. Is the way you see the situation factual? Instead of listening to countless warnings regarding hits, you can study the evidence by monitoring and evaluating your own transfer activity. You will be able to determine if your hits have been successful. If so, you will also be able to establish the optimal time to utilise them.

In the context of FPL, for the majority of the time, hits are portrayed in a negative light. The negativity surrounding a hit is a common theme and warnings are routine. It's not very often that you see or hear positive comments highlighting the possible benefits of taking a hit. The message that you see or hear is clear; do not take a hit under any circumstances. One specific article refers to a four-point deduction as "seriously damaging". The author of a further article suggested that the top one percent of managers rarely take hits, while another claimed that the top 1k-2k do not take any hits. My research didn't support these observations. On the contrary, there is growing evidence to show that the use of hits is becoming more widespread. When referring to taking a hit, many refer to the term "unless absolutely necessary", but then don't go on to define what that means. There are no fixed rules to say what is absolutely necessary and what is not. Everyone will have a different interpretation of that statement. All teams are different and many factors are team-dependent.

Some players who have accumulated a significant number of points deductions throughout the season may have suffered as a consequence. Conversely, there will be those who have gained a considerable number of points by taking hits. Another group will confirm that their hits have neither been beneficial nor a hindrance. The important factor is to monitor the effectiveness of the additional transfers that you make. Many managers do not do that and merely assume that their hits are unsuccessful because of the negative perception associated with them. Not only will you learn if your hits have been a success, but importantly, the circumstances in which they have been beneficial.

This raises an interesting question. Are there more negative mentions about hits because more players have experienced a net loss rather than a net gain, or is there a tendency for the negative outcomes to stay with us longer than the positive outcomes? Do we actually remember the negative outcomes more than the successful outcomes? Many studies suggest that we are more likely to remember negative events as opposed to positive experiences. It's likely that many will recollect their negative outcomes while they let the good moments lapse. Many will recall vividly those instances where they left 40 points on their bench or incurred a 12-point deduction which proved unsuccessful. However, how often does the same manager remember the 28-point gain from taking a 12-point deduction, or when a player was auto-subbed into their team with 18 points? When our hits are a roaring success, we do not acknowledge and cherish those moments. Needless to say, we can all recall the occasions which produce a disappointing outcome.

As discussed in Part 4, FPL is a game consisting of both skill and luck. Undoubtedly, skill is the biggest component, but Lady Luck does play its part. There are plenty of those what-if and if-only moments throughout the season. In terms of FPL, the word 'variance' springs to mind. You will clearly be able to recall the instances from last season when luck somehow bypassed your team. Yet, you will have no recollection of those occasions when you were fortunate to get the rub of the green. It seems a lot easier to remember the bad times as opposed to the good times. There is a tendency for the negatives to remain with us a lot longer - many days of reflecting on what could have been.

You question whether some managers are stuck in a time capsule and haven't adapted to change. Perhaps years of negative spin have driven many managers into sidestepping hits at all costs. Convinced that their no hits policy will reap dividends. As a part of my research, I discovered the 'Zero Hit Club', a group of managers who have made a concerted effort to avoid hits at all costs. They managed to navigate through an entire season without succumbing to temptation and have taken no hits. They deserve recognition for achieving such a difficult task. During the 2020/21 season, two Top One Hundred Managers didn't take a hit and there were others at various ranks who did likewise. In contrast, at the conclusion of the following season, I found it difficult to identify any members of the Zero Hit Club. Every Top One Hundred team incurred at least one four-point deduction. Actually, it was apparent that the average number of point deductions had increased considerably in comparison to the previous season. With the game evolving, I ask whether some risk-averse managers are missing out on the opportunity to maximise their points potential. Taking a hit should not become common practice, but there are certain situations where the opportunity to maximise points is on offer. A prime example being double Gameweeks.

At the conclusion of each campaign, some will reflect on their performance. They will presume that had they not taken X hits, they would be X points better off. Consequently, they would have achieved a far higher rank. Would that be the case though? Many do not keep an up-to-date record of their transfer activity. Therefore, monitoring your transfers is paramount. Not only will you obtain a true reflection of their effectiveness, but it will also be beneficial for your future transfer activity. You will be able to determine if your hits produced an immediate or long-term net gain or loss, and if your transfer dealings were effective. For example, if you incurred a 64-point deduction over the season, after evaluating your hits, you may discover that you only suffered an immediate net loss of 12 points. Conversely, you may have benefited from a net gain of 28 points. Many assume that taking a hit always produces a negative outcome. That is not the case. In reality, monitoring hits for a minimum of five Gameweeks will give you a more of an accurate picture of their success or failure.

My research uncovered some startling findings. Many teams incurred a substantial number of point deductions, yet still managed to achieve an excellent rank. For example, during the 2020/21 season, numerous teams finished with a remarkable rank inside the top 20k, despite collecting 252 in point deductions. Some will argue that those teams could have done even better had they not taken so many hits, but that's not necessarily true. It's feasible that those managers only managed to perform so well and achieve their rank purely by taking hits. The team that finished 75th in the world in the following campaign accumulated 152 in points deductions. It didn't stop their march to the top. Actually, some will suggest that their hits ensured a top 100 finish. You will find similar examples in Part 8 of the book.

With an ever-growing number of participants and fierce competition, you could ask if opinions are beginning to change. A new type of manager who is far more proactive in their search for points. A player who is willing to abandon the 'take no hits' advice that has been forcefully put forward in the past. Are we now witnessing a more dynamic manager who refuses to be risk averse and seeks innovative ways to boost their points tally? Managers with a higher risk appetite. Perhaps the game is heading towards a new norm with a new type of player emerging. Someone who is abandoning their safety-first strategy.

Armed with more information, they are prepared to be more proactive in searching for additional points by utilising hits at the appropriate time. This theory is supported by the fact that recently multiple hits seem to be rife. It's now common to see managers openly share their hit experiences on social media. An influx of content creators ensures that players are becoming more knowledgeable.

There is a wealth of information available to help managers improve their game and succeed. It's been suggested that content creators with big profiles are becoming more aggressive with their use of hits. That being the case, are these two factors the catalyst for more managers taking hits?

You could question whether the reluctance by some to take a hit could be hampering their progress. Perhaps a risk-averse approach doesn't guarantee success. Some will suggest that the lack of ambition shown and being over-cautious could be having an adverse effect on their performance. The lack of hits in certain circumstances may actually be depriving managers of valuable points, an exceptional rank or winning a mini-league. Their progress is stalling. Who is to say that a play safe policy is beneficial?

Countless managers will just assume that their hit(s) were unsuccessful purely because of the negative perception associated with them. There is nothing set in stone to say that making additional transfers will produce a negative outcome, neither is there any evidence to suggest that this is the case. There is overwhelming evidence to show that you can be very successful if you use hits wisely. When considering hits, it's important to keep an open mind and give them serious consideration. Treat each one in isolation. Monitoring the effectiveness of your transfers will enable you to determine if your transfer strategy is effective.

Potential Drawbacks

There are potential drawbacks when taking a hit. Occasionally, regardless of the amount of planning and preparation that you undertake, unexpected events can and do occur. For example, there is a necessity to start planning well in advance for a double or blank Gameweek. However, once you start utilising your free transfers to prioritise blank or double GW assets, circumstances can quickly change. Every transfer has the potential to backfire. Problems can arise, most notably when one of the new additions, that you specifically targeted, becomes unavailable prior to the Gameweek commencing.

One of the golden rules of FPL is to leave your transfer(s) until as late as possible. Ideally, it's always advisable to conduct your transfer(s) after the press conferences. This will allow you to act on any snippets of information, which will drastically reduce the chances of a wasted transfer. It's disheartening to discover that the player you have just signed has sustained a midweek training injury and is now unavailable. It could be a significant injury which will rule the player out for a prolonged period. Realistically, if the player is unavailable, one of your crucial free transfers would have been wasted. Worse still, a points deduction was incurred for no reason. Additionally, you may also need to acquire a replacement, which could cost you a further points deduction.

Regardless, every week, without fail, many make early transfers. As soon as a new Gameweek commences and the official site re-opens, the transfer merry-go-round starts. Some make transfers even before a ball has been kicked. It's definitely a risky strategy, as a lot can happen in between weeks. Players not only need to survive the current Gameweek, but then avoid any training ground injuries or illness.

A valid reason to make an early transfer is to beat an expected overnight price change when you have the exact funds to complete the signing. It's frustrating to miss out on a player if you discover that you're 0.1m short after a price increase. However, early transfers shouldn't become a habit, as you are taking a calculated risk. Fortunately, there are several websites which monitor price fluctuations. These include both fantasyfootballfix.com and fplstatistics.co.uk.

Besides injury issues, there is also the dreaded rotation - something despised by all FPL managers. With numerous cup competitions, and the strengthening of squads, rotation is inevitable. Some teams are more prone to rotation than others. In past seasons, we have become accustomed to expecting some rotation, particularly with Pep Guardiola at Manchester City. However, during recent seasons, rotation has been taken to a new level with more clubs rotating players more often. It's highly likely that those teams involved in multiple competitions are more prone to rotation.

An in-form player with favourable fixtures can attract a great deal of interest within the FPL community. It's likely that they will become a much sought-after asset. Expectations are great and it's not a case of whether they are likely to score a goal or create an assist, but how big their haul is going to be. Suddenly, many managers are tempted to jump on the bandwagon and their ownership rockets. Some may have already used their free transfer, so the possibility of a hit is on the cards. A classic example from the 2020/21 season being Riyad Mahrez. In BGW36, Manchester City faced struggling Newcastle Utd and the in-form Mahrez hadn't played for two games. He was a certain starter.

Many signed City assets specifically to target the Newcastle game, but Mahrez was by far the most popular pick. Some even felt confident enough to entrust him with the armband. Everyone waited in anticipation for the dreaded team announcement an hour before kick-off... Mahrez was on the bench! The one consolation for distraught managers was the fact that Mahrez didn't make a five-minute cameo appearance and hence could avail of their substitutes bench. Many knew the risks involved, but they were still convinced that Mahrez would not only start the game, but they were also confident of seeing a big return on their investment. Rotation is an FPL nightmare and there were a significant number of unnecessary hits taken that week. Considering rotation during your decision-making process, and leaving your transfers as late as possible, are wise moves.

When Not to Take a Hit

For some managers, the temptation to take a hit is overwhelming and they take hits when they're not a viable option. Many are accruing needless points deductions. There are various reasons for this and most are avoidable. For example, emotionally led, knee-jerk, rage and impromptu transfers are common. There are also transfers through the 'fear of missing out' (FOMO). Another prime example being one week 'punts', a speculative transfer when chasing points. In the process, a reliable player is needlessly replaced. Some prematurely cast aside dependable players, while others aspire to build their perfect team. It's key to analyse the player that you are replacing and not just the player that you are signing. It's inevitable that at some stage during a season, some will make needless transfers for no specific reason.

Some conduct emotionally led transfers when they are not in the right frame of mind to do so. For example, through frustration, anger, or intoxication. FPL is a game to be enjoyed, but if you wish to succeed, hits can severely dent your chances if not deployed for valid reasons. Making frivolous transfers and hitting dizzying heights are not compatible. Utilising your free transfer to replace an underperforming player with an in-form player is understandable, but would it justify taking a hit for that purpose? If hits are used sparingly and purely for specific purposes, it's likely that the number of unnecessary points deductions will be greatly reduced. By eradicating futile hits and targeting those occasions which are likely to produce net gains, in all likelihood you will benefit from more green arrows. I would suggest that the options highlighted are not viable options.

From my research, there is considerable evidence to indicate that numerous transfers are made at short notice, without any prior research or serious consideration. Managers are making knee-jerk, rage transfers, or transfers through fear of missing out. Many of the transfers are a spur-of-the-moment reaction to a poor performance by an underperforming player or team. Generally, the transfers are made during a match or soon afterwards. It's common for managers within the FPL community to refer to completing a rage transfer - a transfer made in anger. Typically, these are the occasions when a transfer does backfire. Apart from being a poor transfer, it could also cost you four valuable points. There is a tendency for FOMO transfers to be conducted as we approach a Gameweek deadline.

To gauge how widespread knee-jerk or rage transfers are, I conducted two polls amongst the FPL community on Twitter. One at the conclusion of the 2020/21 season and again the following campaign. I asked participants if they had completed similar transfers during the season without any prior planning. Unsurprisingly, the outcome of the poll supported my suspicions. Some 48% of participants confirmed that they had made such a transfer during that season. Notably, the poll was conducted amongst an audience largely made up of committed managers. A similar poll amongst a wider group of players may have produced an even greater percentage of players participating in these types of transfers. The findings from the second poll, conducted in the 2021/22 season, were more startling. On this occasion, 62% of respondents confirmed that they had made a knee-jerk or rage transfer during the season.

A factor that does influence transfer activity is the fear of missing out (FOMO), particularly on social media. Hence, beware the 'Twitter Bubble'. Just because something is discussed on Twitter, it doesn't mean to say that it is representative of the entirety of FPL. FOMO is a real phenomenon which accounts for many unnecessary hits weekly. FOMO is the psychological term for the "pervasive apprehension that others might have rewarding experiences from which one is absent". It's characterised by the "desire to stay continually connected with what others are doing" (Przybylski et al., 2013).

The English dictionary provided by Oxford Languages describes FOMO as "anxiety that an interesting or exciting event may currently be happening elsewhere, often aroused by posts seen on social media". For those with a tendency to experience FOMO, social media can be a very persuasive and dangerous place to be as we approach a Gameweek deadline. Groupthink comes into play, and you could easily be influenced by other players and ongoing bandwagons. Suddenly, the pressure is on for you to follow suit. Przybylski et al. (2013) suggest that "Social networking sites create many opportunities for FOMO, they offer a view into an endless stream of activities in which a person is not involved." While Jonathan K. J. (1998) suggests "psychological dependence on social media can lead to FOMO."

Herd mentality or groupthink is a phenomenon which explains the process by which an individual's behaviour or beliefs conform to that of the majority. The FPL Twitter community is a group of committed enthusiasts with the sole aim of being a successful manager. However, it is an ideal place for players to incorporate the views of others as their own beliefs. Often, some players decide to conform to the decision made by the masses. An outcome that they may not have made themselves had they not been a part of that community. For example, it is common to see managers requesting assistance from fellow players by seeking advice regarding their team, transfer or captaincy selections. Some may even run a poll to identify the most popular player to sign or who to captain. The opinion of others may influence their judgement. Consequently, their original selection will be discarded and their planned captaincy or transfer selections switched to another player recommended or selected by the majority.

There is a tendency for some to internalise what the prevailing view is amongst the FPL community. Undoubtedly, many make regular transfers to conform to the template team. Some are merely happy to follow the majority. Presumably, there is a sense of security if you are a part of the crowd - a safety in numbers mentality. Occasionally, the majority will get it wrong. However, it's likely that the wisdom of the majority will get it right on most occasions. Weekly, many succumb to FOMO - the fear of missing out on an imaginary haul. Some players become the topic of conversation amongst the FPL fraternity and are perceived as essential. A bandwagon emerges and gathers momentum throughout the week, culminating in many taking the plunge. Having already used their free transfer, some will be tempted to take a hit. They complete an unplanned, knee-jerk signing purely because they do not want to miss out on the 'must-have' asset. This is not a wise move; every transfer deserves serious consideration before confirmation. Planning ahead and conducting effective research will ensure that you complete the optimal long-term transfer.

Another influential factor is effective ownership. Some will consider the implications of EO, in particular, of not owning or captaining a player who is likely to have a high EO. They will sign the highly owned player solely to safeguard their rank. Prior to DGW36 of the 2021/22 season, FPL Theorist conducted a poll which produced an interesting outcome. Some 59% of participants confirmed that EO had influenced their decision-making. It is common to see the FPL community discussing transfers instigated by FOMO. This is most prevalent as we approach a Gameweek deadline. To determine how widespread FOMO is, I conducted a poll amongst the FPL community. Managers were asked if, at any point during the 2020/21 season, they had taken a hit through FOMO. Remarkably, 75% of participants confirmed that they had completed a FOMO transfer. A similar poll conducted the following season produced a startling outcome. Incredibly, 87% of participants confirmed that they had completed a FOMO transfer.

Social media is a powerful tool, and this outcome highlights how influential the platform can be. It is evident that some players can be easily influenced in their decision-making process and have their judgement swayed by others. Some make transfers without considering the long-term implications. From my research, there is evidence to demonstrate that the majority of knee-jerk or FOMO transfers are not successful. Additionally, such transfers are needlessly wasting a valuable free transfer or, even worse, a four-point deduction.

It's evident that herd mentality is widespread within the FPL community and it may also be prevalent amongst other FPL players. Consequently, it's highly likely that some are taking unnecessary hits which will have an adverse effect on their performance. The frequency of these types of transfers is unknown. However, it is clear that with better planning and more thoughtful transfers, the number of hits being taken can be significantly reduced. I would recommend making a concerted effort not to make impromptu transfers. Every transfer should be considered in isolation and each one judged on merit. Transfers need to be thoroughly researched and supported by a good decision-making process. Additionally, ignoring the masses and playing your own game will be beneficial. Do not be guided by countless other managers. If you require a second opinion, then confide in a 'buddy'. Someone who you have confidence in, can be relied on, and provides sound advice.

Making Additional Transfers

My research uncovered a variety of reasons why managers take hits. Some of those reasons are obvious, whilst some are bizarre. The most common reasons for making additional transfers are straightforward, and you can understand why managers take a hit under those circumstances. We will now discuss the most common reasons as to why hits are taken and differentiate between those occasions which can be beneficial or those which are not viable.

Quality of Player

Whilst conducting my research, I received a lot of interesting responses to polls and surveys. Some of those responses may well have answered some of my questions in relation to why hits are becoming more acceptable within the game. For example, managers were asked what was the main reason for them taking a hit. FPL Hopper (@FplHopper) responded:

"I think that hits are becoming more aggressive due to PL squads, now being more reliable, having more quality, etc. In the earlier years, in the 06/07 season, I finished 6,187 overall. I made less than 20 transfers all season. The standout was keeping my strike force of Rooney, Mc Carthy and Berbatov for the full 38 Gameweeks. Throw in the likes of Gerrard and Lampard, there were very few changes I wanted or needed to make. Squads were rotating less back then."

The Premier League is regarded as the best league in the world and attracts many of the top players. Consequently, we are served with some quality football by an array of stars. Squads have not only expanded, but the quality of player has improved. Rotation is now a common theme. Astonishingly, during the 2021/22 season, there were 737 players to choose from on the official FPL site. A remarkable number which provided an enormous number of different player permutations when selecting your 15-man squad. Undoubtedly, the quality of player and football on offer has improved considerably since the inception of FPL.

186

Mini-Leagues: Prizes

Occasions arise when you are fighting to win a mini-league, many of which attract prizes. A poll was conducted amongst the FPL community to ascertain if managers thought FPL had become more competitive. If so, is it now more difficult to achieve a top 10k finish? FPL Hopper responded:

"A lot of cash leagues are enticing people to seek help online. They find 'the community', they then stumble across the 'template' which leads to very similar teams throughout. How do you break it when they are practically the same? I see guys at work now who have improved a lot over the years. I know a lot of these blokes don't watch football. Yet I see them ranked at 25k come Christmas, the template is intact and a TV of 106.1m. They lurk and they copy."

FPL Hopper raised a really interesting point regarding the emergence of cash leagues and their popularity. Given the rewards on offer, are prize leagues a motivating factor? An incentive for managers to become more knowledgeable and adopt a more aggressive approach to hits? Many actively seek to improve their game by analysing statistics, watching more football, YouTube videos, listening to Podcasts, etc. While others learn from content creators who are active on social media and on dedicated FPL websites. Just imagine, the end of the season is in sight and you are within touching distance of the top team. Undoubtedly, you browse through your rival's team. It looks very similar to yours. If things remain the same, you have no chance of overtaking them. Time for some desperate measures and a classic winner-takes-all scenario. Some would certainly be tempted to take a hit under these circumstances, or even to play a mini-wildcard. At least it will give you a realistic chance of winning the league. Conversely, if you are sitting comfortably on top of the league with your nearest rival 10 points behind, you may hold firm and avoid a hit. Let them take the hit and do the chasing.

There is clear evidence to suggest that players are becoming more knowledgeable, and the presence of cash leagues may well be a motive for managers to succeed. To gauge the popularity and possible impact prize leagues are having on hits, a poll was conducted amongst the FPL community. To ascertain if managers are taking hits to gain rank in a cash-based mini-league, they were asked if they had taken a hit during the 2020/21 season for this reason. Surprisingly, 43% of respondents confirmed that they had taken a hit for this purpose. Striving to win a prize-league may be a motivating factor in the upward trend of making additional transfers.

Gain Rank

Regardless of prize-leagues, some make additional transfers to gain rank or improve their standings in mini-leagues. I examined data from the 2017/18 season and there was a marked increase in the number of hits being taken as the season evolved. However, it's noteworthy that the majority of DGWs do normally occur in the second half of the season when the European competitions are in full swing. My research confirmed that approximately two-thirds of Triple Captain and Bench Boost chips are utilised in the second half of the season. Similarly, with additional transfers. Countless managers chase points towards the latter end of the season, as they make a concerted effort to finish the campaign and their mini-leagues strongly. One final push for success. Hence, the popularity of hits during the latter stages of the season.

Perfect Team

Another group of managers aim to be perfectionists. They use their transfers in pursuit of unattainable excellence, as no stone is left unturned in their pursuit of perfection. Weekly, their aim is to build the perfect team. Their desire is to field the strongest possible XI on paper, regardless of cost implications. They crave every player that has either passed the eye test, or any in-form players regarded as crucial. A bandwagon is in full swing and they target the players deemed essential, regardless of whether it means replacing one of their most consistent performers or not. In reality, there is a good likelihood that this type of manager will regularly dabble in the transfer market. For some, the temptation is too much. If it means incurring point deductions to attain perfection, so be it.

Ideally, we would all like to aspire to build the perfect team, but it's not realistic. A 15-man squad should suffice. Occasionally, there will be the necessity to utilise an enabler if one of your regular starters is absent. However, instead of playing an enabler, some will sign a player who is perceived as essential amongst the FPL fraternity. You could question whether some are actually complicating matters by 'over-managing' their teams in pursuit of perfection. There is a tendency for some to overthink their captaincy and transfer selections, despite there being a standout player who is the obvious choice. Instead, they jump from player to player, targeting in-form players and plumb fixtures. Perhaps a more realistic and consistent approach to managing a team could be more beneficial, and reduce the number of unnecessary transfers being made. A strategy of avoiding hits and relying on your squad could be more advantageous. What is the perfect team and what's to say that the 'perfect team' will outperform your current team? There are no guarantees in FPL. Serious consideration should be given to every transfer with form, fixtures and the likelihood of a successful outcome being influential factors.

Chasing Points

There is a tendency for some to jump from one premium asset to another to chase points - a simple case of targeting the player who has the better fixture. This approach may pay off in the short-term. However, the downside is that you are either using one of your 34 valuable transfers, or incurring a points deduction. Occasionally, the term 'fixture proof' is referred to. A term usually used in connection with a premium asset who is always likely to deliver points irrespective of the opposition. This is more likely if they are on penalties or set pieces. The issue is whether you really need to incur points deductions to jump between assets if you have important fires to put out? Chasing assets with favourable fixtures means that the more pressing issues which need your attention may be neglected. Your transfers are a valuable commodity and it could be argued that the focus of your transfer activity should be on tackling your weakest link. There is the option to solve your Achilles heel by replacing them with an in-form player with favourable fixtures. Failing to address your squad weaknesses will catch up with you and you're likely to lose points as a consequence.

Gain Team Value

A topic that divides opinion is building team value. An important strategy which allows you greater flexibility later in the season. It is a positive tactic which will enable you to have more buying power. Building funds will allow you to focus on quality players to strengthen your squad, players that you would otherwise be unable to afford. The strategy is particularly popular between Gameweeks 2-12, when prices are most volatile. The aim is to target in-form players who are likely to experience an increase in price. Typically, premium assets also see their value rise relatively quickly. In addition to building team value, managers can also conform to the template team.

The argument for targeting players and building team value is that the extra funds will enable you to improve the quality of your squad as the season evolves. Those players will then reward you by generating additional FPL points. Over the long-term, the extra points will more than compensate for the point deductions incurred. I personally think that building team value is good practice. However, some will take a hit purely to gain team value. Unless the incoming players are going to be a permanent fixture in your team or given the armband regularly, then taking a four-point deduction to gain minimum value over a short-term is not a viable option. Alternatively, using your free transfers, or utilising your WC1, to build team value is a smart move. Besides re-shaping your team and pinpointing favourable fixture swings, you can also target in-form players that are a part of the template team and will increase in value.

Template Team

Including numerous differentials in your GW1 team is a recipe for disaster and is likely to have a detrimental impact on the rest of your season. A popular tactic is to conform to the template team - a hypothetical team of players which emerges containing the most popular players. Each season, a template team is formed early and as the season progresses, there is a tendency for that team to evolve. Conforming to the template team during the early part of the campaign will enable you to build a solid foundation that will keep you in contention. Utilising free transfers to conform to the template team is beneficial, but taking hits to do so is questionable. Newly signed players may pay for themselves over the long-term. However, it's unlikely that many would actually retain those players for any period of time. There are several websites which provide details of the template team. An informative website which will undoubtedly assist you in managing your team is www.livefpl.net.

Premium Absentees

Some opt to take a hit to replace one of their premium assets who has sustained a long-term injury or collected a three-match suspension. Consideration should be given to replacing them at the earliest opportunity. A substantial sum is invested in the player, so you wouldn't necessarily want a high-valued player sitting on your bench for any period of time. That money could be re-invested to strengthen your team elsewhere. Additionally, in the meantime, their value is also likely to decrease. Ideally, replacing an injured premium asset by utilising a free transfer is optimal. However, you may have more pressing issues, like injuries, inactive and underperforming players that need your attention. Premium assets consistently deliver points, therefore taking a hit in these circumstances is likely to pay for itself more often than not.

In-Form Players

Many will be tempted to take a hit on a standout performer who has hit a purple patch. A bandwagon will emerge and a price increase is inevitable. Meanwhile, you're methodically trying to get your house in order by replacing injured or underperforming players using one FT per GW. By the time that you're in a position to sign the player, they could have lost form or face a difficult run of fixtures. Since becoming your transfer target, they have accumulated a substantial number of points and gained value. Having missed their points hauls, you now discover that they are being abandoned by many and their price is dropping. You have missed the boat. In these circumstances, many would consider taking a hit to sign the player while they are in-form, increasing in value and before they lose their appeal. It's highly likely that the four-point deficit would be recovered plus more. That may be an occasion where doing nothing costs you more than taking a hit.

Speculative Transfers

Some are inclined to take a one-week punt purely on the basis that they believe the player that they sign will significantly outscore the player that is being replaced. The player is perceived as essential, although there is nothing to suggest that the new acquisition will perform markedly better than the outgoing player. Disappointing statistics and no recent standout performances doesn't instil confidence, but the idea is there. Some will seek a second opinion and may be advised by others to "go with your gut". Speculative transfers can easily be avoided to reduce the number of unnecessary hits. If it's an in-form player with favourable fixtures, going to be a long-term addition, or will be given the captaincy, then such a transfer becomes more viable. Otherwise, it's a gamble which could prove costly.

Put 'Fires Out'

With only one free transfer allowed per Gameweek, those managers with an injury crisis or a number of underperforming players may find revamping their team slow and arduous. The weak links need addressing and players need replacing. In the meantime, those managers could be missing out on valuable points by not signing the standout performers as they seek to tackle their pressing issues. By the time their issues are resolved, their intended targets are no longer delivering points. Many managers will be tempted to take a hit not only to address their problems but also to benefit from the in-form player when they still have enticing fixtures.

Additional Transfers: Optimal Time

Having considered my research findings, making additional transfers could be a viable strategy to optimise your potential points. If used wisely, hits can enhance your game and give you an advantage over your rivals. We will now discuss the merits of taking a hit and highlight those favourable occasions, which offer the best opportunity to deliver extra points.

Double Gameweek

Probably the most popular reason for taking a hit is to attack a double Gameweek. Acquiring DGW assets in exchange for a points deduction can be a wise investment. In the context of FPL, double Gameweeks can be an absolute game changer in terms of a manager's overall rank. They provide you with an outstanding opportunity for your team to produce a substantial score. A score that will secure a green arrow and has the potential to turbo charge your climb to the top. Planning for a forthcoming double Gameweek is key.

Occasionally, some double Gameweeks are arranged at relatively short notice. This prevents managers having sufficient time to recruit an adequate number of DGW assets by using free transfers alone. You could activate your Free Hit chip or Wildcard, but you may wish to keep those valuable chips for a more suitable occasion. This is a great example of why holding two free transfers in reserve is such a favourable tactic. Alternatively, in these circumstances, many will be inclined to take a hit to bolster numbers. Especially if you are considering playing your Bench Boost chip. A great tactic is to deploy your second Wildcard the week before a DGW. The benefits could be two-fold. Besides giving you the opportunity to strengthen your team in readiness for the DGW, it can also set your team up for the remainder of the season. I make reference to your WC2 purely because it's unusual to experience a DGW during the first half of a season.

Ideally, the best possible preparation is to sign as many DGW players as possible with a view to activating your Bench Boost chip in a big double Gameweek. If you do manage to fill your entire squad with DGW players, and you utilise your BB chip, your team could theoretically play 30 fixtures. Potentially, your starting team could feature in 22 games and your bench players in a further 8 fixtures. A squad capable of producing an impressive score. Realistically, the more DGW players that you play, the higher your points potential. Typically, a DGW can generate a significant number of points, and scores in the region of 150-170 are not uncommon. If a player manages to play in both games, a four-point deficit for a hit is likely to be offset by their appearance points alone. This is more likely if the player has a high ceiling, two favourable fixtures, or will be your captain. If you don't have your BB available, fielding a strong team consisting of DGW players should still give you an advantage over many teams. When contemplating a hit under these circumstances, there are a few issues to consider. Form, fixtures, captaincy, long-term hold, high ceiling and rotation are all influential factors.

Season after season, players will step up and produce a mega-points haul out of nothing. It's more likely to occur during a double Gameweek purely because of the extra game. For example, listed below are the biggest point hauls for the 2021/22 season. You will note that the top seven scores were all achieved in a DGW. They offer a fantastic opportunity to enhance your points total.

Player	Points	Gameweek
Kevin De-Bruyne	30	DGW36
Matty Cash	29	DGW28
Mo Salah	28	DGW26
Raheem Sterling	28	DGW36
Sadio Mane	26	DGW26
Kai Havertz	26	DGW28
James Maddison	25	DGW37
Gabriel Jesus	24	SGW34
Mo Salah	24	SGW9
Mason Mount	24	SGW9

Over recent seasons, there has been a significant amount of re-scheduling and a notable increase in the number of double Gameweeks in comparison to a typical season. Players encountered six double Gameweeks and one triple Gameweek during the 2020/21 season. In TGW35, Manchester Utd were confronted with the unenviable task of playing three games within the space of five days. It was a welcome bonus for managers as it provided the ideal opportunity to score extra points. However, planning for such Gameweeks was exceedingly challenging. The 2021/22 season was record-breaking, with eight BGWs, seven DGWs and six Gameweeks, which were both blank for some teams and a double Gameweek for others. Despite the fact that managers received an extra FH chip, the increased number of DGWs undoubtedly contributed to a record points total set by the eventual winner, Jamie Piggot. Remarkably, 2,009 managers beat the points record set by Michael Coone in the previous season.

My research confirmed that many managers had been more aggressive over recent seasons, with a marked increase in the number of additional transfers being made. Presumably, extra DGWs was a contributing factor. This finding is not only supported by statistics, but numerous managers confirmed that they had taken hits to target the many double Gameweeks on offer. Prior to DGW26, I conducted a poll on this very subject. Some 53% of participants confirmed that they had taken a hit that GW purely because it was a double Gameweek. While a further 19% confirmed that they intended to take a hit that GW regardless. Maximising the number of DGW assets that you play during a double Gameweek and deploying your Bench Boost chip in such a week is optimal.

Field A Full-Strength Team

There are specific occasions when taking a hit to supplement your squad with the intention of fielding a complete team is a viable option. For example, to negotiate a blank Gameweek, when you have multiple injuries or suspensions, and when playing your Bench Boost chip. Especially if it's a double or triple Gameweek. Managers have experienced 15 blank Gameweeks over two seasons, which has tested the managerial skills of players of all abilities. Trying to field a full-strength team during a blank Gameweek, while trying to contend with multiple injuries and Covid cases, also made it very challenging. Particularly without taking a hit. Several blank Gameweeks were in close proximity to one another and with different teams having different schedules, juggling your team was crucial. It emphasised the importance of your planning. The more groundwork that is conducted, the less likelihood of incurring points deductions. However, on occasions, late withdrawals, etc. don't give you sufficient time to resolve the problem. That's when hits become an option.

Many will activate their Free Hit chip to tackle a blank Gameweek. However, those without their FH chip, or who wish to retain their chip for a more appealing GW, will consider additional transfers. When contemplating whether to take a hit under these circumstances, it is worth considering the minus two debate and the additional benefits that go with it. Supplementing your depleted team may help you to consolidate or even improve your rank. Some will take a gamble and tackle a Gameweek without sufficient bench cover, or even worse, a full-strength XI. Possessing an inactive bench will increase the likelihood of you having to take a hit to field a full-strength team in these circumstances.

A major problem arises when you encounter a blank or double Gameweek in consecutive weeks. This scenario occurred in TGW35 and BGW36 during the 2020/21 campaign. It proved a turbulent time for managers. Some managed to field a full-strength XI for one of the weeks but not the other. Managers were better prepared for TGW35, but the following week many encountered problems and hits were abundant. A considerable number of managers had failed to prepare for both types of Gameweeks and consequently had to take hits to bolster their team. Therefore, planning for such eventualities decreases the chances of you incurring point deductions. It is important to try to build a squad that is capable of covering both types of Gameweeks adequately.

A similar situation arises when managers struggle to field XI if their squad is decimated by a spate of injuries, illnesses or suspensions. To exacerbate the problem, many teams carry a relatively inactive bench. A common practice for managers is to buy cheap enablers to warm the bench - players who see little or no game time. Filling your bench with budget players allows you to direct your funds elsewhere in the team. Although this tactic can pay dividends, it is still a calculated risk. Some prefer to have a very strong starting XI, which is detrimental to their bench. Managers hold benches full of enablers or players that are either injured or suspended. This is particularly common as the season evolves and the demands of players become more noticeable. If you suffer an excessive number of absentees, it will take you some considerable time to resolve the situation by using your free transfers alone. Hence, the importance of dealing with your weaknesses as a priority.

Many were caught out by the global pandemic and found themselves with insufficient bench coverage. Managers faced a dilemma: they could either tackle a Gameweek with an under strength team or incur a points deduction to supplement numbers. You could opt to field a weakened team and hope that you don't lose too much ground. However, logic says the greater the number of players on the pitch, the more likelihood of a bigger points tally. Fielding a severely depleted team could damage your rank, therefore you need to weigh up the pros and cons of tackling a GW without a starting XI.

Some opt to take a hit when playing their Bench Boost chip. This is prevalent during a double or triple Gameweek. Ideally, you would either have played your Wildcard the week prior to a DGW or have planned meticulously in advance for it. If a double Gameweek is arranged at short notice and the fixtures are enticing, some are tempted to make additional transfers to maximise their points potential when deploying their BB chip. Signing a quality asset with two games should repay the points deficit immediately or within a short space of time. More so, if they are in-form or have favourable fixtures.

Captaincy

Captaincy is a crucial aspect of FPL. Therefore, taking a hit on signing a player who is destined to be your captain for the forthcoming Gameweek, or in the foreseeable future, is a viable option. Particularly if the player is due to face an underperforming team or, even better, has a string of favourable fixtures. If you encounter a week where there are no standout captaincy candidates, you have a choice: you can either select one of your premium assets for a difficult fixture or take a gamble and select a differential. Alternatively, you could target an in-form premium asset who has a very favourable fixture or run of fixtures. A hit in these circumstances is both appealing and can be very rewarding. Selecting Haaland or Salah as your captain against the worst performing defence in the league could be very profitable, with the deficit instantly wiped out.

This type of transfer can be very effective and can repay the investment with bumper points and a significant net gain. For example, on six occasions during the 2020/21 season, I took a hit to sign a premium asset with the intention of giving them the armband for that Gameweek. I also viewed the transfers as a long-term benefit. The six Gameweeks in question comprised two singles, three doubles and one triple Gameweek. Listed below are the transfers made and their outcome.

Gameweek	Player	Opponents	Points	Double Points
SGW 9	Fernandes	West Brom	11	22
DGW19	De Bruyne	Palace & Villa	8	16
DGW 26	Kane	Burnley & Fulham	12	24
DGW 27	De Bruyne	Man Utd & Southampton	16	32
SGW 34	Kane	Sheffield Utd	2	4
TGW 35	Fernandes	Villa, Leicester & Liverpool	19	38

This tactic worked out on five of the six occasions, an 83.33% success rate. Although I lost two points on the Harry Kane transfer, my five other transfers produced a net gain of 46 points. Doubling up the points amounted to a healthy 92 points. Therefore, I suggest that targeting a premium asset to give them the captaincy is a very good ploy to optimise your potential points. Bizarrely, my only failure came from Harry Kane, who seemed odds on to pick up a mega haul against Sheffield United. Kane surprisingly drew a blank against The Blades, who at the time were bottom of the league and destined for the Championship. The ideal scenario is to sign an in-form player with a favourable fixture and to give them the captaincy. Such transfers are a viable option and a profitable avenue for collecting additional points.

Additional Benefits

Besides providing you with the opportunity to maximise your team's points potential, it's important to recognise that additional transfers can also provide further benefits. Factors that should also be considered during your decision-making process. If an immediate net gain is achieved, besides boosting your points tally, you have also received a free transfer. The additional transfer has enabled you to make one extra permanent transfer, which has strengthened your team for the long-term. Other possible benefits include the opportunity to change formation, gain squad value and to release funds to finance a future transfer. There is also the option to utilise a hit as part of a mini-wildcard.

Measuring Success

The question is: over what period of time should we measure the success of an additional transfer? I suggest that transfers should be viewed in the context of a long-term project, rather than just chasing short-term gains. It's not as simple as asking yourself if the player that you sign is likely to outscore the player that you replaced by more than four points in the following Gameweek. At the moment, that seems to be the consensus on measuring the success of a hit. How do we determine if a hit has been a success or not? Do you just measure the net gain or loss in the player's first game? Or do you include all the appearances made by your new signing during the remainder of the season? There isn't a set criterion. An alternative means of measurement is more suitable.

Ideally, a player's performance and whether the transfer has been a success or not should be measured over the period that they are deployed in your team and not purely by one game. In the case of long-term signings, that could be impractical, but it does provide an accurate assessment. The player may draw a blank in their first game, but proceed to score a hat-trick in the second game. That should also be viewed as a gain. To obtain a true reflection of the success of a transfer, there is a more accurate and practical means of measurement. A player's performance should be counted over a period of at least five weeks following the transfer. You may have considered the players' fixtures over the following 4-6 Gameweeks as a part of your decision-making process, so why not take those into account?

For example, a successful hit from GW10 of the 2021/22 season. I signed Trent Alexander-Arnold and Ivan Toney to replace Joël Matip and Romelu Lukaku. Taking into account the four-point deduction, there was an immediate net loss of one point. However, after five games, there was a net gain of 44 points. Earlier, I provided you with another successful example when I signed Cristiano Ronaldo and Jarrod Bowen in GW19. The two additional transfers discussed provided my team with an additional 87 points. A considerable number of points from just two transfers. When measuring the success of a transfer, you should abandon the one-game measurement. Instead, you should focus on the bigger picture and an extended run of fixtures. Monitoring a player's performance for at least five Gameweeks following a transfer will provide you with a true reflection of their success.

Additional Transfers: Statistics

Recently, there is growing evidence to suggest that hits are becoming more acceptable in the game. Although there has been an unprecedented number of extra double Gameweeks, it appears as though the number of hits being taken is still on the rise. Below, you will find a table of the average number of point deductions taken by teams at various ranks during the 2021/22 season. As a comparison, I have included the statistics for the previous season. It is noteworthy that both seasons had a high volume of DGWs.

Overall Rank	Average Hits 2020/21	Average Hits 2021/22
Top 100	33.16	47.38
Top 1k	40.64	50.85
Top 10k	46.08	57.32
Top 100k	55.02	67.43
100k - 200k	63.86	73.84
200k - 300k	69.97	76.94
300k - 400k	72.57	82.32
400k - 500k	72.24	77.27
500k - 600k	74.31	83.69
600k - 700k	71.50	79.31
700k - 800k	78.70	76.78
800k - 900k	76.61	78.97
900k - 1m	77.11	81.83
1m - 1.5m	80.13	77.93
1.5m - 2m	73.20	82.22
2m - 3m	78.26	68.97
3m - 6m	83.23	66.42

You will note that there is a significant rise in the number of hits taken by the top 10 categories. That includes managers who were ranked between 1 and 700k. There is a strong correlation between the number of hits taken and overall rank. The number of point deductions increases as one's rank climbs. Although managers were awarded a second FH chip, this would not have impacted on the number of hits taken. If anything, it's highly likely that more additional transfers would have been made had it not been for the second FH chip being made available. Recent seasons have produced a record number of fixture postponements and, subsequently, blank and double Gameweeks. It is likely that some utilised hits to tackle Gameweeks where they were struggling to field a full-strength team. In all likelihood, many managers would have taken hits to maximise their points potential by targeting the DGWs. This may be further evidence of the evolving nature of the game where a new type of manager is emerging, proactively seeking innovative ways to optimise their points potential.

The assumption is that additional transfers are damaging and that avoiding hits will result in a more favourable rank. Conversely, it could be argued that risk-averse managers are overlooking the opportunity to generate extra points. Does a no-hit strategy guarantee success and a higher rank, or is such a stance hindering a manager's progression? There is evidence to show that teams with a substantial number of point deductions can still propel themselves to the summit. My research found that the number of managers who are not inclined to utilise hits across an entire season is relatively low.

Hits not only offer you reassurance in the event of an emergency, they provide you with the opportunity to optimise your potential points. I suggest that hits should not be regarded as a hindrance, but as an effective tool. A means of enhancing your game, which can have a positive impact on your season. If used wisely, they can be used to your advantage over those managers who are risk-averse. A way of getting one step ahead of your mini-league rivals, while also improving your rank. Making additional transfers is all about minimising the risk by conducting thorough research and utilising them at the appropriate times. Focus on those occasions which are most viable and likely to produce a net gain.

Even though there is a correlation between the number of hits taken and overall rank, I would suggest that you keep an open mind with regard to taking a hit. Besides targeting those specific occasions when an additional transfer may be successful, the key to taking a hit is to be judicious and to totally avoid unnecessary, unplanned hits. For example, knee-jerk, rage, FOMO and impromptu transfers that haven't been researched will not have a positive impact. Adopting a strategy of eradicating unnecessary transfers in conjunction with deploying hits to target specific occasions will contribute to your success. Taking a hit routinely should not be considered as normal, but if used sensibly, they can be a valuable tool to have in your armoury.

Part 8: Top One Hundred Managers And The Elite

"If you want to be the best, you have to do things other people aren't willing to do." – Michael Phelps

The top managers achieve excellent ranks because they have the winning formula to succeed. Climbing to the top of the FPL pyramid is in their DNA. FPL is continually evolving, so complacency needs to be resisted. What better way to learn than from some of the greatest managers in the game? A combination of the Top One Hundred Managers and The Elite players provide a fascinating insight into the strategies they have adopted to succeed. Some players go onto become Elite Managers because they are the crème de la crème of Fantasy Premier League. They are the very best managers who have a staggering number of top 10k finishes amongst them. Managers who become elite for a reason. That's because they have the ability to succeed. The Elite Managers consistently perform at the highest level, achieving an impressive rank season after season. They plan their game meticulously, adopt the optimal strategies, pinpoint the standout performers, excel at captaincy picks, know when to attack and defend and when to make additional transfers. They are also adept at critically evaluating their squad and adapting to new information as the season unfolds. The secrets of their success are disclosed.

The performance of the Top One Hundred Managers from the 2021/22 season has been analysed. We will discuss the chip and hit strategies they adopted to succeed. As a comparison, I have included the salient points from my analysis for the Top One Hundred and Elite Managers from the previous season. There is a compelling insight from three top managers who excelled, finishing 3rd, 16th and 110th in the world in 2021/22. In addition, captivating insights from three Elite players are also included. Managers reveal their FPL career backgrounds, discuss their chip and hit strategies, and provide excellent advice. Analysing the performance of some of the best players in the world will enable you to get a better understanding of what is required to succeed in fantasy football.

However, you do not have to be a seasoned campaigner to be successful. My research demonstrates that with the right skills and good fortune, a novice to the game can catapult themselves from obscurity to reach the upper echelons of FPL. A prime example being the runner-up from the 2021/22 season. They achieved their remarkable rank even though it was their debut season. To reinforce the point that the best always rise to the top is the fact that eight of the top 11 managers from that season had previously recorded at least one top 10k finish.

Top One Hundred Managers 2020/21: Salient Points

The Top One Hundred managers comprised players from 35 different countries and just a measly 76 points separated them. It was fascinating to discover that for five managers, it was their debut season. For a further seven, it was only their second season. Considering their lack of experience, they performed admirably. When you delve into their FPL backgrounds, for some, the transformation was remarkable. The eventual winner finished with a rank of 1.34m in 2019/20, while a further 21 managers recorded a rank exceeding 1m. Actually, the team that finished in 32nd place completed the previous season with a rank of 4.51m. Highlighted below are the salient points from the Top 10 and Top 100 Chip and Hit strategies.

Top 10: Chip Strategy

- 90% activated WC1 during the first 10 GWs
    - The only exception was the eventual winner
- 90% utilised their FH to negotiate a BGW & one to target a DGW
- 90% deployed their BB chip to target a DGW & just one in a SGW
- 100% utilised their TC chip to attack a DGW

Top 100: Chip Strategy

- 46% activated WC2 in GW31: It followed a BGW & prior to further double & blank Gameweeks
- 86% used their FH to navigate a BGW & 13 to target a DGW
    - One manager played their FH in a SGW
- 89% used their BB to attack a double/triple Gameweek
- 11% played their BB in a SGW (5 in GWs 37/38)
- 97% managers utilised their TC to attack a DGW or solitary TGW
    - Three managers deployed their TC in SGW38

Top 10: Hit Strategy

- ➤ Average point deductions: 32
- ➤ Highest: 52 points (two players)
- ➤ 90% of managers made more additional transfers in the second half of the season
- ➤ 37.5% of hits taken in the first half of the season were to attack DGW19
- ➤ 75% of hits taken in the second half of the season were to tackle a BGW/DGW/TGW
- ➤ Blank, double & triple GWs accounted for: 15/38 weeks (39.47%)
- ➤ Hits taken in a blank/double/triple Gameweek: (63.75%)
- ➤ Two teams did not take a hit to attack a double/triple Gameweek
    - ○ They were outscored by seven of the other eight teams who did take a hit

Top 100: Hit Strategy

- ➤ 98% of teams took hits
- ➤ Highest: 68 points (two teams)
- ➤ Hits first half of season: 380 (45.57% - Ave Pts deduction 15.20)
- ➤ Hits second half of season: 454 (54.44% - Ave Pts deduction 18.16)
- ➤ Average point deductions: higher for the top 20 than those ranked 21-50

Elite Managers 2020/21: Salient Points

Chip Strategy

- 69.57% of managers activated WC1 between Gameweeks 2-5
- WC2 was deployed either the week of a DGW or the week prior to a DGW/BGW
- 85.09% of managers utilised their FH chip to tackle a BGW
- 10.56% used their FH to attack TGW35, 2.48% for a DGW & 1.96% for a SGW
- 98.76% of managers deployed their TC chip to target a DGW/TGW
- 1.24% used their TC chip in a SGW (GW37 & GW38)
- 87.65% of managers utilised their BB chip to attack a DGW/TGW
- 19 managers deployed their BB chip in a SGW (12 in GWs 37 & 38)

Hit Strategy

- Average point deductions: 48.41
- Ave hits per manager first half of the season: 5.94 (Equates to 23.77 Pts)
- Ave hits per manager second half of the season: 6.16 (Equates to 24.64 Pts)
- 963 hits taken during the first half of the season
- Comprised: 640 hits (-4) 124 hits (-8) 25 hits (-12)
- 998 hits taken during the second half of the season
- Comprised: 650 hits (-4) 150 hits (-8) 16 hits (-12)
- 1,035 hits (52.78%) were utilised in a blank, double or triple GW

Summary

There is clear evidence to show that the majority of the top managers utilise their WC1 early. This suggests that their strategy was either to gain team value, conform to the template team, or to navigate a favourable fixture swing. It could have been a combination of several factors. Many teams activated their WC2 just after BGW29. This coincided with a significant fixture swing. Furthermore, the research suggests that the majority of Elite managers activated their WC2 to reset their teams in order to tackle the many blank and double Gameweeks towards the latter end of the season. Those planning to deploy their Bench Boost in a double Gameweek opted to activate their Wildcard the week prior to that Gameweek. Others, who were not playing their BB chip, opted to use their WC2 the week of the DGW.

There is overwhelming evidence to show that the vast majority of the top managers utilised their Free Hit chip to tackle a BGW, and their Bench Boost and Triple Captain chips to target a double or triple Gameweek. It is also evident that the leading managers prioritise their hits to negotiate the numerous blank and double Gameweeks that feature heavily towards the latter end of the season. I would strongly recommend that you consider applying the same strategy.

Top One Hundred Managers 2021/22

"The key to success is to focus our conscious minds on things we desire not things we fear." – Brian Tracey

The leading teams achieved their excellent rank on merit. They outperformed nine million rival teams over a challenging 38 Gameweek period. After countless hours of meticulous planning and tinkering, they demonstrate the necessary skills to succeed. In this section, we will evaluate the hit and chip strategies adopted by the Top One Hundred Managers for the 2021/22 season. The analysis will enable us to identify the most popular and optimal time for the best players to utilise their chips. In addition, we will learn when additional transfers were made and discover whether they were beneficial or a hindrance to their performance. The Top One Hundred Managers represented 33 different countries, which affirms the games' global appeal. The data below highlights the number of managers per country that achieved the enviable rank.

Country	No. of Teams
England	29
Sweden	11
Norway	10
Ireland	7
USA	5
Poland	3

Each of the following eight countries had two managers who made it into the Top 100:

- Australia, Canada, Egypt, India, Malaysia, Nepal, New Zealand & Serbia.

Each of the following 19 countries had one manager who made it into the Top 100:

- Bangladesh, Bosnia-Herzegovina, Denmark, Finland, Germany, Hong Kong, Isle of Man, Lebanon, Libya,

213

Maldives, Myanmar, N. Ireland, Qatar, Saudi Arabia, Scotland, Singapore, South Africa, Syria & Wales.

Salient Points

- ➢ The winner: overall rank of 4.06m in 2019/20 & 230k in 2020/21
- ➢ First season: 4 managers - (2nd, 23rd, 71st & 92nd position)
- ➢ No previous top 10k finish: 66 managers
- ➢ Rank exceeding 1m in 2020/2: 6 managers
- ➢ One manager: 5th season - first overall rank inside 1m
- ➢ One manager: 5th season - previous best rank 806k
- ➢ One manager: 15th season - first overall rank inside 100k

The salient points should provide you with plenty of optimism and encouragement in your quest for glory. There is nothing to stop you from achieving your ultimate goal and climbing to the top of the FPL pyramid. My research has confirmed that players with differing abilities and experience can reach the upper echelons of FPL. Nothing is impossible. It is now common to see teams jumping from obscurity to the summit. Whether you are a novice, or a seasoned campaigner who has never registered a top rank, there is overwhelming evidence to demonstrate that it's achievable.

"The pessimist sees difficulty in every opportunity. The optimist sees opportunity in every difficulty." – Winston Churchill

The overall winner for the 2021/22 season was Jamie Pigott who scored an incredible 2,844 points. Remarkably, 164 more points than the previous best, set by Michael Coone during the preceding season. One can assume that the number of fixture postponements and the record number of double Gameweeks contributed to Jamie's exceptional score. In an unprecedented move, managers were provided with a second Free Hit chip, to help deal with the significant number of fixture postponements and new challenges emerging. In all likelihood, the extra chip also contributed to the record points total. Unbelievably, 2,009 managers beat the previous best score of 2,680 points. Undoubtedly, the game has become more competitive since its inception. A significant increase in the number of participants, the availability of information and more knowledgeable players has ensured that the competition is fierce. It will be interesting to see how the game develops in future years. A list of the previous winners of FPL with their winning scores is listed below.

Season	Name	Points
2002-03	Graeme Haddow	1,940
2003-04	Muir O'Connor	2,151
2004-05	Andy Tomlins	2,253
2005-06	Tommy Wilson	2,326
2006-07	Mike Dolan	2,268
2007-08	John Frisina	2,466
2008-09	Sir Moult	2,264
2009-10	Jon Reason	2,668
2010-11	Chris McGurn	2,372
2011-12	Sam Pater	2,414
2012-13	Matt Martyniak	2,472
2013-14	Tom Fenley	2,634
2014-15	Simon March	2,470
2015-16	Dimitri Nicolaou	2,458
2016-17	Ben Crabtree	2,564
2017-18	Yusuf Sheikh	2,512
2018-19	Adam Levy	2,659
2019-20	Joshua Bull	2,577
2020-21	Michael Coone	2,680
2021-22	Jamie Pigott	2,844

"I really think a champion is defined not by their wins, but how they can recover when they fall." – Serena Williams

Top One Hundred Managers 2021/22: Chip Strategy

The strategies which you adopt in FPL are crucial. To help understand the strategies adopted by the Top One Hundred Managers, their playing records for the 2020/21 and 2021/22 seasons were analysed. Do the strategies adopted by the best managers hold the secret to their success? The aim was to identify the optimum time to activate each chip. Establishing when the very best play their chips will give us a clue as to when that time is. I wanted to ascertain if there was a specific trend and why managers played their chips when they did. My findings shall be highlighted under the heading of each chip.

Wildcards

During the first half of the season, there were just three weeks where at least 10 Wildcards were activated (SGWs 5, 7 & 8). The favoured time to utilise the first Wildcard was in Gameweek 8, when 55 were activated. This not only coincided with the first international break of the season, but there was also a favourable fixture swing for several of the top teams. Playing their WC1 at this time allowed managers to benefit from price increases over the break and conform to the template team. In addition, in-form players with good fixtures could be targeted. It also enabled managers to configure their team for the Gameweeks ahead.

Similarly with the second Wildcard. Only three weeks attracted more than 10 activations. They were DGWs 26, 34 and 38. Two of the Gameweeks had 14 fixtures and the other 11 fixtures. The Wildcard not only set teams up for those weeks, but it enabled managers to take advantage of the many double Gameweeks that were imminent. There was a distinct pattern, with the majority of players activating their chip a week or two prior to a DGW. Many activated their chip in DGW26 with a view to deploying their BB chip in DGW28. Likewise, DGW28 was popular, allowing managers to deploy their BB in DGW29. Finally, many activated their second

Wildcard in DGW34 with a view to playing their Bench Boost in DGW36.

Remarkably, 87 managers activated their WC2 in a double Gameweek and a further four in a combined double/blank Gameweek. Just six activated their chip in a single Gameweek and three in a BGW. Surprisingly, no Wildcards were activated in the biggest DGW of the season. That was DGW36, which comprised 16 fixtures. Presumably, this was because managers preferred to deploy their Bench Boost chip instead. There is compelling evidence to show that the vast majority of managers utilised their second Wildcard either the week of a double Gameweek, or a week or two prior to a DGW. Those managers who didn't activate their WC2 during a double Gameweek, opted to attack that Gameweek by playing their Bench Boost and Triple Captain chips instead.

Free Hit

During the first half of the season, just four Gameweeks attracted at least 10 Free Hit chips. They were BGW19 (14 chips), D/BGW27 (41), DGW28 (17) and BGW30 (12), which consisted of four games. Traditionally, the FH chip is used to navigate a blank Gameweek. However, due to the unusually high number of double and double/blank Gameweeks on offer, some decided to activate their chip to attack these weeks. Similarly, with the extra Free Hit chip that was made available to managers. The most popular weeks to deploy FH2 were BGW30 (20 chips), D/BGW33 (13) and D/BGW37 (53). Of the 200 Free Hit chips available, 119 were deployed to tackle a combined double/blank Gameweek (59.5%), 47 were used to navigate a blank Gameweek (23.5%), 33 were utilised to attack a double Gameweek (16.5%). Just one was deployed in a single GW (0.5%) and that was on the final day of the season.

Bench Boost

Only four Gameweeks attracted more than 10 Bench Boost chips. Three of those weeks were double Gameweeks and the other was a D/BGW. They were DGW36 (42 chips), DGW28 (21), DGW29 (13) and D/BGW33 with 11 chips. Double Gameweek 36 had the most fixtures during the season (16), DGW28 comprised 14 games, whilst there were 13 fixtures in DGW29. Unsurprisingly, 78 managers played their BB chip to attack a double Gameweek and a further 14 deployed their chip in a double/blank Gameweek. Six chips were played in a single Gameweek and two in a blank Gameweek. My findings were consistent with those from the previous season. There was overwhelming evidence to demonstrate that the leading managers prefer to deploy their Bench Boost chip to attack a double Gameweek.

Triple Captain

Incredibly, all 100 managers activated their Triple Captain chip over four Gameweeks. All but one team activated their chip in a double Gameweek. DGW26 attracted 68 chips, 24 were played in DGW29, seven in DGW36 and just one chip in single GW38. Conclusive evidence that the best managers utilise their TC chip to attack a double Gameweek. Of the 200 Bench Boost and Triple Captain chips available, seven (3.5%) were deployed during the first half of the season. The remaining 193 (96.5%) were activated in the second half of the season.

Top One Hundred Managers 2021/22: Hit Strategy

There is a general perception that the top managers succeed purely because they avoid taking hits and that doing so is a suboptimal strategy. However, this isn't necessarily true. There is conclusive evidence to demonstrate that the vast majority of the better-performing managers take hits each season. For example, all but two teams made at least one additional transfer during the 2020/21 season. In the following campaign, all 100 teams took at least one hit. In all likelihood, teams are successful because managers plan meticulously, adopt the best strategies, play their chips at the optimal time, and select the best available players. They own relatively strong squads which have strength in-depth and perform exceptionally well consistently. They may also have been fortunate to avoid injuries and rotation. Therefore, there wasn't the necessity to take a hit. A winning formula negates the need to make additional transfers.

Firstly, the data for the top 10 managers was analysed and then the Top One Hundred Managers for the 2021/22 season. The statistics were then compared with those from the previous season. I examined their transfer activity, the number of additional transfers made, and when they took those hits. My aim was to establish if the hits taken had contributed to their success and whether there was a distinct pattern over the two seasons. What was the key to their success? Below, you will find details of the points deductions incurred by the top ten managers in the world over both seasons. Displayed are the number of points deductions taken by each team during each half of the season, plus the total number over the season.

Overall Rank	2020/21 GWs 1-19	2020/21 GWs 20-38	2020/21 Total Hits	2021/22 GWs 1-19	2021/22 GWs 20-38	2021/22 Total Hits
Team 1	-12	-24	-36	-12	-28	-40
Team 2	-8	-8	-16	-20	-32	-52
Team 3	-4	-28	-32	-12	-24	-36
Team 4	0	0	NO HITS	-8	-40	-48
Team 5	-8	-4	-12	0	-16	-16
Team 6	-8	-28	-36	-12	-36	-48
Team 7	-12	-36	-48	-28	-48	-76
Team 8	-12	-40	-52	-12	-20	-32
Team 9	-24	-28	-52	-12	-40	-52
Team 10	-8	-28	-36	-20	-44	-64
			Total: 320			Total: 464
			80 Hits			116 Hits

Despite both seasons having a notable number of double and blank Gameweeks, it is clear that there is a sizeable difference in the number of hits taken between both seasons. An extra 36 hits were taken during 2021/22 in comparison to the previous season. The average number of point deductions incurred by the top 10 teams jumped from 32 to 46.40. The highest number of additional transfers made by a top 10 team in 2020/21 was 13 transfers (52 Pts). In the following season, that number rose to 19 transfers (76 Pts). One team didn't take a hit in 2020/21. In contrast, all 10 teams made at least one additional transfer during the following campaign. The least number of additional transfers made by a top 10 team was 4 (16 Pts).

It was noteworthy that all Top One Hundred teams incurred point deductions during the 2021/22 season, ranging from four to 152 (38 hits). Three teams incurred a substantial number of point deductions. However, it did not prevent them from attaining an exceptional rank. Their final rank along with the number of point deductions is shown below.

Overall Rank 2021/22	Points Deductions
33	92
72	108
75	152

The other notable feature is the fact that considerably more hits were taken in the second half of both seasons in comparison to the first half of each season. Further evidence to suggest that managers utilize hits to attack double – and navigate blank – Gameweeks. The top 10 teams took 24 hits (30%) in the first half, and 56 hits (70%) in the second half of the 2020/21 season. During the following season, 34 hits (29.31%) were taken in the first half and 82 (70.69%) in the second half of the season. More or less an identical breakdown from the 2020/21 season.

This is clear evidence to demonstrate that you can reach the FPL summit despite incurring a substantial number of point deductions. My research over two seasons uncovered examples of such teams. Making a large number of additional transfers did not prevent numerous teams from achieving a brilliant rank. Many teams accumulated point deductions in excess of 100 points. For example, in 2020/21, the team who finished with a rank of 7,088 incurred 204 in points deductions (51 hits). The team placed 2,347th made 38 additional transfers (152 points deductions). Below are the statistics of the average number of point deductions incurred by specific groups within the Top One Hundred teams. The contrast between the two seasons is remarkable. There is a significant increase in the average number of points deductions incurred per group during the 2021/22 season.

Overall Rank	Average Points Deductions 2020/21	Average Points Deductions 2021/22
1 - 10	32	46.40
11 - 20	38.40	44
21 - 30	27.20	48.40
31 - 40	28.80	51.60
41 - 50	29.40	49.20
51 - 60	38.40	54
61 - 70	45.60	39.60
71 - 80	26	58
81 - 90	38	40
91 - 100	29.60	41.20

The statistics below indicate the number of Top One Hundred teams finishing in a specific point deduction range each season. The number of point deductions per range is displayed along with the number of teams included in that specific points range. There is a marked difference between both seasons. There is a sizeable 'swing' after the 30-40-point group. It's noteworthy that the number of teams making more than 10 additional transfers jumps from 36 in 2020/21 to 64 teams in 2021/22.

Points Deductions	Number of Teams 2020/21	Number of Teams 2021/22	
0	2	0	
Less than 30	41	18	
30-40 Inc	21	18	9 with 40
40-50	18	23	
50-60	11	24	6 with 60
Over 60	7	17	

Despite there being slightly more DGWs during the 2021/22 season, the data suggests that hits are becoming more prevalent and are widespread throughout the game. A cautious, risk-averse approach is becoming less popular and the number of risk-seeking, proactive managers is on the rise. Contrary to what's purported in much FPL literature, there is overwhelming evidence to demonstrate that the majority of top managers are not risk averse. They are utilising hits for specific types of Gameweeks and for particular purposes. The most popular being to attack a DGW, to sign a player and give them the captaincy, or to field a full-strength team. Furthermore, it is evident that some take hits in a concerted effort to climb rank in the latter stages of the season. That's regardless of whether it's a single Gameweek or not.

The desire to succeed is attracting more hits and they are becoming more acceptable in the game. When FPL returns to some form of normality, it will be fascinating to study similar data. With the number of double and blank Gameweeks returning to their normal levels, it will be possible to establish if the trend continues. Will the popularity of hits continue to grow? Below are some interesting statistics that I uncovered whilst analysing the 2021/22 Top One Hundred teams. Displayed is the number of point deductions incurred in a specific timescale.

➤ Team 25: 20 Pts in DGW26 (7 transfers)
➤ Team 29: 16 Pts & 12 Pts to attack DGWs 26 & 29

- ➢ Team 31: 28 Pts - final 5 GWs
- ➢ Team 32: 32 Pts - final 6 GWs
- ➢ Team 46: 24 Pts - final 6 GWs
- ➢ Team 49: 32 Pts - over seven consecutive Gameweeks
- ➢ Team 52: 24 Pts - final two GWs
- ➢ Many teams took a 12, 16 or 20 Pt deduction to attack DGW26

The Top One Hundred Managers took a total of 1,161 hits during the 2021/22 campaign. The average number being 11.61 transfers, which equates to 46.44 points per manager. 378 hits were taken in the first half of the season (32.56%) and 783 hits were taken in the second half of the season (67.44%). Two Gameweeks did not attract any hits, while 17 weeks attracted more than 30 additional transfers. Two of those Gameweeks were single GW4 when 52 hits were taken and SGW38 when 53 hits were taken. It's likely that a significant fixture swing in GW4 accounted for the high number of hits taken at that time. In all likelihood, those who took a hit in GW38 did so to attack the final Gameweek. One late surge to try to reach their desired rank, or overhaul their mini-league rivals. The table below displays the Gameweeks which attracted more than 30 hits, the type of Gameweek, number of hits taken, and the number of games. D/BGW denotes a Gameweek where some teams had two fixtures while others had no game.

Gameweek	Number of Additional Transfers	Number of Games
BGW16	59	9
BGW17	51	7
BGW18	50	4
BGW19	41	7
BGW20	40	7
D/BGW21	75	10
D/BGW22	39	11
DGW26	93	14
D/BGW27	36	9
DGW28	34	14
DGW29	112	13
D/BGW33	37	12
DGW34	55	11
DGW36	58	16
D/BGW37	37	12

As in the previous season, there is clear evidence to demonstrate that the Top One Hundred Managers employ hits to target a DGW and to strengthen their teams in a BGW. Notwithstanding that GW36 was the biggest double Gameweek of the season, the two most popular weeks were DGWs 26 & 29. Presumably, DGW36 wasn't the most popular week for hits because many managers had activated their Wildcard. Furthermore, 42 managers deployed their Bench Boost and a further seven their TC chip. Additionally, many deployed hits during the final Gameweeks to target a strong finish to the season.

An Insight: Top One Hundred Managers 2021/22 & The Elite

"If football has taught me anything it is that you can overcome anything if you love something enough." – Lionel Messi

The Top One Hundred Managers and the Elite Managers are the type of player we all aspire to be. We crave success and seek to reach the next level. They're at the top of their game and are the best of the best. Whether they finish as a Top One Hundred Manager or as an Elite Manager who consistently performs at the highest level. I have had the pleasure of communicating with six of the best managers in the world to analyse their FPL careers. They provide a fascinating insight into their FPL background, managerial style, career highlights, plus their chip and hit strategies. In addition, they outline what changes to the game they would like to see implemented, if any. The amount of time spent playing FPL, plus their source of FPL information is also disclosed. Finally, they offer some top advice.

Undoubtedly, we all wish that we could emulate their achievements and we can learn a great deal from these exceptional players. They provide a wealth of useful information. I congratulate each manager on their magnificent performances and I would like to thank each of them for contributing to this book. The focus is on three managers who finished 3rd, 16th and 110th during the 2021/22 season to add to some excellent finishes in previous seasons. A further three managers can be regarded as Elite Managers, with 19 top 10k finishes between them. Sit back and enjoy a summary of their career highlights whilst you soak in some great FPL tips. First up is the 2021/22 world number three, Brett Taylor. Brett finished just two points behind the second placed team, and 14 points behind the eventual winner. A fantastic achievement.

Name: Brett Taylor (@FPLEchidna)
Country: Australia
OR 2021/22: 3

Career History:

"I have been playing FPL since the 2006/07 season but have only played 'seriously' for the last five seasons. That is when I discovered the FPL community and its tools. Most of the insight will be drawn from my 3rd place finish."

Chip Strategy:

"The most common wisdom suggests saving chips until the second half of the season when blank and double Gameweeks occur; my experience confirms this theory. My success in 2021/22 was in large part a result of my navigation of the fixture chaos caused by Covid-19. I used regular transfers and chips to maximise the number of fixtures my team played, by targeting 'doublers' and avoiding 'blank' players. Across the season, I deployed 488 players, including DGW players, as two but not including captaincy as an extra player. As a reference, 38 GWs x 11 players = 418; plus four for a standard Bench Boost = 422. So, by targeting DGW players (especially with chips), I gained an extra 66 rolls of the dice above the baseline.

"I was one of several managers who used the WC26, FH27, BB28 and TC29 strategies. The number of fixtures that my players played during this run (not including captaincy as extra) were 22, 14, 25, & 20. A total of 81 games. This path's success was dampened by the fact I missed Salah's DGW26 haul with my Triple Captain chip. The fact that I still managed to finish 3rd overall speaks to the quiet power of fixture maximisation. Away from the blank and double Gameweeks, there are perhaps three noteworthy points about my first Wildcard in GW7. I timed it for major fixture swings in favour of Chelsea and Man City. I played it from a position of strength (rank 146k). I stacked my team with safe, long-term 'no regret' picks, such as Dias, Rudiger, Mount, Saka, Raphinha and Toney. Not

226

all of these picks succeeded, but the point was that I knew they wouldn't be dropped or rotated and therefore wouldn't require a transfer out any time soon. This freed up my subsequent transfers for the higher impact moves which catapulted me to success."

Hit Strategy:

"I've heard people talk about hits in terms such as 'use as few as possible' or 'aim for about X per season'. I think these outcomes are downstream from the principle which should guide hit use: always use hits whenever they pay you back at least the four points! The inverse is of course also true: never use hits when they won't pay themselves back. The art, then, is predicting whether a hit will earn a net gain in expectation. This calculation can be obvious or elusive. There are several situations where hits are likely to be worth it in the immediate term. If a hit 'buys' an extra fixture (by bringing in a DGW player or removing a blank/flagged player), it's likely to pay itself straight back (since most good players average four points for a decent fixture). If you captain the player that you're hitting in, they also have more capacity to return more of your points straight away. That's assuming that the new pick is superior to your other options.

"It's also worth taking a hit if it's likely to pay itself back in the longer term, although this can be harder to calculate. Think about how long you're likely to own the new players, how they're likely to score in those fixtures and how this stacks up compared to your path without hits. Weigh up your need to make other transfers now or in the near future. A good time to take a hit might be when you need to redistribute your budget around your team in a way which would be impractical or inefficient without multiple simultaneous transfers. For example, I took a 12 and 8 point deduction in GW29 and GW35. In both cases, I was bringing in a new premium (Kane & KDB, respectively) who both had extra fixtures coming up and who I would captain. In both cases, one of the transfers was downgrading a mid-priced forward to a 4.5m player to free up funds. These examples illustrate some of the above principles working in combination.

"However, even a successful hit is not necessarily reflective of 'optimal' play. Successful hits are good but even better is making the same moves with free transfers as a result of good planning, and effective play. I played just one hit between GW5 and GW29, rising from 166k to the top 50. I rolled my transfer often during this golden run, which allowed me to react to fires and change formations without hits. That said, it is normal to think that most seasons will be marked by phases where there are more beneficial transfers to make than free transfers available. Hits should be framed as a valuable tool in the elite manager's kit rather than a casual's vice or admission of failure."

Changes:

"I noticed the mood for change growing in the last off-season, but I, for one, think that FPL ain't broke. Maybe I would say that as I nearly won it! As I write this, the 2022/23 game has launched and I would say that player prices should have increased across the board. That change would make the template less obvious and force more interesting and challenging decisions. I also think that the deadline should be at least two hours before the first kick-off. This would remove any disadvantage for players who can't be logged on and make moves based on early team news. This would make FPL fairer and more accessible for managers in different time zones around the world. Also, those that have unavoidable work or care responsibilities. On the same note, upcoming price changes should be transparent and published on the FPL site. Where possible, equalising the information available to all managers levels the playing field. It returns more of the outcome to the use of in-game skill."

Time:

"A useful way to think about time invested in FPL might be in two buckets: research and leisure. Research is what I call the required time invested in playing the game to the standard I want. For example, following team news, reviewing data, watching highlights, planning and making my actual decisions. Leisure is everything on top, such as following the FPL community on Twitter, consuming or creating content and developing my analytical skills. I enjoy FPL as a hobby, beyond the pursuit of a high rank. Of course, there is a lot of overlap between the two but the distinction is useful. If FPL becomes too much, I know I can strip back a lot of Twitter use and Podcasts without compromising on my baseline commitment to playing 'seriously' for the whole season. Thankfully, the research component has become a lot less time-consuming due to ever-improving community tools. These make key information more readily available, liberating time for decision-making.

"It's worth noting that I also play a Fantrax draft league with friends. Monitoring an even larger player pool, including the less-fancied teams, is required. So, the answer to 'how many hours a week' is probably too many. I justify this by the social and intellectual dividends it delivers on top of the competitive game itself. The games were valuable outlets during the Covid-19 lockdowns, which were quite long and strict in Melbourne. I play with the knowledge that it can be made manageable when necessary."

Information:

"FPL Review has become my most valuable resource, although I haven't tested and compared other points prediction models, so I make no comment about their relative merits. I don't follow the model blindly; I use it to sense check decisions I'm already leaning towards, or to narrow the scope of possible moves to reduce cognitive load. Above all, Review saves a lot of time I used to spend trawling and aggregating data I used to do manually, such as in the Fantasy Football Scout members area or on Fbref or Understat. I do still use the Scout team news page and fixture ticker. I use FPL Statistics for price changes, LiveFPL for rank info and FPL Optimized for Gameweek analysis. Podcasts that I listen to are The FPL Wire, Planet FPL, FPL Black Box, The Athletic FPL Podcast, FPL Optimized and Who Got The Assist.

229

"On Twitter, I try to follow the most practically useful accounts, such as Ben Crellin and Colm Hayes for injury news and manager quotes. There are many others. I don't use a transfer planning spreadsheet or maintain any of my own models. I jot down the thoughts of future moves in the Notes app on my phone/laptop. I watch at least a short highlights package of nearly every match, more often a 20-minute 'mini match', all of which is available on-demand by the Premier League's Australian broadcast platform."

Top Advice:

"Think about thinking. Study economics, behavioural psychology and decision-making. Get at least a basic grasp of statistics and probability. Read about football tactics and sports analytics. Learn from the many generous experts in the FPL community."

Name: David Addison (@_SexyWater_)
Country: Canada
OR 2021/22: 16

Career History:

"I have been playing FPL for four seasons and I have made steady progress from 530k, 71k, 41k to my 16th place finish in 2021/22. In my first year, I was way too focused on price rises and took too many hits. In my second year, I discovered Twitter and YouTube and started watching more games on TV. It's easy to say that my 16th place finish is my career highlight. I'm learning that it may be a once in a lifetime rank, although it won't stop me trying. Although my final position was 16th, I actually tied for 14th (on points). My highest rank during the season was 3rd and that was in GW36. I ended up being number 1 in Canada and I won three mini-leagues (Newcastle Utd, FPL Mate & FPL Tips). I also came 2nd in Always Cheating Super League and 5th in the FPL BlackBox mini-league. I am a Newcastle Utd supporter and I also enjoy American Football. My team is The Green Bay Packers."

Chip Strategy:

"I try to be optimal. I rely on the work done by FPL content creators, who do a wonderful job of breaking down schedules and chip strategies. I do like to be aggressive and I will use chips early if needed. Activating your Wildcard between Gameweeks 4-8 gets you ahead of the crowd and builds team value early. I generally save my Free Hit chip for a double Gameweek. I aim to use my Bench Boost a week after activating my second Wildcard and target a double Gameweek towards the end of the season. The 2021/22 season was something different with the amount of double Gameweeks and we are unlikely to see anything like that again."

Hit Strategy:

"I'm totally fine with hits. A -4 here and there works well on smart moves with a multi-week outlook. My favourite tactic is to hold one of my free transfers until it's time for a mini-wildcard, 3 transfers for a -4. I don't mind taking a -8 when needed, but a -12 seems unnecessary. Anything more than this is trying too hard. Often, when I don't know whether to make a transfer or not, it pays to hold the transfer even though it's going against my aggressive nature. I took a -8 in Gameweeks 37 & 38. I needed to do this in order to make up ground on the people in contention. It didn't allow me to win the title, but these bold moves helped me win the Canada and NUFC titles. I was more interested in going up in rank rather than holding rank. Go big or go home!"

Changes:

"I really enjoy the game and I absolutely love the format. I enjoy the stock market approach to player values and the entire pool of players being made available. I wouldn't change too much as I like the game as it is. I know there's a growing sentiment to reduce or eliminate chips. I don't agree with this, I think they make things spicy! As with the Wildcard, I would make two Free Hit chips as standard. I'm not a huge fan of the Bench Boost chip but I do enjoy planning for it."

Time:

"Generally, I spend approximately 3-5 hours per week playing the game."

Information:

"I get my information from a variety of different sources. I use the FPL Community on Twitter and I'm also in a Twitter chat group with fellow Canadian players. I watch YouTube content from FPL Mate and Let's Talk FPL. I also listen to a couple of Podcasts, Always Cheating and Planet FPL."

Top Advice:

"Have fun, it's a game with outcomes you have zero control over. Don't let negativity get into your head. Trust your gut."

Name: Adrian Ilioski (@FPLOlympian)
Country: Australia
OR 2021/22: 110

Career History:

"I have been playing FPL for eight seasons. My first four seasons were played very casually and intermittently, whereas my last four seasons were played more competitively. I was rewarded with an impressive rank of 10.9k in my first competitive season, and this motivated me to continue playing FPL in a competitive nature, achieving ranks of 24k and 16.5k in the following two seasons. In the most recent season (2021/22), I achieved my best overall rank of 110th in the world. This happened to be the season where I started doing quite a significant amount of my own FPL research and analysis. I also finished 1st in the Australian Twitter League, which is a competitive League created by @fplplannerau for all FPL Twitter managers from Australia and New Zealand."

Chip Strategy:

"When it comes to chip usage, I tend to develop my own strategies that cater to my own specific team, as opposed to following the herd. Even if it feels like 90% of managers are planning to wildcard in week X. I certainly won't be afraid to Wildcard in week Y if it better suits my team. In fact, last season I used most of my chips at a different time to what was considered the most popular time amongst FPL managers. I found it crucial not to develop any FOMO with chips and to stick to the long-term plan as opposed to spontaneously deciding to use your chips in any given week, or when other managers are doing so to avoid a red arrow. Whilst you may suffer a small red arrow in a week when many other managers are using a chip, this rank can easily be made up two or three-fold when you use your chip in a later week that is more suited to your team. FPL is a 38-week marathon, so I tend to avoid letting a red arrow in any given week deter me. I have the tendency to save my chips relatively late in the season where possible, as I tend to avoid making short-term transfers that may backfire and force me into an early wildcard for instance. In fact, last season I had five chips remaining to use in the final 12 Gameweeks of the season, allowing me to play more aggressively than other managers. My rank was rewarded with this patient chip strategy approach in the latter stages of the season."

Hit Strategy:

"I would classify myself as a very hit-averse manager, so I intend to avoid hits unless I am confident that the minus four will repay itself almost instantly. Most of my hits come during the DGW period, as trading a single Gameweek player for a DGW player theoretically becomes a minus two as opposed to a minus four, from appearance points alone. I had only taken two hits prior to GW26 last season, but as the season became more chaotic with the DGWs, I was not afraid to play aggressively and take more hits. In fact, I had taken a total of 32 points in hits from GW26 until the end of the season. I consider this to be a lot for my standards. The lure of the DGWs was certainly a contributing factor. Also, as a general rule, I try to avoid taking anything more than a minus eight in a given week, no matter the circumstances. I also favour rolling transfers as much as possible when there are no fires to put out, and I would consider this a power play. In fact, I rolled my free transfer a total of 12 times last season. This allows more flexibility with restructuring your team without the need to take hits, as your transfer options open up exponentially with two free transfers as opposed to one. Especially when taking a hit-averse approach."

Changes:

"If I had to change something about FPL, it would be the transparency surrounding price changes. In previous seasons, I had the tendency to make panic transfers to avoid being priced out of a particular move, and I placed heavy reliance on third-party price change predictors. These served me well for a few seasons, but last season it appeared that price changes were much less predictable and more randomised. In my opinion, FPL should implement a price change tracker on their website to ensure a level playing field. Last season, I avoided early transfers entirely due to the chaos surrounding Covid and the random postponements. In fact, I have made every single transfer in the 24 hours before the deadline, ensuring that all press conferences were completed before making any moves. For the first time, I did not let price changes rush my decisions last season. I valued information over team value, and I certainly did not regret taking this approach."

Time:

"Most of my spare time in the week goes towards FPL. This includes watching live football or catching the highlights, researching, analysing data and creating content. This usually takes up 10-15 hours per week."

Information:

"Prior to joining Twitter, I consumed much of my FPL content through YouTube and FFScout. When running poor on time, I found that Podcasts were an efficient way to absorb content as you can listen while going about your daily life. Upon joining FPL Twitter, I found myself being exposed to a lot more information, allowing me to view concepts from different perspectives as Twitter is filled with such a variety of opinions. The important thing is to filter out any bias when making decisions for your own team and not to blindly follow any bandwagons without reason. I now find myself doing my own research and coming to my own conclusions. I still utilise a lot of the FPL Twitter content, but I also take advantage of fBref, FotMob and Playmaker for free stats. Drafthound is good for odds to help with those tricky 50/50 decisions. Team Planners are also a very effective way to navigate your future moves. I find these very useful as a long-term Planner."

Top Advice:

"Consume as much information as possible but also do your own research to eliminate any external bias and to ensure the information is relevant to your specific team and situation. Whether you have an aggressive or conservative play-style, you should not let others change the way you play the game. Whilst it is important to utilise EO, you should not let it control your decisions. So, if you believe a low EO differential will outscore a very high EP player, then follow your gut. There is nothing worse than seeing your gut call haul while you go for the safe high EO option out of fear. Finally, do not make any decisions or transfers when angry or emotional through FPL. Give yourself a few hours or days to cool off and come back with a clear mind. Remember that the season is 38 weeks long, so there is always a way to claw back a red arrow."

Name: David (@DayvyFPL)
Country: South Africa
OR 2021/22: 3,190

Career History:

"I started playing FPL after seeing my friend alter his team on his phone one day in high school. I asked him "what's that?" and the rest is history. I started my first season in GW10 and I managed to win my friend's mini-league. I was hooked. I have played for a total of 6 seasons (including the first one) and I have 3 top 6k finishes - more specifically, 22 in 2018/19, 5.4k in 2019/20 and 3.1k in 2021/22. I am a member of FPL General's Elite 64 mini-league after winning his community League in 2018/19. During the 2022/23 season, I was inducted into the FPL Review's Elite 1000. My career highlight must be the season where I finished 22nd. It's one of those things that you don't realise at the time, but now looking back, it was a ridiculous finish."

Chip Strategy:

"Going off past seasons, I have always seemed to prolong my first Wildcard for as long as possible. In 2018/19 and 2019/20 I used the chip on the last possible Gameweek. However, this has now changed and I use it whenever the team needs it (I probably prolonged it as the team was strong in both seasons). In terms of the Triple Captain and Bench Boost chips, I am a sucker for a double Gameweek and I have historically used those chips in such Gameweeks. I generally like to use the Free Hit chip in a blank Gameweek but I have used it aggressively in a double Gameweek previously. The second Wildcard usually comes into play before the double/blank Gameweeks in the latter part of the season."

Hit Strategy:

"I like to describe myself as a 'conservative' manager, but I would say more about the logic I use when making transfers and not in the usual description of not taking hits. If I believe a transfer is worth taking a hit, then I go for it. In determining whether a transfer is worth a hit, I usually go for a few factors. The first is if I'm going to captain the player that I transfer in. I always find it easier to take a hit for a captain, as you are reducing the time needed to 'pay back' the hit by captaining them and receiving double their points. The second is whether the player that I am taking out is injured. Sometimes people forget about their benches, so if an injured player can be replaced by a bench option, you can still get points. Let's just say that you don't have a bench or that the bench options are unreliable, then taking a hit for an injured player is a lot easier as you are now replacing 0/1 points with, hopefully, a good asset. The last factor and probably the hardest one to quantify is projected/predicted points. There are various models/algorithms that help predict a player's future points, but generally I look at fixtures. If I predict the player that I'm bringing in will score more than four points in the future over the player I'm taking out, then I will take a hit. You may have to be a bit patient with the last factor as the hit may pay off in a longer time period than expected."

Changes:

"I really do like the way FPL is setup. I would say the player prices for the 2022/23 season were a bit weird and made great options quite easily attainable. Saying that, the 'Template' didn't have the best start to the season with most going for five Premium defenders. I think the one thing that I would change is price change transparency as this is a massive part of the game and is hidden from the eyes of many managers. I can't tell you how many times the more casual players in my friend's group have said "oh, he rose in price" or "I can't afford the moves because a player rose or dropped in price". I feel this needs to be corrected."

Time:

"To be honest, probably too many! I do feel that the hours I do spend on FPL are different to most people, as I do create FPL content on YouTube. However, FPL is definitely my main hobby. I have always watched and loved football, so I think that I would be spending time on it anyway, even if I didn't create content. I am probably always thinking about FPL and whether it be transfers that I want to make or watching the Champions League. I'm always thinking what a particular game means to an upcoming Gameweek".

Information:

"Since starting to take the game seriously, I have been using Football Fantasy Fix. I enjoy their price change predictor, predicted points algorithm, Opta stats sandbox and the new Elite XI team reveal tool. The one place where I also find information is 'FPL Twitter'. It's not a set site but there are a vast number of FPL accounts that you can find. I would say the most useful information is the 'set in stone' news such as selection rumours, press conference and injury news. There have been endless times where an 'in-the-know' account has tweeted something that is super useful for FPL. An example of this could be that there is a rumour circulating that a certain player is injured and then they end up missing the upcoming game. I would definitely recommend creating a Twitter account for anyone who wants to take FPL more seriously. I do not usually use betting odds (on clean sheets, goal scorers, etc.) as I have found differences in the betting odds to my own thinking and therefore, I don't find them too useful."

Top Advice:

"My number one piece of advice to anyone playing FPL is to please remember, at the end of the day, it is just a game! If you are not enjoying it or find that it is taking away your enjoyment of football (something that I have experienced in the past), and most importantly, if it is affecting your everyday life - then stop playing. FPL is meant to be fun and if you are not having fun then I would either retire the game or change the way you play it."

Name: Tom Stephenson (@FPL_Badgers9)
Country: England
OR 2021/22: 22,133

Career History:

"I am currently in my 16th season of playing FPL with a highest finish of 375 in 2019/20. I have achieved 6 top 10k finishes and 14 consecutive seasons with a finish under 36k. In terms of leagues, I am currently in the Elite 64 which is run by FPL General, The Great and the Good run by Fantasy Football Scout's FPL Greyhead and in FPL Analytics Elite 64 League Division 1. The latter requires a combination of good overall finishes and Massive Data and Expected Goal ranks.

"I ended the 2021/22 season 9th in the Fantasy Football Scout's Hall of Fame, having dropped from second the previous season due to a rank of 22k. It is fair to say it is very competitive at the top of these rankings and hard to stay there. I also appreciate that I probably have had a lot of luck to have got there in the first place and that doesn't last forever. In terms of playing FPL for all these years, the biggest achievements have been getting to the top of various Hall of Fame rankings, something I never dreamed could be possible. I have also been invited to appear as a guest on a host of amazing podcasts, such as Meet The Manager Series with Joe from Fantasy Football Scout and the FPL Wire by Zoph and Lateriser."

Chip Strategy:

"I would say patience is the most important quality when playing FPL, given that there will always be players scoring highly who you do not own in any given Gameweek. One needs to try and not overreact and chase the points already scored. If I have plans in place, then I try to stick to them. At the same time, I do believe that sometimes there is a need to be aggressive in correcting issues with my team and I will even use my Wildcard in Gameweek 3 or 4. The one big advantage of this is buying good players that were not obvious before the season started, before they go up in price quickly. The start of the season is when transfer activity is at its most extreme, given there are still so many active players.

"The biggest skill for me in FPL is knowing when to be patient, and less frequently when to be aggressive. It is definitely a very hard balancing act. I also now spend more time thinking about captaincy, given it is such a big part of the game. I will even contemplate taking hits to bring in the right captain if needed. I will try and plan a few GWs ahead to consider who I want as my captain, and it is always good to have two big hitters to pick from. Another focus is on building value in the early part of the season. I will look to get on bandwagons quickly, and even make early transfers or even take hits if I feel I need certain combinations of players and could be priced out. Later in the season, I try to be much more patient and not make early transfers, valuing information gained over price rises. I usually have a core of set players in my team that I will try and keep for long periods. They could be big hitters that I need for the captaincy, or they may just be under-priced players who are good value long-term. I will move other players around based on fixtures. I like to identify blocks of good fixtures, perhaps somewhere between 4-6 games and try to target these blocks."

Hit Strategy:

"Over a season I probably take between 5-10 hits. If there are more double Gameweeks then this would be at the higher end. I used to take more hits, but from experience, I think they do not pay off often. With good planning, they can generally be avoided. It is probably less fun to play like this, but I believe it helps to achieve a better rank."

Time:

"I really wouldn't like to calculate how much time I spend on FPL. Watching football and playing FPL are my main hobbies and there must be many hours a week I spend on both. But it is something that I really enjoy, and I wouldn't change anything. I just try and bear in mind that there will be many highs and lows in playing FPL, and that a good slice of luck is always needed to do well."

Information:

"Two years ago, I joined Twitter, initially to help me get early team news that was becoming an important way to stay ahead of the crowd in any given Gameweek. I would say that Twitter is less useful for this now given the change in time of the deadline, but there is still a wealth of information to be gleaned. The hardest thing is knowing who and what to listen to and it is easy to get information overload and then find it hard to make decisive decisions. I still love being part of the FPL community on Twitter though, and I enjoy joining in with events like the Scouts Community tournament.

"I listen to a host of podcasts throughout the week, including Blackbox, The FPL Wire, Burning Questions, Planet FPL, Above Average FPL and The Green Arrow. I often listen to Let's Talk FPL Andy for his deadline stream, given he is so good at getting early team news and such a good manager himself. I have membership for FFScout and I sometimes look at player comparison tools, heat maps, fixture tickers, etc. I also look at data on FBref, such as player and team expected goal involvements. I also have membership at FPL Review and the Transfer Algorithm run by Mikkel Tokvam.

"A few years ago, I would have said that I was an eye test manager. That has definitely changed to more of a hybrid approach. I just cannot watch that many full games and highlights do not give you a complete picture. So I use various analytical tools to help me view and try to understand what has happened in games. Also, using FPL Review allows me to look at transfer strategies. Sometimes it highlights players that I may have not thought about, or just helps me to make a 50/50 decision on who to bench."

Finally, we come to another long-standing elite manager who is well known by many amongst the FPL Community. Like Tom, Abdul has an exceptional career history. Displaying skill over a prolonged period.

Name: Abdul Rehman (@FPL_Salah)
Country: Scotland
OR 2021/22: 3,231

Career History:

"I have been playing FPL since the 2007/08 season. One of my friends casually invited me to start playing and to join a mini-league which consisted of a few friends. At the time, I didn't have a clue about the game, but after the first Gameweek I was hooked. In my first season, I started playing in Gameweek 2 and, despite the late start, I still managed to win our mini-league. This really got me into it as I thought that I was great at the game (even though I wasn't). The bragging rights between mates were the top tier. It was the second season in which I really got serious. I found Fantasy Football websites, which at the time were extremely niche - almost cult-like. I have since managed four top 1k finishes and six top 5k finishes. At the time of writing, I sit as the 16th best manager in the world, according to the Fantasy Football Scout Hall of Fame."

Career Highlight:

"I have a few FPL career highlights which I am very grateful for. Making a career out of this financially over the last few years has almost been a dream come true. I write and make videos for Fantasy Football Hub, have appeared on the Fantasy Football show and the Premier League Fanzine show as a pundit during the 2021/22 season. I have also recently signed up with The Athletic and I will be producing content for them this season (2022/23). Working with seasoned presenters such as James Richardson, Kelly Somers and Jules Breach has been pretty cool. I am in the Elite 64 League, which was founded by FPL General (Mark McGettigan). I am also ranked 22nd by the FPL Research all time rankings."

Chip Strategy:

"Since chips were introduced my chip strategy has always been quite template, as it works. I have used my Bench Boost in the big double Gameweeks towards the end of the season and after activating my Wildcard. I have used my Free Hit chip during a big blank Gameweek and my Triple Captain chip in a double Gameweek. This strategy has been pretty successful for me and I don't see the need to diverge from it just to be different. I'm not saying it's the only way to use your chips because managers have used them in different ways to good effect."

Hit Strategy:

"I am very hit averse and try my utmost not to take a hit. I think many overestimate how valuable taking a hit is. I usually take approximately 3-5 hits per season, usually around double Gameweeks or when I have been hit badly with injuries, etc."

Changes:

"Not much. I would probably tweak the bonus point system a bit. Things like no negative BPS for yellow cards, forwards not being punished for losing the ball or shooting off target. Generally, I think the game is fine and it appeals to both casual and hardcore managers."

Time:

"I spend a lot of time trawling through statistics rather than on my actual team. I'm not sure that I can put a number on it. I am always picking up pieces of information, whether researching for an article, trawling through Twitter or watching games."

Information:

"Most of the statistics I get are from Fantasy Football Hub, more specifically their OPTA stats tool. It's great for looking at multiple stats and easily comparing. I also use Fbref and Understat a fair bit. When looking at my actual FPL team decisions, I consult fplreview.com for most Gameweeks."

Top Advice:

"My five tips: 1. Stats over eye test. Look at xG stats and use the eye test as a secondary source of information.

"2. Don't 'points-chase' by making 'knee-jerk' transfers: This is a very common mistake made by managers new to the game. I was guilty of this a lot in my early days of playing. It's very tempting to transfer a player who has just scored a brace, but you also need to look at who you are removing. Don't transfer out good proven players for last week's points. FPL is about chasing next week's points. Even when things go wrong, for example, a bad Gameweek, always keep a cool head, take a step back and assess throughout the week.

"3. Always wait as late as possible before making transfers. This may be hard for some, especially the less engaged managers. If I was to only give one piece of advice for a successful season this would be it. Waiting for as long as possible means you will have gained the most information that's available. In a typical season, there will be midweek games, injuries and illnesses. Therefore, holding out until after all the press conferences are completed, gives you an advantage. Making transfers early in the week could bite you in more ways than one. Don't worry about team value. It's extremely overrated.

"4. Don't take risks on captains, as they are one of the most important aspects of the game. Hitting your Captain consistently will go a long way in getting you a good rank. It can even paper over the cracks of a poor team if you get it right more often than not. Captain the 'obvious' player each Gameweek.

"5. Fixture over form. Historical data has shown that fixtures most definitely matter even for the best players in the world. Pay very close attention to fixtures and target good and proven players for teams who have a good run of games."

"Success is not only for the elite. Success is there for those who want it, plan for it, and take action to achieve it." – Jim Brown

Conclusion

"You've got to beat the best if you want to be the best." –
Trent Alexander-Arnold

The overriding principle of playing Fantasy Premier League is to enjoy the game. It is an utterly immersive football prediction game designed for football fans; a game which has an enormous global appeal. Players not only have the satisfaction of watching exciting Premier League football, but participate in a gripping fantasy football game which runs alongside the live action being played out on the field. FPL has transformed the way fantasy managers watch games. FPL is an emotional rollercoaster. Players ride the highs and suffer the lows, but reenergise and go again. Acknowledging that you will experience both emotions will help you to cope with the inevitable disappointments and joyous moments.

This book was designed to incorporate all the main aspects of the game. The aim was to focus on the key topics and disseminate the most helpful information. Guidance which will help to develop your game and assist you in your quest for glory. Furthermore, my research over two seasons was conducted to ascertain the best strategies to adopt and the optimal time to play your chips, etc. There is a high level of consistency between the findings from both the 2020/21 and 2021/22 seasons. The findings are also compatible with, and reinforce, the strategies adopted by many of the game's outstanding players. Tactics that have enabled them to repel fierce competition to reach the upper echelons of the game.

It is evident that to climb to the top of the FPL pyramid, managers need certain attributes and skills. They need to be highly motivated, possess a sound temperament and be patient. A player who is very knowledgeable, adopts effective strategies, uses forward thinking, and also has a slice of good fortune on their side. Research by O'Brien et al. (2021) found a consistent level of correlation between managers' performances over seasons, suggesting a persistent level of skill. Researchers found that the leading managers performed very strongly. They found that the top managers built an initial squad to take advantage of the fixtures. This suggests a high level of preparation. The same level of planning was also apparent when utilising their chips. Their planning was far more thorough than those with a lower rank. Effective planning will also reduce the necessity to make additional transfers.

My research confirmed that there is a strong correlation between the number of captaincy points and overall rank. Data shows that the number of captaincy points achieved decreases as your rank declines. For example, at the conclusion of the 2021/22 season, 12 of the top 13 teams with the highest number of captaincy points achieved a top 7k rank. It was evident that there was a significant increase in the average number of captaincy points achieved by players at all ranks between the 2020/21 and 2021/22 seasons. There was a marked jump in the number of points accumulated by the Top One Hundred Managers. The additional double Gameweeks, extra Free Hit chip and more knowledgeable managers may have all been contributing factors. There is a tendency for the stronger managers to select a proven in-form premium asset as their captain. Especially if they have a favourable fixture or run of appealing games.

It was noteworthy from the research that the average number of bench points collected dropped considerably between the 2021/22 season and the previous season. This included players at various ranks up to 6m. The data suggests that the increased number of fixture postponements and unavailable players led to managers being more dependent upon their bench. The top 1k managers accumulated more bench points than any other player. In all likelihood, this is due to those players being more knowledgeable, engaged and owning stronger squads.

The most successful managers will adhere to the template team throughout the majority of the season. However, at some stage there is the necessity to select some differential players to separate yourself from the crowd. Knowing when to attack and when to defend is key. There is evidence to demonstrate that the outstanding players hold their chips until the latter stages of the season. Recently, two-thirds of all chips have been deployed in the second half of a season. For example, during the 2021/22 campaign, of the 200 Triple Captain and Bench Boost chips available to the Top One Hundred Managers, 193 were played in this period of time. Manager's aim to utilise their chips to attack the double Gameweeks on offer and navigate the blank Gameweeks.

The optimal time to utilise your Triple Captain and Bench Boost chips is in a DGW. For example, 99 of those managers activated their Triple Captain chip in a double Gameweek. Similarly, with the Bench Boost chip, 92 played their chip in a double or double/blank Gameweek. Usually, the most popular time to deploy your Free Hit chip is to negotiate a big BGW, although it is team dependent and the chip can be extremely profitable if used to target a DGW. For example, 86 of the Top One Hundred Managers and 85% of Elite managers deployed their chip in a blank Gameweek during the 2020/21 season. In the following campaign, 83% of Top One Hundred Managers utilised their Free hit in either a blank or a combined blank/double Gameweek.

The most popular time to activate the first Wildcard is during the opening 10 Gameweeks of the season. Typically, the first international break between GWs 8-9 appears to be the preferred time. Similarly to the chips, the majority of managers retain their second Wildcard until the latter stages of the season. Their aim is to build their perfect squad to tackle the impending double and blank Gameweeks. The optimal time to activate the Wildcard is a week prior to a big DGW and then to deploy the BB chip during that double Gameweek.

The data confirms that there is a strong correlation between the number of point deductions incurred from additional transfers and one's overall rank. The number of point deductions increases as one's rank falls. That is, the outstanding teams took fewer hits than those teams who were not performing so strongly. The optimal strategy is to plan your transfers in advance and utilise your free transfers. However, most teams will encounter situations where it's difficult to sign their preferred targets and replace injured or underperforming players, etc. using free transfers alone.

There is overwhelming evidence to demonstrate that hits are utilised by the leading managers and they can be an effective tool if used wisely. All Top One Hundred Managers made at least one additional transfer during the 2021/22 season. The average point deductions were 47.38%. Actually, one team incurred a points deduction of 152 (38 hits) and they eventually finished the season in 75th place.

This reaffirms that it's possible to achieve a memorable rank irrespective of incurring points deductions. In the preceding season, one team finished with an exceptional rank of 7k besides incurring 204 point deductions (51 hits). Two thirds of all additional transfers were made in the second half of the season to coincide with the double and blank Gameweeks.

I suggest that hits can be advantageous if used judiciously for specific reasons. Targeting the most appropriate occasions, while eradicating unnecessary transfers, will enhance your game. Minimising the element of risk is key. Hits can be effective when going on the offensive in a double Gameweek. Likewise, supplementing your team when you are unable to field a full XI can be a viable option. Additionally, hits can be productive if you acquire an in-form premium asset to entrust them with the captaincy.

Double and blank Gameweeks attract many hits. For example, during the 2020/21 season, double and blank Gameweeks accounted for 39.47% of Gameweeks. 63.75% of hits taken by the top ten managers were in these types of weeks. A group of Elite Managers utilised 52.78% of their hits in a double or blank Gameweek.

The research confirmed that there is a tendency for many top managers to employ hits in the final weeks of the season to target a strong finish. Most notably, the research revealed that there was a significant increase in the number of hits taken by players at all ranks in 2021/22 in comparison to 2020/21. There is a growing trend, with evidence available, to suggest that the number of hits being taken is on the increase.

Generally, the exemplary players rise to the top of the global rankings each season. They achieve that for a reason. However, the research produces compelling evidence to demonstrate that it's possible for inexperienced players to succeed. You do not have to be a seasoned campaigner to be successful. Remarkably, for four of The Top One Hundred Managers in 2021/22, it was their debut season.

Astonishingly, one finished as the eventual runner-up. If you have the dedication, skill, good fortune and motivation, you can proudly sit at the FPL summit. A novice is more than capable of reaching the upper echelons of FPL and this should offer plenty of encouragement to those who are new to the game. Undoubtedly, players will learn from their experiences and become a better player as a consequence. There is nothing stopping you being a part of the crème de la crème of Fantasy Premier League managers.

I hope that you have enjoyed reading this book as much as I have enjoyed writing it. Hopefully, you have found the content both interesting and beneficial. Regardless of your experience or ability, the aim was to provide readers with the 'tricks of the trade'. General tips, the best strategies to adopt, and research findings that you will find invaluable for your future success. Guidance which will help you deal with every eventuality that you encounter in the game. Acquiring this new information should enable you to build a strong foundation and improve your game.

We all adore the beautiful game and Fantasy Premier League. Although we strive to perform to the best of our ability and succeed, don't forget that FPL is only a game. Pleasure is paramount and we yearn for those joyous weeks when our team breaks through the 100-point barrier. A colossal score ensures a green arrow and a significant jump in rank. Those are the special moments that we play the game for. Good luck in chasing green arrows and your quest for the coveted title and glory.

"If you don't believe that you are the best, then you will never achieve all that you are capable of." – Cristiano Ronaldo

Acknowledgments

Writing this book has been a very challenging, yet very satisfying and rewarding, experience. This project has been an amazing journey which I have thoroughly enjoyed. There are a number of people who deserve a great deal of praise for helping me fulfil this ambition. None of this would have been possible without the support and encouragement of my family and friends.

To Matt Whelan (FPL Obsessed) who I have had the pleasure of communicating with over a number of years. He has made a significant contribution to this project by proofreading the manuscript, and assisting in the publication process. His professionalism is exemplary, and he is willing to offer sound advice if the need arises. Matt has worked tirelessly to bring this project to fruition. I cannot express my gratitude enough. Thank you, Matt, for your commitment.

A deserving mention goes to Dan Bennett for agreeing to write the Foreword for this book. Dan is an Elite Manager who has been playing the game since the 2007/08 season. In that time, he has achieved one Top 1k finish, six Top 5k finishes and three Top 10k finishes. Dan is a top personality amongst the FPL community and he currently produces content for Fantasy Football Fix. Thank you, Dan.

Finally, a very special thank you to those FPL experts who have kindly contributed to this venture. A combination of Top One Hundred and Elite Managers from around the globe who have excelled in Fantasy Premier League. Managers we all aspire to be. They have all provided an invaluable insight into the thought processes and strategies that they have adopted in order to be successful. Your contributions are greatly appreciated and no doubt many players will learn from your expertise. Thank you, Brett Taylor, David Addison, Adrian Ilioski, David (@DayvyFPL), Tom Stephenson and Abdul Rehman. Here's to many more successful seasons.

Glossary of Terms

This is a comprehensive, but not exhaustive, list of terms that are used in official Fantasy Premier League, on social media, and within this book.

Assist
An assist in FPL has a wider meaning than an assist awarded by the Premier League. An assist can be awarded for a pass or cross in the build up to a goal, even if an opponent gets a touch before the goal is scored. However, that touch must not significantly alter the intended destination of the ball. A player can also earn assist points if they win a penalty, which is then converted. Each assist generates three points for the player.

Auto-Substitute
If one of your starting team doesn't play any minutes, the player will be automatically replaced by your first suitable substitute. This is on the proviso that it does not lead to an invalid formation. For example, an eighth attacking player cannot replace your third defender.

Bandwagon
The act of following popular transfer trends. Generally, in-form players who are attracting increasing support. Typically, a player who was not previously highly owned.

Bench Boost (BB)
One of five chips that managers can play on one occasion during the season. The Bench Boost enables the points of your entire 15-man squad to count in the Gameweek that it is played.

Blank
When a player completes 60 minutes and scores two appearance points or less in a single game, they are deemed to have 'blanked'. Whether a midfielder picking up an extra point for a clean sheet counts as a blank is open to debate.

Blank Gameweek (BGW)

A standard Gameweek consists of 10 scheduled fixtures. A blank Gameweek comprises nine fixtures or less. Usually, fixture postponements are caused by cup commitments or inclement weather.

Bonus Points System (BPS)

The BPS utilises a range of statistics supplied by Opta that capture actions on the pitch to create a performance score for each player. These include points for actions such as successful dribbles, interceptions or chance creation, which otherwise would not contribute to a player's score. The players with the top three BPS in a given match receive bonus points - three to the highest-scoring player, two to the second best and one to the third. The BPS system applies to every Premier League game that is played.

Burning a Transfer

If a manager has two free transfers and fails to use one of them, they are deemed to have 'burned a transfer'. That transfer will be permanently lost.

Bus Team

A term made prominent by the Always Cheating FPL Podcast. Refers to setting up your team for the following Gameweek at the earliest opportunity. Doing so avoids missing out on your optimal team if you were unfortunate enough to be 'hit by a bus'. In a wider context, if, for whatever reason, you are unable to select your team later in the week, e.g., due to work commitments, at least your team is set. Selecting your team early will allow you to select your strongest XI and the optimal captain. You can update your team if the need arises.

Captaincy (C)

Each Gameweek, one player is selected as your captain. That player scores double points during that GW. A vice-captain is also selected, so in the event that your captain doesn't play, your vice-captain will fulfil that role. If neither play, then you will not benefit from double points from any other player.

Chips

Chips are a valuable tool with the potential to enhance your team's performance throughout the season. Only one chip can be played per Gameweek: Wildcard (x2), Free Hit, Bench Boost and Triple Captain chip. The chips allow you the opportunity to boost your score or change your team. A temporary change via your Free Hit or permanently via your Wildcard.

Clean Sheet (CS)

Clean sheet bonus points are awarded to goalkeepers, defenders and midfielders when the team they play for doesn't concede a goal. This is on the proviso that the player completes at least 60 minutes of the game. A player substituted after 60 minutes, without conceding a goal, will still be awarded the bonus points, even if their team goes on to concede a goal.

Dead-Ending

Managers often 'dead-end' their teams in the run-up to activating their Wildcard. Specific players are targeted for short-term benefits. For example, a player who is likely to feature in a double or blank Gameweek who you do not want to keep long-term. They are then likely to be sold when the Wildcard is activated.

Differential

A differential is often defined as a player that is owned by fewer than 5% of managers (TSB). Your own definition may vary based on what you are trying to achieve. Some regard a player with less than 10% ownership as a differential. They provide an opportunity to gain rank over your rivals.

Double Gameweek (DGW)

A Gameweek with more than the 10 scheduled fixtures, with some teams playing two games in a week. Typically, they are rearranged games caused by previous fixture postponements. Rotation allowing, a DGW player has the potential to score points in both games.

Doubling/Tripling Up
Owning either two or three players (maximum permitted) from the same team.

Effective Ownership (EO)
Effective ownership equals the percentage of managers who started the player, plus percentage captained and triple captained. This summed percentage gives you an indication of the effect this player has on the average. If a player has an EO of 150%, it means that every point he scores raises the average by 1.5 points. The metric can help you determine the impact that various players will have on your rank should they collect returns.

Enabler(s)
An enabler or 'bench fodder' is generally a cheap player who is purchased purely to release funds. The additional funds will allow you to invest your budget in more desirable and productive assets. It's unusual to find many enablers who are regular starters for their respective clubs. Therefore, they normally occupy a sub-spot on your bench.

Essential
A player is regarded as essential if that player has hit a purple patch and is consistently delivering returns/points. They have become a desirable asset and are perceived by many as an integral part of their team going forward. It is believed that they should feature in all FPL teams.

Expected Assist (xA)
Opta defines the 'Expected Assist' metric as follows: Expected assists (xA) measures the likelihood that a given pass will become a goal assist.

Expected Goal (xG)
The Expected Goals' metric measures the quality of a chance by calculating the likelihood that it will be scored from a particular position on the pitch during a particular phase of play.

Expected Value (EV)

The key concept is the idea that we can estimate the percentage chance of several outcomes before a ball is kicked. The EV is determined by probabilities and discounts luck and the events which take place during a match. EV reflects the mathematical potential of a player and how many points they can theoretically achieve. Each element that contributes towards points and the risks involved (e.g. goals, assists, clean sheet, bonus points, game time, cards, etc.) and probabilities are assigned to outcomes for each of these elements. EV models predict a point prediction for each player. Luck is ignored, since EV holds sway over the long-term.

Eye Test

Watching matches to make a decision on potential targets. Players who have performed well are deemed to have passed the eye test.

Fixture Difficulty Rating (FDR)

The ranking of a player's fixtures in terms of how difficult it is likely to be on a scale of 1-5. One being the easiest fixture (green) and five the most difficult (red). The FDR is based on a complex algorithm. A set of formulas process key Opta data variables, along with each team's home and away form (past 6 matches), in order to generate a rank for the perceived difficulty of each Gameweek opponent. The FDR is designed to assist FPL managers in planning their transfer and team selection strategy. The ratings are reviewed on a weekly basis.

Fixture Proof

The term fixture-proof refers to a player (usually a premium asset) who is able to produce a good performance and deliver FPL points regardless of the opposition. The likes of Mo Salah and Erling Haaland are good examples of fixture-proof players.

FPL Review

FPL Review is a website which deals exclusively with data modelling for Fantasy Premier League. For more information, please visit www.fplreview.com where a full explanation for each metric is provided.

Free Hit (FH)
One Free Hit chip is available per season and it cannot be used in conjunction with any other chip. The FH allows you to make unlimited transfers for one Gameweek. At the next deadline, your squad will revert back to how it was at the start of the Gameweek.

Free Transfer (FT)
Managers are allowed one free transfer per Gameweek. If unused, the FT can be carried over (rolled) to the following week so that you will have two free transfers available. You cannot hold more than two free transfers at any one time.

Gameweek (GW)
A term used to describe a round of Premier League fixtures (normally 10 games per GW). There are 38 Gameweeks throughout the season, with a total of 380 fixtures.

Ghost Ship Teams
Teams that at some point during the season become inactive. As the season evolves, there is a tendency for some managers to give up managing their teams.

Haul
It is generally regarded that a player picks up a haul when they register multiple returns. A double-digit haul occurs when a player accrues 10 or more points in a Gameweek.

Hit (Additional Transfer)
A hit is a term for making an additional transfer. Each transfer made in addition to your one free allocated transfer per Gameweek. Each hit will cost your team a four-point deduction. For example, if you make three transfers in a GW and you only have one FT, the two additional transfers will incur an eight-point deduction. The points will be deducted at the start of the Gameweek.

ICT Index
The ICT index stands for Influence, Creativity and Threat. Players are ranked on their underlying statistics for how they compare to other players in the same position.

In The Bank (ITB)
The amount of spare funds that are available to a manager to invest in their 15-man squad.

Knee-Jerk
Often described in the context of knee-jerk transfers. This is when you make a spontaneous decision without thinking through your actions and with limited information.

Mini-League
Private leagues that any manager can set up. You may invite other players to join your league, or you may be invited to join a different league using a set code provided when the league is being set up.

Nailed (On)
A player who is expected to start a match unless they are injured or unavailable. Ideally, it is desirable to own as many nailed-on players as possible.

Out of Position (OOP)
A player who has been registered on the FPL website in a certain position but finds himself playing for his team in a different position. For example, a player who is classified as a defender finds himself playing in a more advanced midfield role. Hence, there is the potential for them not only to benefit from clean sheet points but also the possibility of scoring more attacking returns by playing in that more advanced role.

Overall Rank (OR)
The rank/position of your team in the main Fantasy Premier League. Your team is automatically entered into the league upon registration and you will compete against every other registered team.

Premium Asset
A player who is in the upper price bracket of their playing position. For example, Trent Alexander-Arnold in defence (7.5m), Mo Salah (12.5m) in midfield and Erling Haaland (12m) as a forward.

Purple Patch
An FPL player experiences a purple patch if they benefit from a run of success or luck. They register a significant number of returns and points. Typically, many players will run into/out of form as the season evolves.

Rage Transfer
An impromptu transfer is usually completed during or shortly after a game in response to an underperforming player or team. For example, a reactive response by a disgruntled manager after seeing one of their strikers miss two 'open-goals'.

Returns
Returns are points generated by a player who either produces a goal, an assist, a clean sheet or bonus points. They are deemed to have earned a 'return'.

Rotating Players
A pair of goalkeepers or defenders who will be rotated by FPL managers depending on the difficulty of fixtures/form, etc.

Rotation-Proof
A player who is more or less guaranteed to start every Premier League game, unless unavailable.

Set-and-Forget
The term is used to describe a player that you own who is likely to be a permanent feature in your team/squad. You're likely to retain their services for a prolonged period unless they sustain a long-term injury. Generally, the term refers to a goalkeeper or a premium asset.

Single Gameweek

Refers to a player (or team) who has just the one fixture in a specific Gameweek.

Squad Value

Each manager starts the season with a squad value of 100m. Depending upon the number of purchases or sales, a player's price will rise or drop as the season evolves. Therefore, your squad value will also fluctuate. The value of your squad and money in the bank are displayed on your points page on the official FPL site.

Template

A hypothetical team comprising the most highly owned players. It is usually made up of the highest-scoring players. It is common to see a template team form at the start of a season and evolve as the season progresses. fpllive.net can provide you with a template reading for your team. This will enable you to determine how 'template' your team is.

Threemium

A team which includes three premium assets. Selecting three expensive assets is difficult to achieve without compromising in other areas of your team.

Triple Captain (TC)

One Triple Captain chip is available per season. When activated, your captain will score treble points rather than the double points in a normal Gameweek.

Teams Selected By (TSB%)

You will find the popularity and ownership of a selected player on the FPL website. Their profile page discloses their TSB ownership. For example, if Mo Salah's TSB is shown as 54%, it means that he is owned by and features in 54% of all teams.

Underlying Statistics

The data that FPL managers base their decisions on. These can include goals, assists, clean sheets, number of shots, ICT Index, etc. As well as expected metrics (xG, xA, xGI, xCS, xGC, etc).

Upside Chasing

Selecting high impact players who have the potential to gain your team a significant climb in rank in a short space of time. Targeting players that have the highest ceiling and are more likely to score a big points haul. There is a tendency for managers to jump between premium assets based on form and fixtures.

Wildcard (WC)

Two Wildcards are made available to managers per season. One to be played in each half of the season. Generally, GW19 is the cut-off. The Wildcard allows you to make unlimited transfers during the week it is activated without incurring any points deductions. The transfers made will be permanent.

About The Author

Paul Rogers has a background in the legal profession, mainly based in London and South Wales. He has a law-based degree (BA) plus has attained further legal qualifications through university. A part of his studies included Forensic Psychology. Paul has also completed an extensive range of legal courses. Much of Paul's work was based on criminal court cases and he has worked for both the prosecution and defence. He was due to start a Masters' degree in Criminology and Criminal Justice before being diagnosed with a rare condition.

Paul has a sporting background and has participated in numerous sports. He has played rugby union to a very high level. Paul is a passionate football fan and he finds nothing more pleasing than watching his local team. He has been a Cardiff City season ticket holder and is a Bluebirds fanatic, experiencing both the highs and lows of the club. He has followed his team on numerous visits to Wembley Stadium plus enjoyed their promotion to the Premier League on two separate occasions. Whilst employed in London, Paul became a keen follower of Tottenham Hotspur and regularly attended home matches.

Paul joined the FPL community on Twitter prior to the start of the 2020/21 season. One of his passions is writing, and he has written articles both for FPL Connect and The FPL Way. He regularly contributes to the FPL community with relevant FPL threads. In December 2021, Paul had his first book published, *Taking A Hit: The Key To Success plus The Top One Hundred Managers and The Elite*. The book proved very successful. Paul completed the 2020/21 season with an overall rank of 29k in the world - comfortably inside the top one percent of players. He can be followed on Twitter: (FPL Bluebird @Cardiff_FPL).

Reference List

Banchera, A. and Damasio, A.R. (2005) *The somatic marker hypothesis: a neural theory of economic decision.* Games and Economic Behaviour 52(2):336-372. doi:10/1016/j.geb.2004.06.010

Bar-Eli, M., Azar O. H, Ritov, I., Keidar-Levin, Y. and Schein, G. (2007) *Action bias among elite soccer goalkeepers: The case of penalty kicks* Journal of Economic Psychology. 28 (5): 706-621. doi:10/1016/j.joep2006.12.001

Baron, J. and Hershey, J. C. (1988) *Outcome bias in decision evaluation.* Journal of Personality and Social Psychology, 54(4), 569-579. https://doi.org/10.1037/0022-3514.54.4.569

Brand, M., Grabenhorst, F., Starcke, K. Vanderkerckhove, MM. and Markowitsch, HJ. (2007)
Role of the amygdala in decisions under ambiguity and decisions under risk: evidence from patients with Urbach-Wiethe disease. Neuropsychologia. 2007;45(6):1305-1317.

Evans, Dr L. (2022) *Study Finds Avid Fantasy Football Fans Face Mental Health Risk*
Available at: https://www.bbc.co.uk (Accessed: 21 November 2022)

Fantasy Premier League (2021) *FPL champion's tips: Plan ahead with transfers*
Available at: https://www.fantasy.premierleague.com (Accessed: 6 June 2021)

Jonathan, K. J. (1998) *Internet Addiction on Campus: The Vulnerability of College Students.* CyberPsychology and Behaviour. 1 (1) 11-17. doi:10/1089/cpb.1998.1.11

LeBlanc, A., Kenny, D.A and O'Connor, A.M (2009) *Decisional Conflict in Patients and Their Physicians: A Dyadic Approach To Shared Decision Making* Medical Decision Making. 29 (1) 61-68. doi: 10.1177/0272989x08327067 ISSN 0272-989X PMID 19196706 S2CID 30171455

O'Brien, J. D, Gleeson, J. P. and O'Sullivan, D. J. P. (2021) Identification of skill in an online game: *The case of Fantasy Premier League*. https://doi.org/10.1371/journal.pone.0246698

Oxford English Dictionary (online ed.). Oxford University Press.

Przybylski, A. K. et al. (2013) *Motivational, emotional, and behavioral correlates of fear of missing out. Computers in Human Behavior*. 29 (4): 1841-1848 doi:10.1016/j.cbh.2013.02.024

Slovic, P. (1987) *Perception of Risk*. Science 236: 280-285. doi:10/1126/science.3563507

The Scout: Fantasy Premier League (2021) *FPL rotation: Pair up to secure run of home matches*. Available at: https://www.fantasy.premierleague.com (Accessed: 19 November 2021)

Tversky, A. and Kahneman, D. (1973) *Availability: A heuristic for judging frequency and probability*. Cognitive Psychology 5 (2): 207-232. doi:10.1016/0010-0285(73)90033-9

Zeelenberg M., Van den Bos K., Van Dijk E., Pieters R. (2002). *The inaction effect in the psychology of regret.* Journal of Personality and Social Psychology, 82, 314-327. doi:10.1037/0022-3514.82.3.314

Printed in Great Britain
by Amazon

29591897R00155